THE 30 DAY MBA

IN MARKETING

2ND EDITION

For many of the topics in the book there are direct links to the free teaching resources of the world's best business schools.

There are also links to hundreds of hours of free video lectures given by other distinguished Business School professors, from top schools including Cranfield, Wharton, Chicago, Harvard and CEIBS (China Europe International Business School).

From the Hass School of Business (**www.haas.berkeley.edu/haas/video_room**) you will find links to lectures by star marketing outsiders such as Steve Wozniak, co-founder of Apple Inc, speaking about entrepreneurship and his experiences during the early days of Apple.

You can download Duke University's top ranking Fuqua School of Business's lecture material on forecasting; a vital aid to anyone preparing sales projections.

Link into Cranfield's School of Management's Research Paper Series and see the latest insights in global supply chain logistics, or watch Harvard's Professor Michael Porter – a leading world proponent of business strategy methodology – outline his ideas.

You can find a list of all these resources online and interspersed within the chapters. Visit **http://www.koganpage.com/product/the-30-day-mba-in-marketing-9780749474980**.

THE 30 DAY MBA

IN MARKETING

2ND EDITION

YOUR FAST TRACK GUIDE TO
— BUSINESS SUCCESS —

COLIN BARROW

KoganPage

LONDON PHILADELPHIA NEW DELHI

First published in Great Britain and the United States in 2011 by Kogan Page Limited
Second edition 2016

2nd Floor, 45 Gee Street
London EC1V 3RS
United Kingdom
www.koganpage.com

1518 Walnut Street, Suite 1100
Philadelphia PA 19102
USA

4737/23 Ansari Road
Daryaganj
New Delhi 110002
India

ISBN   978 0 7494 7498 0
E-ISBN   978 0 7494 7499 7

British Library Cataloguing-in-Publication Data

A CIP record for this book is available from the British Library.

Library of Congress Cataloging-in-Publication Data

Barrow, Colin, author.
  The 30 day MBA in marketing : your fast track guide to business success / Colin Barrow. – Second edition.
      pages cm
  ISBN 978-0-7494-7498-0 (paperback) – ISBN 978-0-7494-7499-7 (ebk)   1. Marketing–Study and teaching.   2. Marketing–Management.   3. Master of business administration degree.
I. Title.   II. Title: Thirty-day MBA in marketing.
  HF5415.B3587 2016
  658.8–dc23
                                                                              2015034004

Typeset by Graphicraft Limited, Hong Kong
Print production managed by Jellyfish
Printed and bound by CPI Group (UK) Ltd, Croydon CR0 4YY

CONTENTS

10   **Marketing and the law**   193

11   **Marketing plans and budgets**   210

12   **Additional core general MBA subjects**   224

LIST OF FIGURES

LIST OF TABLES

Introduction

- What the holder of an MBA in Marketing knows
- Why *you* need that knowledge too
- How to use this book
- Planning your 30 day learning programme

The Master of Business Administration (MBA) is widely regarded as the solution to the apparent lack of professionalism in many aspects of management as well as providing a recognized qualification for business managers. Accountants, engineers, scientists, actuaries, chemists, psychologists and a host of others in and around the organizational world have bodies of knowledge and accrediting associations that ensure that those practising in the field meet at least some minimum criteria. The MBA to some extent addresses that problem for business and now over 2,000 institutions around the world turn out hundreds of thousands of MBAs each year.

The MBA has been around for nearly half a century but business schools, where these degrees are minted, have been around a good deal longer. The honour of being the world's first business school is usually said to go to Ecole Spéciale de Commerce et d'Industrie (now ESCP Europe), established in Paris in December 1819, with Jean-Baptiste Say, who coined the word 'entrepreneur', as its first professor of economics.

In the United States, the first business school was Wharton, founded in 1881 by Joseph Wharton, a self-taught businessman. A miner, he made his fortune through the American Nickel Company and the Bethlehem Steel Corporation, later to become the subject of the earliest business case studies. Harvard Business School, a comparative latecomer, opened in 1908 with a faculty of 15 and launched a Management Masters programme two years later. By 1922 Harvard was running a doctoral programme pioneering research into business methods using the case study method, an approach that was to become its trademark and widely emulated throughout the business school fraternity. The UK was late into the business school game.

The Administrative Staff College at Henley, now the Henley Business School, established in 1945 as the civilian equivalent of the Military Staff Colleges, was a business school in all but name. It took a further decade or so before the long-held belief of politicians and business leaders that management was an inherited ability, a view reinforced by the heavy concentration of family run businesses, diminished. Three Business Schools, each part of a university but with considerable autonomy, were established at Manchester (1965), London (1966) and Cranfield (1967). The Work Study School, which evolved to become Cranfield School of Management, actually opened in 1953.

Aside from ESCP, business schools took a while to catch on in Europe, but they have caught up fast with over 70 institutions offering post graduate business degrees in Germany alone. As Table 0.1 below shows, the MBA has been embraced with enthusiasm the world over.

With the growing complexity of business it rapidly became apparent that there was a need for a more specialized business degree rather than the all-singing, all-dancing general MBA. While that was fine for giving an overview, anyone wanting to go deeply into a particular disciplinary area as a management practitioner needed something with a bit more substance. And so the specialized MBAs were born.

The MBA in Marketing, the subject of this book, goes under various titles. Initially the subject started out as a specialization within the general MBA. Edinburgh runs an MBA with a 'Specialism in Marketing'. The pathways to a Marketing MBA are, as you would expect from such a subject, innovative and varied. WPP, for example, a world leader in advertising and marketing services, offers a number of Marketing Fellowships on MBA programmes to groom future leaders in the marketing needs of their clients. Business schools from Aberdeen to Vienna now offer MBA 'marketing pathways' to promote a comprehensive understanding of the role of marketing management in consumer and industrial markets and service industries. Silberman College of Business, in Madison, New Jersey, has segmented the market further and offers MBAs in Marketing that further specialize in areas such as Database and Interactive Marketing, International Marketing, and the Management of Advertising.

What is interesting about this ranking table (Table 0.1) is that the overall ranking and that for the Marketing specialization are not quite the same. London Business School, which ranks 2nd in the world MBA league, slips to 7th place when it comes to Marketing, whilst Northwestern University, Kellogg, 14th in global ranking, is in first place for Marketing.

TABLE 0.1   Top Ranked World Business Schools FT Global Rankings 2015 and TopMBA 2014 Ranking for Marketing (teaching, research and learning resources drawn on for this edition)

School	2015 World Rank (FT) And for marketing( )*	Country
Harvard Business School	1 (2)	United States
London Business School	2 (7)	United Kingdom
University of Pennsylvania: Wharton	3 (3)	United States
Stanford Graduate School of Business	4 (6)	United States
INSEAD	4 (4)	France
Columbia Business School	6 (8)	United States
MIT Sloan	8 (13)	United States
University of Chicago: Booth	9 (14)	United States
University of California at Berkeley: Haas	10 (11)	United States
IE Business School	12 (5)	Spain
Northwestern University: Kellogg	14 (1)	United States
IMD	20 (26)	Switzerland
Duke University: Fuqua	21 (16)	United States
Saïd (Oxford)	22 (22)	United Kingdom
Dartmouth College: Tuck	23 (21)	United States
Indian Institute of Management, Ahmedabad	26 (17)	India
SDA Bocconi	26 (12)	Italy
The Indian School of Business	33 (29)	India
Cranfield School of Management	45 (46)	United Kingdom
Kelley School of Business, Indiana University	62 (37)	United States

*TopMBA (http://www.topmba.com/mba-rankings/specialization/marketing#.)

What is the content of an MBA in Marketing and what use will it be to you?

There isn't a major listed company that doesn't employ a clutch of MBAs. Last year McKinsey hired 188, BCG, 138, Deloitte, 119, JP Morgan, 103 and Amazon 94. Further down the league, Google took on 63, Microsoft, 54 and Apple, whose founder Steve Jobs famously flunked college, took in 29 MBAs mostly from Duke University's Fuqua School, where Apple's current CEO Tim Cook had earned his MBA.

Apple is by no means an exception in having an MBA for CEO. At the last count, 165 Fortune 500 companies were run by MBAs. John S Watson (Chevron), Jeffrey R Immelt (GE) and Margaret Cushing Whitman (better known as Meg), who runs Hewlett-Packard and before that was CEO of eBay for 10 years, topped this league. One school alone, the Harvard Business School, produces an incredible 12 graduates who are among the top 50 best paid CEOs in corporate America last year with an MBA. An impressive 40 of the 100 best paid CEOs in corporate America last year have an MBA, according to the Forbes list of America's Highest Paid Chief Executives.

Anyone who wants to play a more rounded role in shaping and implementing the direction of the organization he or she works in but are inhibited by his or her lack of detailed marketing knowledge will find that reading this book will equip him or her to take part in the strategic decision making on an equal footing with MBA graduates, while feeling at ease in the process. It places MBA marketing skills within reach of all professionals in large and small organizations in both the public and private sectors, providing them with a competitive edge over less knowledgeable colleagues.

Marketing basically comprises a number of disciplinary areas, each with a number of components. The disciplines contain the tools with which you can effectively analyse a business's marketing situation, drawing on both internal information relevant to the business and external information on its markets, competitors and general business environment as a prelude to deciding what to do.

The emphasis here in the contents of this book is on the terms 'concepts' and 'tools'. The business world is full of conflicting theories and ideas on how organizations could or should work, or how they could be made to work better. They come in and out of fashion, get embellished or replaced over time. A good analogy would be the difference between the limited number of tools a carpenter, for example, has in his or her toolbox, and the infinite number of products that could be made from those same tools. The ultimate success of the product the carpenter makes is partly down to his or her skills in using those tools and partly down to the world he or she find themself operating in at a particular moment in time. A glance in a carpenter's toolbox will reveal an enduring range of common robust implements – screwdrivers, pliers, spanners, smoothing planes, saws and hammers.

In business, for example, there is no such thing as an optimal capital structure, or the right number of new products to bring to market, or whether or not going for an acquisition is a winning strategy. What is best in terms of, say, the ratio of growth generated from existing products and services as opposed to, say, that coming from new products or entering new markets varies with the type of organization and the prevailing economic conditions and the competitive environment. That ratio will be different for the same organization at different times and when it is pursuing different strategies. Layering an inherently risky marketing strategy, say, diversifying, with a risky financing strategy, using borrowed rather than shareholders' money, creates a potentially more risky situation than any one of those actions in isolation. But whichever choices a business makes, the tools used to assess marketing strengths and weaknesses are much the same. It is the concepts and tools to be used in those disciplines that this book explains and shows you how to use to comprehensively assess a business situation.

The MBA Marketing core disciplines

There are a small number of core subject areas that comprise the subject matter of an MBA Marketing programme. Many business schools eschew some vital elements within these disciplines as they are considered either too practical, or too unattractive from a research or career prospective, or more skill- or art-orientated than academic. A prime example is the field of selling, which fits naturally into the marketing domain but – much to the surprise of MBA students – often fails to appear on the syllabus. There are thousands of professors of marketing, distribution and logistics, market research, advertising, industrial marketing, strategic communications and every subsection of marketing, but there are no professors of selling. Yet most employers and students feel that an MBA's value would be enhanced by a sound grounding in selling and sales management.

The irreducible core MBA Marketing syllabus that you will find in the programmes of top business schools is as follows:

Introduction to marketing: How it all began, defining the marketing concept, marketing's role in the internet era, understanding markets – consumers, B2B, the marketing mix – the core concept of marketing strategy.

Buyer behaviour: Understanding customers, how consumers make decisions, how business buyers make decisions, researching markets, desk and field research methods, relationship marketing.

Marketing strategy: Generic option – focus, differentiation and cost leadership, segmentation – methods and procedures, market share, product and service positioning, to brand or not to brand, targeting markets, competitor analysis.

Products and services: Defining the product or service, understanding the product or service mix, the product life-cycle model, quality positioning, extending the product service line, launching new products, the new product or service adoption cycle, protecting intellectual property.

Promotion and advertising: Communication strategies, advertising media defined, deciding on the promotional mix, public relations, sales promotion, personal selling, using databases, effective website strategies, measuring advertising effectiveness, social media.

Place and distribution: Marketing channels and how they add value, retail, wholesale, and direct routes to market, vertical marketing systems (VMS), horizontal marketing systems, distribution strategy criteria, choosing channel partners, marketing logistics.

Pricing: Cost-plus pricing, break-even pricing, value pricing, competition pricing, skim vs penetration strategies, sealed bids and tenders, product-mix pricing, real-time pricing models, segmented pricing, negotiation and its role in pricing, handling foreign exchange risk.

Managing the marketing organization: How a marketing organization behaves, marketing strategy vs structure, systems and people, structures, the options – functional, matrix and strategic business unit (SBU), recruiting and managing the marketing team, planning for change.

Mathematics for marketing: Essential statistics to understand marketing data, sales forecasting and prediction techniques, inventory management, marketing decision tools and probability, marketing scheduling – Gantt, critical path management (CPM), profit margins and product or service profitability calculations, analysing marketing investment decisions.

Marketing and the law: Handling data, advertising standards, labelling, consumer protection, selling on credit, distance selling and online trading, returns and refunds, collecting money, the environment, marketing ethics.

Preparing the marketing budget and plan: Setting marketing goals, using growth matrices – Ansoff, Boston, GE and others, setting the marketing budget, variance analysis, using marketing planning software, macroeconomic indicators for marketing decisions, marketing acquisition/merger strategies.

Additional core general MBA subjects: Accounting, finance, organizational behaviour and strategy.

The main uses of MBA marketing knowledge

Marketing and an appreciation of customers and competitors are common threads that run through all decisions and unless a manager has a sound grasp of the subject he or she will always be a junior partner in major operating decisions, particularly those of a strategic nature. Having this wider marketing knowledge base will open up more and diverse career options.

Specialist marketing knowledge as covered here in this book or in a business school equips the student to get a thorough understanding of marketing theory and practice and to master the skills needed to use marketing tools essential to implementing, interpreting and influencing marketing performance. With these skills a student can:

- gain the marketing analysis and strategic perspective needed to interact effectively with top management as a partner in making key business decisions;
- play a full role in marketing planning, control and competitor analysis;
- be able to take part effectively in acquisition strategies, including buying, selling and joint ventures;
- be able to prepare business plans and financial projections;
- know where to find detailed information on any business or market anywhere.

MBA marketing knowledge can also open up opportunities for career development and change in a wide variety of areas including business analysis, mergers and acquisitions. Tepper School of Business at Carnegie Mellon, consistently ranked amongst the top business schools in the world, lists destinations for its marketing graduates in over 200 companies, from Abbott Laboratories (pharmaceuticals), through Apple, Google, Yahoo! and of course Microsoft. Other career paths for marketing MBAs include consulting, banking and public services including hospital management, trade bodies, the UN and the World Bank. The University of Oxford's Saïd Business School lists a number of 'tree hugging' destinations for its graduates including running a charity in Africa. The school also offers Skoll Scholarships, funded by eBay co-founder Jeffrey Skoll, that pay the tuition and living expenses for five students each year who are pursuing careers in social entrepreneurship, an increasingly popular destination for MBAs specializing in marketing for the non-profit sector.

How this book is organized and how to use it

Each chapter in the book covers the essential elements of each of the core disciplines in a top MBA Marketing programme. There are links to external readings and resources, online library and information sources, case examples and self-assessment tests so you can keep track of your learning achievements.

For many of the topics there are direct links to the *free* teaching resources of the world's best business schools. There are also links in the book to hundreds of hours of *free* video lectures given by other distinguished business school professors from top schools including LBS (London Business School), Imperial, Oxford and Aston. You can download Duke University's top-ranking Fuqua School of Business's lecture material on forecasting, a vital aid to anyone preparing sales projections. Link into Cranfield School of Management's research paper series and see the latest insights into marketing, or watch Professor Malcolm McDonald, a leading world proponent of marketing planning methodology, outline his ideas.

Depending on your knowledge of marketing, you should plan to spend about two days on each of the 12 areas. You should draw up a timetable spread over the time period allocated for your 30 day MBA in Marketing, say 12, 24 or 36 weeks. Then mark out the hours allocated for each subject, not forgetting to leave an hour or so for the test at the end of each subject. You will also need to build in a couple of days for revision before you take your final exam.

The subject areas within each chapter correspond to what you would find in the syllabus at major business schools in terms of theoretical underpinning and the practical application of that theory that you would pick up from fellow students.

The final chapter, 'Additional general MBA subjects', contains the basic tools that an MBA graduate will use or need to refer to more or less every working day. Every MBA student, whether he or she takes a general programme or one that specializes in a particular disciple, as this book does, will be required to study the four core disciples: Marketing (the subject of this book), Finance and Accounting, Organizational Behaviour, and Strategy. Depending on your knowledge in these areas, you should plan to allocate the remaining six of your 30 day learning plan to these areas.

The case study method

Pioneered by Harvard and championed by schools such as Cranfield, which hosts the European Case Study Clearing House, Bocconi (Milan), Esade (Barcelona) and INSEAD (Paris), the case study teaching method is de rigueur. Business schools use the case study as a vehicle for applying and testing out the theories their students are studying in class. The logic for this is impeccable. By studying a business at a particular moment in time, students are forced to grapple with exactly the kinds of decisions and dilemmas managers confront every day. The case method brings into the classroom the opportunity to analyse a complex situation, where all the relevant facts are not available, and persuade others to your point of view.

Of course, if you weren't in the classroom you would be in your own organization, evaluating a business opportunity if you plan to start a business, or looking outside at other enterprises for new career prospects. In short, you would have no need of a case study. You would even have to hand an infinite supply of people whose views differed from your own to debate the options with.

This book contains a selection of shorter case studies that will give you a flavour of the case study method.

Additional online learning resources

At the end of each chapter you will find two new sections which, if used, will extend and cement your learning. In 'Online videos lectures' you will find topical and relevant classroom or lecture theatre presentations and discussions. With a few exceptions these are free and delivered by faculty members of leading business schools. Some of those from business schools are by way of an entire course of anything up to 20 or so lectures. These can comprise everything you would receive had you attended the class in person, teaching notes, handouts and discussion forums using the latest in peer-to-peer social learning tools. Most of the lectures are available all the time, but some of the full courses run periodically, up to four times a year. Some courses will enable you to earn a Certificate of Achievement, or you can just audit the course. Delivery is usually via a virtual 'classroom' open 24/7 where everyone is accepted.

The courses are often delivered by one of the two main MOOCs (Massive Open Online Courses) platforms. These courses are free for everyone but some courses have a fee for verified certificates but are free to audit.

Coursera (www.coursera.org)

Founded at Stanford in 2012, their mission is to 'provide universal access to the world's best education'. They are 'an education platform that partners with top universities and organizations worldwide, to offer courses online for anyone to take, for free'. There are over a hundred universities offering lecture courses including Stanford, IE Business School, Yale, Princeton, Northwestern, Rutgers, Duke, Copenhagen, Tokyo, HEC Paris, Columbia and Ludwig-Maximilians-Universität München.

EdX (www.edx.org)

Founded by the Massachusetts Institute of Technology and Harvard University in May 2012. Over 400 courses are on offer from universities including: MIT, Harvard, Berkeley, Caltech, Georgetown, the Sorbonne, Peking, IIT Bombay, Rice, Kyoto, Columbia, Australian National and Cornell. EdX's goal is to 'offer the highest quality courses from institutions who share our commitment to excellence in teaching and learning'.

There are many other MOOCs course providers and often universities that participate in Coursera or EdX programmes run their own MOOCs through their university website. It has to be said that such offerings are not easy to find. A better route to further supplementing the lectures and courses offered here is to use the MERLOT 11 (**www.merlot.org**) 'Search Merlot' tab. The letters stand for Multimedia Educational Resource for Learning and Online Teaching. The MERLOT project began in 1997 at the California State University Center for Distributed Learning. For students the search facility is all you really need to know about.

Online video case studies, 80 or so in number, include an eclectic mixture of business-school-based presentations, often by entrepreneurs and senior managers of business and other organizations. Some are critiques made by journalists on TV and others are student analysis of business behaviour and performance. Apple's Steve Jobs, Amazon's Jeff Bezos, Airbnb's Nathan Blecharczyk appear here alongside less flattering critiques of Walmart's labour policy, Union Carbide's handling of the Bhopal gas tragedy and Nike defending its position on corporate responsibility. These case studies complement those in the text.

Introduction to marketing

1

- Measuring markets
- Understanding customers
- The marketing mix
- The internet challenge
- Richness and reach combined

Business schools didn't invent marketing but they certainly ensured its pre-eminence as both an academic and practitioner discipline. *Principles of Marketing* and *Marketing Management*, seminal books on the subject by Philip Kotler (*et al*) of Kellogg School of Management at Northwestern University have been core reading on management programmes the world over for decades. The school's marketing department has rated at the top in all national and international ranking surveys conducted during the past 15 years.

Marketing is defined as the process that ensures the right products and services get to the right markets at the right time and at the right price. The key word in that sentence is the word 'right'. The deal has to work for the customer because if they don't want what you have to offer the game is over before you begin. You have to offer value and satisfaction, otherwise people will either choose an apparently superior competitor or, if they do buy from you and are dissatisfied, they won't buy again. Worse still, they may bad-mouth you to a whole mass of other people. For you, the marketer, being right means there have to be enough people wanting your product or service to make the venture profitable; and ideally those numbers should be getting bigger rather than smaller.

So inevitably marketing is something of a voyage of discovery for both supplier and consumer from which both parties learn something and hopefully improve. The boundaries of marketing stretch back from inside the mind of the customer, perhaps uncovering emotions he or she were themself barely aware of, out to the logistic support systems that get the product or service into the customer's hands. Each part of the value chain from company to consumer has the potential to add value or kill the deal. For example, at the heart of the Amazon business proposition are a superlatively efficient warehousing and delivery system and a simple zero-cost way for customers to return products they don't want and get immediate refunds. These factors are every bit as important as elements of Amazon's marketing strategy, as are its product range, website structure, Google placement or its competitive pricing.

Marketing is also a circuitous activity. As you explore the topics below you will see that you need the answers to some questions before you can move on, and indeed once you have some answers you may have to go back a step to review an earlier stage. For example, your opinion as to the size of a relevant market may be influenced by the results achieved when you segment the market and assess your competitive position.

Understanding markets

All products and services have markets that comprise consumers. However, there are two fundamentally different types of markets. The first is consumer markets where the product or service is largely bought and used by the same person, or someone close to them, for personal satisfaction rather than financial gain. The second is business-to-business (B2B) markets where both parties to the transaction expect to make money and both may simply be in the chain that links to end-consumers. A food processing company making pizzas would buy ingredients from other businesses and sell to outlets such as supermarkets or other retailers. They in turn would sell to someone who actually eats the pizza. It could of course be that they merely bought the product for some other family member to consume. Markets can be complicated, messy affairs and the marketer has to get an understanding of all the forces at work along the path from materials to end consumption or use.

Consumers

The same product or service can be used for a variety of purposes, by different end-consumers to gain quite different satisfactions or to meet quite different needs. Marketing to consumers requires getting under their skin to see what their needs, desires, preferences and aspirations are: all the subjects of later chapters. Also, of course, where they will buy – online or offline – and how much they are prepared to pay, factors that are influenced by their socioeconomic and educational background, amongst other factors.

The problem for the marketer is that markets don't stand still and the most profitable path may move from selling B2B to end-consumers as markets mature and develop.

Business-to-business markets

Although apparently invisible to the end-consumer, the B2B market is bigger, more diverse, complex and profitable than the consumer market. To return to our pizza buyer, before that is available in the retail outlet dozens of businesses have played their part in the process. The cheese topping alone, just one of several ingredients that are assembled in the final pizza product, goes through many business hands before it gets to the retailer. Take milk, for example. Cows have to be bred, fed, kept healthy and warm, milked efficiently and that milk distributed from dairy to units for further processing. These business-to-business transactions involve farmers, fertilizer companies, milking equipment manufacturers, builders, transporters and cheese processors, amongst others.

Marketing in the internet era

Exactly when the internet was born, like so many enabling technologies – steam, electricity and the telephone, for example – is a subject for conjecture. Was it 1945 when Vannevar Bush wrote an article in *Atlantic Monthly* cocerning a photo-electrical-mechanical device called a Memex, for memory extension, which could make and follow links between documents on microfiche? Or was it a couple of decades later when Doug Engelbart produced a prototype of an 'oNLine System' (NLS) which did hypertext browsing editing, e-mail and so on? He invented the mouse for this purpose, a credit often incorrectly awarded to Apple's whiz-kids.

Some date the birth as 1965 when Ted Nelson coined the word 'hypertext' in 'A file structure for the complex, the changing, and the indeterminate', a paper given at the 20th National Conference, New York, of the Association for Computing Machinery. Others offer 1967 when Andy van Dam and others built the Hypertext Editing System.

The most credible claim for being the internet's midwife probably goes to Tim Berners-Lee, a consultant working for CERN, the European Organization for Nuclear Research. In June–December of 1980 he wrote a notebook program, 'Enquire-within-upon-everything', that allowed links to be made between arbitrary nodes. Each node had a title, a type and a list of bidirectional typed links. 'Enquire' ran on Norsk Data machines under SINTRAN-III. Berners-Lee's goal was to allow the different computer systems used by the experts assembled from dozens to countries to 'talk' to each other both within CERN itself and with colleagues around the globe.

The record of the internet's meteoric growth has been tracked by Internet World Stats (**www.internetworldstats.com/stats.htm**) since 1995 when just 16 million people, representing 0.4 per cent of the world's population, were online. By the last quarter of 2014 that had grown to 3,035,749,340 users, some 42.3 per cent of the planet's population. Whilst the United States still leads the field with 87.7 per cent internet penetration, over a quarter of

Africans are now connected, a third of Asians and half of those in the Middle East and Latin America and the Caribbean.

So what's new?

In later chapters, particularly Chapter 2 when we look at the works of Maslow, the argument is advanced that consumer needs are enduring and only the means of satisfying them changes. While this gives a sense of stability to the whole subject of marketing, the internet has substantially changed everything by changing the traditional trade-off between giving customers what they want and what it is economically viable to provide.

But for the first decade or so, the internet looked as though the only thing it could reliably deliver for the business world was a colossal collapse in value. In the years to 2002–03, investors in internet businesses lost hundreds of billions of dollars. Many of the first generation of internet start-ups had nothing unique about their offer other than that it was 'on the net'. Any new entrant to a market with nothing particularly distinctive to make it better in the customer's eyes will end up competing on price. New and small businesses are less able to win price wars than bigger and better-established competitors. Arguably the first business to sell books on the internet was offering nothing new into a mature established market. The same was true of food retailers offering product on the net. Most customers for books and groceries already had a wide choice of products available close to them and available at convenient times. The only sector that the internet might have appealed to was rural populations who were not so well supplied. But the drawback here was that rural populations were less likely to be on the internet and had less spending power than people in urban areas. The result was a price war with few people in such sectors making any profit even after the best bit of a decade in the market.

Richness vs reach

The internet has largely changed the maths of the traditional trade-off between the economics of delivering individually tailored products and services to satisfy targeted customers and the requirement of businesses to achieve economies of scale. The near-impossible second-hand book that had to be tracked down laboriously and at some cost is now just a mouse click away. The cost of keeping a retail operation open all hours is untenable but sales can continue online all the time. A small business that once couldn't have considered going global until many years into its life can today, thanks to the internet, sell its wares to anyone anywhere with a basic website costing a few hundred dollars and with little more tailoring than the translation of a few dozen key words or phrases and a currency widget that handles its payments. The internet has made real what in the 1970s Marshall McLuhan, a Canadian visionary of marketing communications, called the 'global village'.

FIGURE 1.1   Richness vs reach

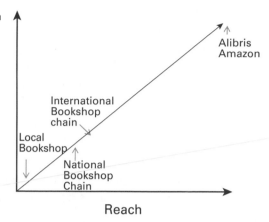

Richness

- Bandwidth or amount of data that can be transmitted
- Ability to customize product or service to an individual buyer's needs
- Interactivity between 'buyer' and 'seller'
- Reliability of the service
- Security of data and transaction processes, including payment systems
- Currency – how current the data is
- Operating hours 24/7
- Ease with which languages can be added to facilitate global reach

Alibris
Amazon

International
Bookshop
chain

Local
Bookshop

National
Bookshop
Chain

Reach

- Number of people/customers who can be approached
- Geographic spread
- New intermediaries in the distribution channels

The book business is a powerful illustration of the way a product and its distribution systems endure in principle while changing in method over the centuries. From 1403 when the earliest known book was printed from movable type in Korea, through to Gutenberg's 42-line Bible printed in 1450, which in turn laid the foundation for the mass book market, the product, at least from a reader's perspective, has had many similarities. Even the latest developments of in-store print-on-demand and e-book delivery, such as Amazon's Kindle, look like leaving the reader holding much the same product. What has, however, transformed the book business is its routes to market, the scope of its reach and the new range of business partnerships and affiliate relationships opened by the internet. The Alibris case is a powerful example of how the internet has affected the way in which marketing strategy is developed and implemented.

CASE STUDY   Alibris.com

Alibris is one of the premier rare and out-of-print book sites on the internet. Started in 1998 they were a pioneer in the field of bringing first editions, signed books and other rare and antique treasures to a wider market via their website using their network of trusted Sellers from around the world. By 2015 the company was still vibrant, but in a fiercely competitive marketplace. Amazon raised the stakes when in December 2008 they bought out AbeBooks, founded three years before Alibris, by two couples from Victoria. AbeBooks remains a stand-alone operation with headquarters in Victoria, British Columbia, Canada, and a European office in Dusseldorf, Germany.

Unsurprisingly, Alibris took corporate shelter too. On 23 February 2010 Alibris announced that it was acquiring Monsoon, Inc, an Oregon-based marketplace selling solutions company. Alibris is an online marketplace for sellers of new and used books, music and movies that connects people who love books, music and movies to the best independent sellers from 45 countries worldwide. It offers more than 100 million used, new and out-of-print titles to consumers, libraries and retailers.

Alibris was founded in 1998 out of the germ of an idea that had been bugging Richard Weatherford, a bookseller who loves old books and new technology. After teaching college for a number of years, Dick turned to selling antiquarian books via specialized catalogues from his home near Seattle, a city that would also become home to Amazon.

Alibris is a business that could only exist in the internet era. The richness of information on hard-to-find second-hand books and its global reach marrying tens of thousands of sellers with hundreds of millions of buyers can only be delivered online. The company built specialized sophisticated low-cost logistics capabilities from the start to allow orders to be consolidated, repackaged, custom invoiced or shipped overseas at low cost. Because Alibris collects a great deal of information about book buying and selling, the company came to be able to offer both customers and sellers essential and timely market information about price, likely demand and product availability. By 2015 Alibris had assembled a galaxy of stars in their business partner network. All the usual suspects – Amazon, Barnes & Noble, Blackwell, Follett and Foyles – alongside a score of names known mainly to the rare book buying aficionados.

Intelligent data abounds

Marketers have always had an appetite for data. Anything that helps get a handle on customer needs, preference, buying patterns or spending power is all grist to the mill. But the internet has added two important twists to information gathering. In the first instance the information can be assembled in real time. That means the information is current and so probably more valid than that gleaned weeks or months ago when different circumstances might have prevailed. Just imagine a stockbroker trying to gauge share buyers' opinions in June 2009 when shares slumped, based on data assembled weeks or even days before.

Breaking down barriers and levelling the playing field

One of the criteria for a successful marketing strategy is to ensure that new entrants can't enter the market easily or at least without at least as much cost as you have incurred. The internet era has levelled the playing field between big established businesses and new market entrants. In many cases the heritage investment made by the early players in a market, however entrenched they seem, counts for little. Lloyd's of London had been in the insurance business for over 300 years when direct marketing via the internet and telephone all but swept it away.

CASE STUDY   Moonpig

In April 2015 Cranfield MBA Nick Jenkins had reason to be excited about a new stage in his life. He was joining *Dragons' Den*, the long-running Bafta-nominated BBC show that sees novice entrepreneurs pitch for start-up funds. When Nick, 46, launched Moonpig, his online personalized greetings card business in 1999, though quietly confident of success, he had no idea just how big his idea would become. In July 2011, barely 12 years after launching, he sold his business to Photobox – the French owned company who offer online photo albums – for £120 million.

Moonpig itself offers a range of over 10,000 customizable cards to which users can add photographs, names and their own personal message. Thanks in part to being responsible for one of the most annoyingly memorable jingles on TV, the company now has annual turnover in excess £32 million whilst netting £11 million in profits.

Before starting his business Nick had spent eight years in Moscow as a commodity trader for a sugar operation. A death threat nailed to his door after a troublesome deal, combined with a declining enthusiasm for his line of work and a healthy lump sum gained from a buy-out of the trading firm, led Nick back to the UK. There he started an MBA at Cranfield and during the course developed a number of start-up ideas. The idea he honed and wrote a business plan for was Moonpig and within a week of graduating Nick had started to piece the business together.

Nick Jenkins saw that reliance on word-of-mouth promotion is also a desirable attribute in a company's name. He wanted a domain name that was easy to remember and fun enough that customers would want to tell their friends about it. He was looking for a two-syllable domain but couldn't find the right combination available and didn't want to buy one from somebody else. Moonpig – Nick's school nickname – worked. At the time, if you entered it into Google nothing came up, and there was the added advantage that it lent itself well to a logo – it's easy enough to remember a pig in a space helmet.

Clicks and bricks

Of course, the internet business world and the 'real' world overlap and in some, cases take over from one another. Woolworth's, for example, died on the high street in 2009 only to be born again on the internet. Many of the old economy entrants to the e-economy have kept the 'mortar' as well as acquiring 'clicks'. When one national retail chain announced the separation of its e-commerce business, one great strength claimed for the new business was: 'Customers know and trust us and that gives us a real competitive edge.' That trust stemmed from customers being able to physically see what the company stands for. Software produced by a leading UK internet software company plans to offer an intelligent internet tool that reacts to customers' shopping habits by suggesting different sites related to subjects or products they are interested in. In that way it hopes to build a similar level of trust, but over the internet. The firm uses its local stores for 'pick and pack' and delivers locally using smaller vehicles.

Viral marketing

This term was coined to describe the ability of the internet to accelerate interest and awareness in a product by rapid word-of-mouth communications. To understand the mathematical power behind this phenomenon it is useful to take a look at recent communications networks and how they work. The simplest are the 'one-to-one' broadcast systems such as television and radio. In such systems the overall value of the network rises in a simple relationship to the size of the audience: the bigger the audience, the more valuable your network. Mathematically the value rises with N, where N represents the size of the audience. This relationship is known as Sarnoff's Law, after a pioneer of radio and television broadcasting. Next in order of value comes the telephone network, a 'many-to-many' system where everyone can get in touch with anyone else. Here the mathematics are subtly different. With N people connected, every individual has the opportunity to connect with $N - 1$ other people (you exclude yourself). So the total number of possible connections for N individuals $= N (N - 1)$, or $N^2 - N$. This relationship is known as Metcalf's Law, after Bob Metcalf, an inventor of computer networking. The size of a network under Metcalf's Law rises sharply as the value of N rises, much more so than with simple one-to-one networks. The internet, however, has added a further twist. As well as talking to each other, internet users have the opportunity to form groups in a way they cannot easily do on the telephone. Any internet user can join discussion groups, auction groups, community sites and so on. The mathematics now becomes interesting. As David Reed, formerly of Lotus Development Corporation, demonstrated, if you have N people in a network they can in theory form $2^n - N - 1$ different groups. You can check this formula by considering a small N, of say three people, A, B and C. They can form three different groups of two people: AB,

AC and CB, and one group of three people, ABC, making a total of four groups as predicted by the formula. As the value of N increases, the size of the network explodes. See Figure 1.2.

FIGURE 1.2   The mathematics of internet networks

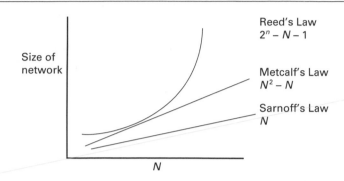

The birth of viral marketing, using the power of Metcalf's Law to the full, has been attributed to the founder of Hotmail, who insisted that every e-mail sent by a Hotmail user should incorporate the message 'Get your free web-based e-mail at Hotmail'. By clicking on this line of text, the recipient would be transported to the Hotmail home page. While this e-mail sent by the company itself would not have had much effect, at the foot of an e-mail sent by a business colleague or friend it made a powerful impact. The very act of sending a Hotmail message constituted an endorsement of the product and so the current customer was selling to future customers on the company's behalf just by communicating with them. The recipient of a Hotmail message learnt that the product works, but also that someone they respect or like is a user. You only have to see how quickly a harmful computer virus can spread in hours and days, to cover the whole world, to see the potential of viral marketing. For a small firm this technique has the added advantage of being inexpensive and easy to execute. Just look at some major sites on the internet to get ideas. Book e-tailors all have links for you to e-mail a friend about a book you have 'stumbled' across on their site. Travel sites encourage you to e-mail a friend any of their special offers that you don't plan to take up. However, the beauty and limitation of viral marketing is that it only works when you are talking about a good product. No one recommends something they don't like using themself.

New world – new threats

Even if firms think that e-business offers few advantages, they could find themselves facing a range of new threats. For example, the competitors that offline businesses face are small and big firms in their own country or area and international firms from elsewhere in the world. With the internet they could now have small firms similar to themselves, but based anywhere in the world, entering their market. Potentially this could put them up against hundreds of new competitors.

Also, their more nimble or forward-thinking smaller competitors could add to their apparent value, in their customer's eyes at least, by having an internet presence. This could be true even if the proportion of business or other activities conducted on the internet is small. Customers are often favourably influenced by irrelevant benefits that they nevertheless think they may one day take advantage of. A vivid example of this phenomenon has been 24-hour retail shopping. Few people actually shop for groceries in supermarkets at two in the morning, but by having a sign saying the shop is open all the time customers will be more inclined to use it anyway than a shop with more conventional opening hours.

So all businesses face new dangers as a consequence of the internet:

● They will have a range of new competitors of all sizes from around the world who can attack their market using the internet.

● An internet presence is now almost mandatory, as is the cost that goes with it. Firms without a presence may appear old-fashioned and out of date compared with other firms who do have websites.

● Firms without an internet strategy and presence will miss out on some business that may only go to firms with an internet presence. This is particularly true of rural markets, where the internet has offered a degree of choice that is otherwise only available in major cities.

● The staff they employ may leave in search of more stimulating places to work.

● They will miss out on the operational cost saving that can be made using e-business, which may make them uncompetitive and so lose out to other firms.

New world – old opportunities

Of course, the internet has not replaced old-world maxims and opportunities. There is as much money in muck – the residue of other commercial activities, successful or otherwise – as there always was. What the internet does provide is a new layer of hidden value, as with any scrap recovery venture.

CASE STUDY   Bargains at Boo.com

In March 2015 Ranker 'the crowdsourced rankings of everything' listed Boo.com as the 6th biggest internet flop of all time (**www.ranker.com/list/10-top-dot-com-flops/ business-and-company-info**). Founded in 1999 by a trio of Swedish entrepreneurs, Ernst Malmsten, Kajsa Leander and Patrik Hedelin, Boo.com was the first truly global internet retailer of fashion and sportswear, or rather wanted to be. Described by *Elle* magazine as the 'literary rock stars of Europe', in August 1997 Kajsa and Ernst set up the internet bookstore bokus.com. A phenomenal hit, bokus. com exceeded all expectations, rapidly becoming the world's third largest online bookstore after Amazon and Barnes & Noble. In February 1996, Patrik Hedelin was retained as financial advisor to bokus.com. and soon after negotiated the sale of the company to Swedish Cooperative KF, one of the largest retail and media companies in Scandinavia.

It was at this point that Boo.com was born. The vision was clear – in the words of one of Boo's founders, to become the world's leading online retailer of fashion and sportswear. The vehicle – a cutting-edge website and a team of dynamic individuals, handpicked from the worlds of fashion, new media, marketing, business, technology and finance. The outcome – 'an awesome virtual shopping experience that we believe surpasses anything that currently exists on the web'. The retail site was complemented by boom, an interactive online magazine bringing together street life, fashion, sport, art and technology from around the world.

Boo sought to become a global brand right from the start, launching simultaneously across Europe and the USA. It also wanted to create one of the most sophisticated internet sites – and as events turned out, this was about all they created.

In less than 18 months, Boo's team burned through the £89 million that their backers, including Bernard Arnault of LVMH, the luxury goods group, Benetton and Goldman Sachs, had put up.

Fast-forward to 2010 and Dan Wagner, who, for just £250,000, picked up the only residual value in the Boo debacle, the technology platform that drove the website, was using it to power Tesco's fashion website and those of TK Maxx and Panasonic. His company, Venda, is a market leader in providing on-demand e-commerce solutions. Wagner was the driving force behind MAID, an early player in the financial information business, securing its listings on the London Stock Exchange and NASDAQ in 1994. An inveterate bargain hunter, Wagner refused to pay £5 million for the Venda name, though he sorely wanted it. After the dot.com crash in 2001 he picked it up for just £12,000.

Online video courses and lectures

Marketing Management Specialization – MBA@Syracuse:
www.youtube.com/watch?v=OdVH0jhdOx4

The Rutgers Mini-MBA: Digital Marketing Program: **www.youtube.com/
watch?v=Eh5i685zmlo**

What Can You Do With an MBA in Marketing? **www.youtube.com/
watch?v=rQdggYxZ1zs**

Online video case studies

Kelley – IU Kelley School of Business MBA – Wake Forest Marketing
Summit 2014: **www.youtube.com/watch?v=3Fzn1T8Exvc**

MBA Career Search at Darden: Marketing: **www.youtube.com/
watch?v=-STQKt6hkpl**

UCD Smurfit MBA – Digital Marketing and Christmas Event at The
Hibernian 2 Dec 2014: **www.youtube.com/watch?v=W6O58UKTe_8**

Buyer behaviour

2

- Appreciating marketing
- Understanding customers
- Qualifying financially desirable customers
- Recognizing benefits
- Researching markets
- Segmenting markets

Customers once upon a time were simply sold products, and the focus of innovative businesses lay in driving costs down so as to widen and open up as big a market as possible. Henry Ford's much quoted 'You can have any color as long as it's black' was part of a determined and successful strategy to build a car for the masses. There is no evidence that Ford actually said those words, but from 1908 to 1927, the Model T assembled at the Piquette Avenue Plant in Detroit churned out 15,000,000 vehicles with little change in its design. This was the longest run of any single model apart from the Volkswagen Beetle. Nevertheless, the 'T' is still recognized as the world's most influential car of the 20th century.

The change in emphasis from selling on price to marketing was captured in the classic *Harvard Business Review* article, 'Marketing myopia' by Theodore Levitt, published in 1960. Levitt, who joined the faculty of the Harvard Business School in 1959 and died in June 2006, went on to produce a score of other thoughtful articles but none that outsold the 850,000 reprints this one ran to.

The thrust of Levitt's proposition was that the difference between marketing and selling is more than semantic. Selling, he claimed, focuses on the needs of the seller, marketing on the needs of the buyer. Selling is preoccupied with the seller's need to convert the product into cash, marketing with the idea of satisfying the needs of the customer by means of the product and the whole cluster of things associated with creating, delivering and, finally, consuming it. He went on to argue that in some industries, the enticements of full mass production have been so powerful that top management in effect has told the sales department, 'You get rid of it; we'll worry about profits'. By contrast, a truly marketing-minded firm tries to create value-satisfying goods and services that satisfy consumers' needs.

The benefit Levitt saw for businesses in moving from an emphasis on mass production and selling across to marketing was that needs endure, while products come and go. He used the railroad as an example of a business that had defined itself too narrowly. At the turn of the century American railroads enjoyed a fierce loyalty amongst astute US investors; European monarchs plunged in, too. The prevailing view was that eternal wealth was assured and no other form of transportation could compete with the railroads in speed, flexibility, durability, economy and growth potential. Even when cars, trucks and airplanes arrived, the railroad tycoons remained unconcerned. If you had told them that in a few short decades they would be broke and pleading for government subsidies, they would have thought you demented. Yet that's what happened and, as Levitt argued, it came about not primarily because of a fundamental change. After all people still travelled and goods were distributed, it was just that these needs were satisfied by other means. (You can download a reprint of this article free at **http://academy.clevelandclinic.org/Portals/40/LHC%20Myopia.pdf**).

One of the few entrepreneurs to grasp this concept is Richard Branson, whose Virgin brand embraces an intercity railway, as well as significant holdings in several airlines. With Virgin Galactic he looks like taking the transportation business to totally new frontiers.

CASE STUDY   dunnhumby

Clive and Edwina, founders of dunnhumby came up with their entire business proposition based on understanding buyer behaviour. Their concept involved retaining and analysing customer data based on behaviour, which would enable companies to deliver marketing that was more relevant to their customers. They approached their employer with the idea but they were not willing to invest their profits in this new concept. Clive was adamant this idea should be pursued and his disappointment in the company's lack of vision led him to resign from the business in order to pursue the vision on his own. As Edwina, who was married to him, recalls, 'I was literally fired 10 minutes later as they felt I would be competing with their business.' She received a substantial payout – enough to dissuade her from claiming unfair dismissal. The result was a new player in the market, dunnhumby, which left CACI playing catch-up in a market they could have dominated from the outset.

The company undoubtedly made its mark when it took on Tesco as a client. The top handful of multinational retailers, Walmart, Metro, Groupe Carrefour, Ahold and Tesco all slug it out around the globe with the all-important aim of capturing a few additional percentage points of market share. To win that extra share retailers have to know more about their markets than their competitors. Tesco's growth in stores in the early years was more art than science. But to be absolutely fair the other retailers operated in much the same way. Jack Cohen, Tesco's founder, based his initial strategy on operating from market stalls which made it easy, cheap and quick to follow his customers rather than requiring them to come to him. But if you want the customers to come to you the strategy has to be based more on science than art. A 130,000ft^2 supermarket costs around £45 million to build and before you get to lay the first brick getting planning and other approvals can set a major retailer back many millions more. So it was hardly surprising for Tesco to want to find ways to understand their customers and encourage their loyalty when so much investment was at stake. Tesco liked the business so much they bought it out for £100 million, leaving the pair to move on to pastures new.

In 2014 they raised £4.7 million ($7.5 million) to fund Starcount (**www.starcount.com**), aiming to do for celebrities on social media what their previous company did for Tesco's Clubcard. By 2015 the Humbys were part of a venture capital team considering buying out dunnhumby from a troubled Tesco that was scrambling for cash.

Understanding customers

Without customers, no business can get off the ground, let alone survive. Knowing something about your customers, what they need, how much they can 'consume', who they buy from now – this all seems such elementary information that it is hard to believe so many people could start without those insights, And yet they do.

There is an old business maxim that the customer is always right. But that does not mean that they are necessarily right for you. So as well as knowing who to sell to, you also need to know the sorts of people that trying to interest will be a waste of scarce resources on your part.

The founder of a successful cosmetics firm, when asked what he did, replied: 'In the factories we make perfume, in the shops we sell dreams.'

Those of us in business usually start out defining our business in physical terms. Customers on the other hand see businesses having as their primary value the ability to satisfy their needs. Even firms that adopt customer satisfaction, or even delight, as their stated aim often find it a more complex goal than it at first appears.

CASE STUDY   Eat 17

Eat 17, founded by Siobhan O'Donnell with her partner Chris O'Connor, his brother Dan and their step-brother James Brundle in Walthamstow, north-west London, may look at first glance like a run of the mill convenience store, but once inside it rapidly becomes evident that the product on offer is very different. First off, Chris is a trained chef and he brings the expertise that ensures their products are fresh and appealing for the whole of the working day. As well as offering independent, artisan and local produce made by small suppliers they have a bakery and pizza restaurant on site and create their own range of ready-meals. Each week they try 20 or so new products adding those that sell to their core product range. This strategy keeps repeat customer visits high and pulls in new ones bored with the more conventional ranges on offer in neighbouring supermarkets. Their latest creation a bacon-based condiment, which they called 'Bacon Jam', flies of the shelves alongside more conventional products provided through their partnering arrangement with the convenience brand Spar. The jam is taking the business in a slightly different direction as it has become a product in its own right now stocked in 3,000 outlets nationwide including Selfridges, Waitrose and Tesco. It has even expanded to a range of five different flavours.

Sales in 2014/15, their seventh year in business, doubled delivering a healthy £1 million plus annual turnover. They have recently bought a former snooker hall on Chatsworth Road in Lower Clapton, taking their investment in the Eat 17 venture to £500,000. Brundle reckons their product offer is the shape of things to come. Customers today expect a different product proposition that relies more on being a destination that people are excited to visit than a chore that simply has to be done to get essential groceries.

Until you have clearly defined the needs of your market(s) you cannot begin to assemble a product or service to satisfy them. Fortunately, help is at hand. An American psychologist, Abraham Maslow, who taught at Brandeis University, Boston and whose International Business School now ranks highly in the *Economist*'s survey of top business schools, demonstrated in his research that 'all customers are goal seekers who gratify their needs by purchase and consumption'. He then went a bit further and classified consumer needs into a five-stage pyramid he called the hierarchy of needs. See Figure 2.1.

FIGURE 2.1   Maslow's hierarchy of needs

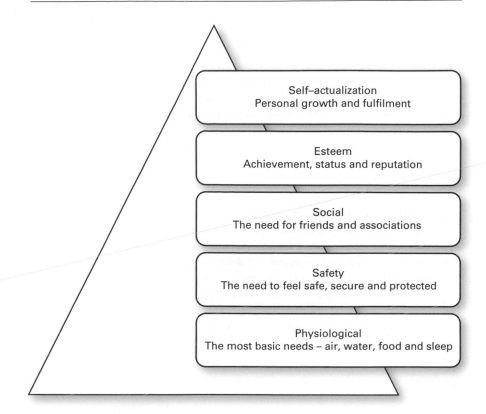

Self-actualization

This is the summit of Maslow's hierarchy, in which people are looking for truth, wisdom, justice and purpose. It's a need that is never fully satisfied and according to Maslow only a very small percentage of people ever reach the point where they are prepared to pay much money to satisfy such needs. It is left to the likes of Bill Gates and Sir Tom Hunter to give away billions to form foundations to dispose of their wealth on worthy causes. The rest of us scrabble around further down the hierarchy.

Esteem

Here people are concerned with such matters as self-respect, achievement, attention, recognition and reputation. The benefits customers are looking for include the feeling that others will think better of them if they have a particular product. Much of brand marketing is aimed at making consumers believe that conspicuously wearing the maker's label or logo so that others can see it will earn them 'respect'. Understanding how this part of Maslow's hierarchy works was vital to the founders of Responsibletravel.com (**www.responsibletravel.com**). Founded in 2001 with backing from Anita Roddick (The Body Shop) in Justin Francis's front room in Brighton, with his partner Harold Goodwin, it set out to be the world's first company to offer environmentally responsible travel and holidays. It was one of the first companies to offer carbon-offset schemes for travellers and boasts that it turns away more tour companies trying to list on its site than it accepts. It appeals to consumers who want to be recognized in their communities as being socially responsible.

Social needs

The need for friends, belonging to associations, clubs or other groups and the need to give and get love are all social needs. After 'lower' needs have been met, these needs that relate to interacting with other people come to the fore. Hotel Chocolat (**www.hotelchocolat.co.uk**), founded by Angus Thirlwell and Peter Harris in their kitchen, is a good example of a business based on meeting social needs. It markets home-delivered luxury chocolates but generates sales by having Tasting Clubs to check out products each month. The concept of the club is that you invite friends round and using the firm's scoring system, rate and give feedback on the chocolates.

Safety

The second most basic need of consumers is to feel safe and secure. People who feel they are in harm's way either through their general environment or because of the product or service on offer will not be over-interested in having their higher needs met. When Charles Rigby set up World Challenge (**www.world-challenge.co.uk**) to market challenging expeditions to exotic locations around the world, with the aim of taking young people up to around 19 out of their comfort zones and teaching them how to overcome adversity, he knew he had a challenge of his own on his hands: how to make an activity simultaneously exciting and apparently dangerous to teenagers, while being safe enough for the parents writing the cheques to feel comfortable. Six full sections on the company's website are devoted to explaining the safety measures it takes to ensure that unacceptable risks are eliminated as far as is humanly possible.

Physiological needs

Air, water, sleep and food are all absolutely essential to sustain life. Until these basic needs are satisfied, higher needs such as self-esteem will not be considered.

You can read more about Maslow's needs hierarchy and how to take it into account in understanding customers on the Net MBA website (**www.netmba.com**>Management>Maslow's hierarchy of needs).

Features, benefits and proofs

While understanding customer needs is vital, it is not sufficient on its own to help put together a saleable proposition. Before you can do that you have to understand the benefits customers will get when they purchase. Features are what a product or service has or is, and benefits are what the product does for the customer. When Nigel Apperley founded his business, internet Cameras Direct – now part of the AIM-listed eXpansy plc – while a student at business school, he knew there was no point in telling customers about SLRs or shutter speeds. These are not the end product that customers want; they are looking for the convenience and economy of buying direct. He planned to follow the Dell Computer direct sales model and good pictures. Within three years Apperley had annual turnover in excess of £20 million and had moved a long way from his home-based beginnings.

Look at the example of product features and benefits in Table 2.1, which has been extended to include proofs showing how the benefits will be delivered. The essential element to remember here is that the customer only wants to pay for benefits while the seller has to pick up the tab for all the features whether the customer sees them as valuable or not. Benefits will provide the 'copy' for a business's advertising and promotional activities.

TABLE 2.1   Example showing product features, benefits and proofs

Features	Benefits	Proofs
Our maternity clothes are designed by fashion experts	You get to look and feel great	See the press comments in fashion magazines
Our bookkeeping system is approved by HM Revenue & Customs	You can sleep at night	Our system is rated No1 by the Evaluation centre (**www.evaluationcenter.com** >accounting software)

Business buyers' needs

When understanding the needs of business buyers it is important to keep in mind that there are at least three major categories of people who have a role to play in the buying decisions and whose needs therefore have to be considered in any analysis of a business market.

The user, or end-customer, will be the recipient of any final benefits associated with the product or service, much as with an individual consumer. Functionality will be vital.

The specifier will want to be sure the end-user's needs are met in terms of performance, delivery and any other important parameters. Its 'customer' is both the end-user and the budget holder of the cost centre concerned. There may even be conflict between the two (or more) 'customer' groups. For example, in the case of hotel toiletries, those responsible for marketing the rooms will want high-quality products to enhance their offer while the hotel manager will have cost concerns close to the top of his or her concerns, and the people responsible for actually putting the product in place will be interested only in any handling and packaging issues.

The non-consuming buyer, who places the order, also has individual needs. Some of these needs are similar to those of a specifier except he or she will have price at or near the top.

Market research

The purpose of market research is to ensure you have sufficient information on customers, competitors and markets so that you can be reasonably confident enough people want to buy what you want to sell at a price that will give you a viable business proposition.

You do not have to launch a product or enter a market to prove there are no customers for your goods or services; frequently even some modest market research beforehand can give clear guidance as to whether your venture will succeed or not.

While big businesses may employ market research agencies to design and execute their research, an MBA should both understand the process and be able to carry out elementary research themself quickly and on a low budget.

The fundamental goals of market research

The purpose of market research from an MBA's perspective is twofold:

1 To build credibility for a business proposition; the MBA must demonstrate first to his or her own satisfaction, and later to that of his or her colleagues, superiors and eventually to financiers, a thorough understanding of the marketplace for the new product, service or strategy. This will be vital if resources are to be attracted to execute the proposal.

2 To develop a realistic market entry strategy for the proposed course of action, based on a clear understanding of genuine customer needs and ensuring that product quality, price, promotional methods and the distribution chain are mutually supportive and clearly focused on target customers.

You will need to research in particular:

- Your customers. Who will buy your goods and services? What particular customer needs will your business meet? How many of them are there?
- Your competitors. Which established companies are already meeting the needs of your potential customers? What are their strengths and weaknesses?
- Your product or service. How should it be tailored to meet customer needs?
- What price should you charge to be perceived as giving value for money?
- What promotional material is needed to reach customers; which newspapers, journals do they read?
- Whether or not your operational base is satisfactorily located to reach your customers most easily, at minimum cost.

Seven steps to successful market research

Researching the market need not be a complex process, nor need it be very expensive. The amount of effort and expenditure needs to be related in some way to the costs and risks associated with the proposition. The market research needs to be conducted systematically following these seven stages:

1 Formulate the problem. Before embarking on your market research you should first set clear and precise objectives, rather than just setting out to find interesting general information about the market.

   So, for example, if you are planning on selling to young fashion-conscious women, amongst others, your research objective could be to find out how many women aged 18 to 28, with an income of over £35,000 a year, live or work within your catchment area. That would give you some idea whether the market could support a venture such as this.

2 Determine the information needs. Knowing the size of the market, in the example given above, may require several different pieces of information. For example, you would need to know the size of the resident population, which might be fairly easy to find out, but you might also want to know something about people who come into the catchment area to work or stay on holiday or for any other major

purpose. There might, for example, be a hospital, library, railway station or school nearby that also pulled potential customers to that particular area.

3   Where can you get the information? This will involve either desk research in libraries or on the internet, or field research, which you can do yourself or get help in doing. Some of the most important of these areas are covered later in this chapter.

   Field research, that is, getting out and asking questions yourself, is the most fruitful way of gathering original information that can provide competitive advantage.

4   Decide the budget. Market research will not be free even if you do it yourself. At the very least there will be your time. There may well be the cost of journals, phone calls, letters and field visits to plan for. At the top of the scale could be the costs of employing a professional market research firm.

   Starting at this end of the scale, a business-to-business survey comprising 200 interviews with executives responsible for office equipment purchasing decisions cost one company £12,000. Twenty in-depth interviews with consumers who were regular users of certain banking services cost £8,000. Using the internet for web surveys is another possibility, but that can impose too much of your agenda onto the recipients and turn them away from you.

   Check out companies such as Free Online Surveys (**http:// free-online-surveys.co.uk)** and Zoomerang (**www.zoomerang.com**), who provide software that lets you carry out online surveys and analyse the data quickly. Most of these organizations offer free trials.

   Doing the research yourself may save costs but may limit the objectivity of the research. If time is your scarcest commodity, it may make more sense to get an outside agency to do the work. Using a reference librarian or university student to do some of the spadework need not be prohibitively expensive. Another argument for getting professional research is that it may carry more clout with investors.

   Whatever the cost of research, you need to assess its value to you when you are setting your budget. If getting it wrong would cost £100,000, then £5,000 spent on market research might be a good investment.

5   Select the research technique. If you cannot find the data you require from desk research, you will need to go out and find it yourself. The options for such research are described later in this section, under 'Field research'.

6   Construct the research sample population. It is rarely possible or even desirable to include every possible customer or competitor in your research. Instead you would select a sample of people, who represent the whole population being surveyed. You need to take

care and ensure you have included the innovators and early adopter segments in your research sample. These will be discussed later, in Chapter 4, but they are particularly important to internet and other highly innovative product categories of firm, whose entire first year's sales could be confined to these groups.

Sampling saves time and money and can be more accurate than surveying an entire population. Talking to all pet owners may take months. By the time you have completed your survey the first people questioned may have changed their opinion, or the whole environment may have changed in some material way. There are two methods of sampling, each having three variants:

- Probability sampling. This is done to statistical rules with each member of the sample population having a known chance of being selected. In simple random sampling a selection is made from the whole of a population, using a method that ensures randomness. This could be achieved by picking names out of a hat or by using random number tables. In the stratified random sampling technique, the total population is divided into subgroups, each of which is treated as a simple random sample. This would be used if certain subgroups of the population could be expected to behave differently but were all important to the study. It is often not possible or practical to get a list of the whole of a population, for example a city, but parts of it can easily be obtained. Area postcodes within the city will be easier to obtain and use. An area or cluster sample is chosen simply by taking a random sample of the postcodes on the list. These are then the people to include in the survey.

- Non-probability sampling. This is used when probability sampling is not possible, such as when no list of the population exists or when the population is not stable over time – for example, an airport booking hall. Convenience sampling includes such methods as calling for volunteers, street interviews and using students as guinea pigs in an experiment. In judgement sampling the researcher selects people or groups of people that they believe will result in a group that is representative of the population as a whole. Quota sampling is a refinement of judgement sampling, where the people sampled represent the overall population in some important respect. For example, if we know that 60 per cent of pet owners are women, then we might construct our sample with that proportion of women in it.

The accuracy of your survey will increase with the sample size. This subject is discussed in Chapter 10.

7 Process and analyse the data. The raw market research data needs to be analysed and turned into information to guide your decisions on price, promotion and location, and the shape, design and scope of the product or service itself.

Desk (or Secondary) research

The business world is awash with information on almost every aspect of business covering everything from what people buy, why and when they buy and how satisfied they are with their purchase. The challenge for an MBA is how to tap into that information. These are the essential starting points.

Libraries

Aside from visiting a library you can identify what information is available in your local library without scouring the shelves. WorldCat (**www.worldcat.org**) claims, with some justification, to be the world's largest network of library content and services letting you search the collections of libraries in your community and thousands more around the world. Entering the term 'market research' into the site's search pane yielded over 1.1 million sources in barely half a second with some 100,000 of those in a downloadable format. Narrowing that down to 'sources of marketing information' delivers 114,000 items, with 5,000 in a downloadable format. WorldCat results often include a direct link to the 'Ask a Librarian' help feature of a library's website. You have to be a member of that library to use that resource.

Major country national libraries often have dedicated business research resources. For example the British Library has a Business and IP Centre (**www.bl.uk/bipc/#**) where they have put together workshops such as 'Beginners Guide to Business Information' and 'Qualitative and Quantitative Research' as well as links to organizations to help you make the most of market research. Courses here range from free to around £25.

Business Insider has a directory of the greatest libraries (**http://uk.businessinsider.com/18-of-the-worlds-greatest-libraries-2014-12**).

Online Newspapers (www.onlinenewspapers.com)

Newspapers and magazines are a source of considerable information on companies, markets and products in that sphere of interest. Virtually every online newspaper in the world is listed here. You can search straight from the homepage, either by continent or country. You can also find the 50 most popular online newspapers from a link in the top centre of the homepage. There is also a separate site for online magazines (**www.onlinenewspapers. com/SiteMap/magazines-sitemap.htm**).

Using the internet

The internet is a rich source of market data, much of it free and immediately available. But you can't always be certain that the information is reliable or free of bias as it can be difficult if not impossible to always work out who exactly is providing it. That said, you can get some valuable pointers as to whether or not what you plan to sell has a market, how big that market is and who else trades in that space. The following sources should be your starting point:

- Google Trends (**www.google.com**>Labs>Google Trends) provides a snapshot on what the world is most interested in at any one moment. For example, if you are thinking of starting a bookkeeping service, entering that into the search pane produces a snazzy graph showing how interest measured by the number of searches is growing (or contracting) since January 2004 when they stared collecting the data. You can also see that South Africa has the greatest interest and the Netherlands the lowest. You can tweak the graph to show seasonality, thus showing that Croydon registers the greatest interest in the UK overall and demand peaks in September and bottoms out in November.

- Google News (**www.google.com**) by selecting 'News' on the horizontal menu at the top of the page under the Google banner. Here you will find links to any newspaper article anywhere in the world covering a particular topic over the last decade or so, listed by year. Asking for information on baby clothes will reveal recent articles on how much the average family spends on baby clothes, the launch of a thrift store specializing in second-hand baby clothes and the launch of an organic baby clothes catalogue.

- Blogs are sites where people, informed and ignorant, converse about a particular topic. The information on blogs is more straw in the wind that fact. Globe of Blogs (**www.globeofblogs.com**), launched in 2002, claims to be the first comprehensive world weblog directory. There are links to over 58,100 blogs, searchable by country, topic and about any other criteria you care to name. Google (**http://blogsearch.google.com**) is also a search engine to the world's blogs.

- Harvard has a useful guide to using web information (**http://usingsources.fas.harvard.edu/icb/icb.do**> Evaluating Sources>Evaluating Web Sources).

Field research

Most fieldwork carried out consists of interviews, with the interviewer putting questions to a respondent. The more popular forms of interview are currently:

- personal (face-to-face) interview: 45 per cent (especially for the consumer markets);

- telephone, e-mail and web surveys: 42 per cent (especially for surveying companies);

- post: 6 per cent (especially for industrial markets);

- test and discussion group: 7 per cent.

Personal interviews, web surveys and postal surveys are clearly less expensive than getting together panels of interested parties or using expensive telephone time. Telephone interviewing requires a very positive attitude, courtesy, an ability not to talk too quickly, and listening while sticking to a rigid questionnaire. Low response rates on postal services (less than 10 per cent is normal) can be improved by accompanying letters explaining the questionnaire's purpose and why respondents should reply, by offering rewards for completed questionnaires (small gift), by sending reminder letters and, of course, by providing pre-paid reply envelopes. Personally addressed e-mail questionnaires have secured higher response rates – as high as 10–15 per cent – as recipients have a greater tendency to read and respond to e-mail received in their private e-mail boxes. However, unsolicited e-mails ('spam') can cause vehement reactions: the key to success is the same as with postal surveys – the mailing should feature an explanatory letter and incentives for the recipient to 'open' the questionnaire.

There are basic rules for good questionnaire design, however the questions are administered:

1 Keep the number of questions to a minimum.

2 Keep the questions simple! Answers should be either 'Yes/No/Don't know' or offer at least four alternatives.

3 Avoid ambiguity – make sure the respondent really understands the question (avoid 'generally', 'usually', 'regularly').

4 Seek factual answers; avoid opinions.

5 Make sure at the beginning you have a cut-out question to eliminate unsuitable respondents (eg those who never use the product/service).

6 At the end, make sure you have an identifying question to show the cross-section of respondents.

Sample size is vital if reliance is to be placed on survey data. How to calculate the appropriate sample size is explained in Chapter 9 in the section headed 'Surveys and sample size'.

Testing the market

The ultimate form of market research is to find some real customers to buy and use your product or service before you spend too much time and money in setting up. The ideal way to do this is to sell into a limited area or small section of your market. In that way, if things don't quite work out as you expect, you won't have upset too many people.

This may involve buying in a small quantity of product to fulfil the order and fully test your ideas. Once you have found a small number of people who are happy with your product, price, delivery/execution and they have paid up, then you can proceed with a bit more confidence than if all your ideas are just on paper.

Pick potential customers whose demand is likely to be small and easy to meet. For example, if you are going to run a bookkeeping business, select five to 10 small businesses from an area reasonably close to home and make your pitch. The same approach would work with a gardening, babysitting or any other service-related venture. It's a little more difficult with products, but you could buy a small quantity of similar items in from a competitor or make up a trial batch yourself.

Market segmentation

Market segmentation is the process that divides consumers into relatively homogeneous behavioural segments identified by some common characteristics that are relevant in explaining and in predicting their likely response to marketing stimuli. For example, a carpet/upholstery cleaning business may have private householders and business clients running restaurants and guesthouses. These two segments are fundamentally different, with one segment being more focused on cost and the other more concerned that the work is carried out with the least disruption to their business. The business market segment is likely to comprise of customers with higher spending power and a capacity for repeat purchasing, so worth enticing to loyalty.

Once a business has subdivided its market by geographic, demographic, psychological, psychographic or behavioural variables, a marketing mix (see Chapter 3) can then be formulated to reach the segment identified in the most effective manner. Market segmentation tries to regain some of the benefits of the closer association with customers which was the strength of traditional business operations before the era of mass production encouraged a 'one size fits all' philosophy.

Origins

Market segmentation can trace its origins back to the 1930s when the prevailing theories of perfect competition and pure monopoly no longer seemed to fit the situation. A new monopolistic theory emerged based around the idea that every firm was in itself in some important way unique. Every business was in effect able to create its own local monopolistic position by offering a product different in some way from others. That differentiation could be based on certain product characteristics, packaging, distribution or the real or imagined value associated with, for example, a brand name. Economists called this process 'product differentiation' and concluded that it resulted in different demand curves for each group of different buyers.

Business managers extended their efforts to create their own monopolistic conditions whilst marketers moved the concept away from 'product' to the more all-embracing term 'market'.

The term and concept of 'market segmentation' have been attributed to Wendell R Smith. In his article 'Product differentiation and market segmentation as alterative marketing strategies', published in *The Journal of Marketing* (1956, 2 (3), pp 3–8), Smith commented: 'Segmentation is based upon developments on the demand side of the market and represents a rational and more precise adjustment of product and marketing effort to consumer or user requirements'.

Twenty-three years later an article 'Retrospective note on market segmentation' published in the introduction to the special edition of the *Journal of Marketing Research* (edited by Smith) indicated that 'the roots of early market segmentation research, carried on almost a quarter of a century ago, can be found in the writings of a group of marketing practitioners and scholars whose undisputed leader was the late Wroe Alderson (1898–1965)'. Anderson's book, *Marketing Behaviour and Executive Action* (1957, Richard Irwin), written whilst he was a professor at Wharton University of Pennsylvania, consolidates his thoughts on this subject.

Methods of segmentation

These are the main ways that market segmentation can be put to working successfully in a business.

Geographic segmentation

When different locations have different needs you can use this form of market segmentation. For example, an inner-city location may be a heavy user of motorcycle dispatch services, but a light user of gardening products. Geographic segmentation was the first type of segmentation to get pressed into service. This was because many companies, particularly small ones either can't afford the cost of extending to national or international distribution channels; or don't have the productive capacity to meet large-scale demand.

Markets can be analysed nationally, regionally or locally using various criteria as a point of differentiation. At the country level, for example, countries can be clustered by their relative GDP (Gross Domestic Product), with the rich industrialized countries in one category, and the developing ones in another. Differences in buying behaviour can also have a local dimension. Food habits, for example, often have regional variations. In Scotland, the consumption of both vegetables and alcoholic beverages are markedly different from that of England and Wales, with the former being lower and the latter higher. Geographic-based segmentation was given a major boost with the introduction by Richard Webber of his ACORN (A Classification Of Residential Neighbourhoods). The system was developed from sociological research into urban deprivation in Liverpool classifying people and households according to the type of neighbourhoods in which they live. ACORN recognized 38 neighbourhood types, identified by a combination of 40 variables including age and household composition, housing type, social and employment status drawn from census data.

Demographic

This consists of dividing the market into groups on the basis of demographic variables such as age, sex, socioeconomic group, family size, income, occupation and education. Philip Kotler, the marketing guru, and S C Johnson, Distinguished Professor of International Marketing at the Kellogg School of Management at Northwestern University, state that 'demographic variables are the most popular bases for distinguishing customer groups'. There have been many critics of demographics who cite research suggesting that variables such as age, sex, income and occupation are poor predictors of behaviour, and as such are of limited value when segmenting markets. But as this data is easy to collect, demographic characteristics are still the basic terms in which most marketers consider the consumer.

A detailed and extensive analysis of the relationship between life cycle and consumption behaviour is presented by Reynolds and Wells in their book *Consumer Behaviour* (1977). Their model is adapted in Table 2.2 below.

TABLE 2.2   Family life cycles

Age	Development level	Stage in the family life cycle
18–34	Early adulthood	1 The bachelor stage: young, single people 2 Newly married couples: young, no children 3 The full nest I: young married couples with dependent children: (a) Youngest child under six (b) Youngest child over six
35–54	Middle adulthood	4 The full nest II: older married couples with dependent children
55+	Later adulthood	5 The empty nest: older married couples with no children living with them: (a) Head in labour force (b) Head retired 6 The solitary survivors: the older single people (a) In labour force (b) Retired

Things have moved on since this study and now further lifestyle categories have been incorporated. Tesco, for example, uses its loyalty card data to uncover six broad segments it considers in every management decision – upmarket shoppers, health-focused shoppers, traditional cookers, mainstream families, convenience shoppers and price-sensitive shoppers. It also has 17 distinct customer groups which include brand loyals, dieters, calorie loaders, adventurous eaters, promotion junkies, ethical, green and so on.

Age, sex and income remain popular as variables with clothing, fashion and food markets relying heavily on these criteria. A study of 2,000 smartphone users by TalkTalk in July 2013 found distinct demographic differences in the owners of different types of mobile phone. iPhone users were more image conscious and spend more on clothes than BlackBerry users but earn £2,500 less on average. BlackBerry owners were the busiest. Android users the most polite and are good in the kitchen.

Indeed as the Victoria's Secret case study on page 47 shows whole businesses can be defined on one demographic alone. The evidence suggests that demographic segmentation works well, even in the digital age. Lyris, in its 2012 Digital Optimizer Survey, found that demographic segmentation of e-mail marketing efforts returned the best results for nearly 40 per cent of the 300 companies surveyed. The highest proportion of any segmentation method used.

Psychographic segmentation

Pioneering research linking psychological factors with consumer behaviour was published by Mason Haire ('Projective techniques in marketing research', *Journal of Marketing*, **14** (5), pp 649–56). In his study respondents were asked to describe the personality and character of the women whose shopping list they examined. They were given two lists which only differed in respect of the coffee listed, one was Nescafe Instant, the other Maxwell House Drip grind (a type of finely ground coffee bean). The respondents were able to characterize these two women with the result that they saw the Nescafe shopper as lazy and a poor household planner and the Maxwell House shopper as thrifty and a good wife.

Since then psychological segmentation, with the name expanded to a more sexy physiographic, has blossomed. This approach divides individual consumers into social groups such as 'yuppies' (young, upwardly mobile professionals), 'bumps' (borrowed-to-the-hilt, upwardly mobile, professional show-offs) and 'jollies' (jet-setting oldies with lots of loot). These categories try to show how social behaviour influences buyer behaviour.

Plummer (see Table 2.3) supplemented demographic measures with indices of activities, interests and opinions to develop the AIO system, profiling consumers on the basis of where they live, how they live and what they aspire to. Similarly, the Stanford Research Institute's VALS system (Values And LifeStyles) identified eight categories of consumer, such as the 'achiever', who is career and work-oriented and favours prestige products, and the older 'struggler', who is more cautious, restrained and brand-loyal.

Forrester Research, an internet research house, claims that when it comes to determining whether consumers will or will not go on the internet, how much they'll spend and what they'll buy, demographic factors such as age, race and gender don't matter anywhere near as much as the consumers' attitudes towards technology. Forrester uses this concept, together with its research, to produce Technographics® market segments as an aid to understanding people's behaviour as digital consumers. Forrester has used two categories: technology optimists and technology pessimists and has used these alongside income and what it calls 'primary motivation' – career, family and entertainment – to divide up the whole market. Each segment is given a new name – 'Techno-strivers', 'Digital Hopefuls' and so forth – followed by a chapter explaining how to identify them, how to tell whether they are likely to be right for your product or service, and providing some pointers as to what marketing strategies might get favourable responses from each group.

TABLE 2.3 Lifestyle dimensions

Activities	Interests	Opinions	Demographics
Work	Family	Themselves	Age
Hobbies	Home	Social issues	Education
Social events	Job	Politics	Income
Vacation	Community	Business	Occupation
Entertainment	Recreation	Economics	Family size
Club membership	Fashion	Education	Dwelling
Community	Food	Products	Location
Shopping	Media	Future	City size
Sports	Achievements	Culture	Stage in life cycle

SOURCE: Plummer, JT (1974) The concept and application of lifestyle segmentation, *Journal of Marketing*, 38 (January), pp 33–37

Behavioural segmentation

This involves dividing potential buyers into clusters by such factors as their usage rate, their brand familiarity and buying patterns, such as weekly or daily shoppers, for example. By using usage rate marketers can focus their efforts on heavy users with loyalty cards, discounts and special offers. Heavy users are usually a more lucrative market and their needs are often different than those of light users. For example frequent fliers could be persuaded to use one airline regularly if they were offered the use of an airport lounge or given periodic class upgrades. Heavy users of certain brands of alcoholic drinks or tobacco can usually be relied on to be brand loyal. So a marketing strategy emphasizing the attractiveness (apparent) of the users of a particular brand can reinforce and reward particular behaviours.

Benefit segmentation

This approach recognizes that different people can get different satisfaction from the same product or service. In 1958, a television commercial featured an excited child running to his mother, exclaiming, 'Look Ma, no cavities!' The product being promoted was Crest toothpaste, which contained a new additive, stannous fluoride. P&G (Proctor & Gamble), one of the first businesses to introduce integrated product and market research teams, launched Crest toothpaste at a market segment that was not seduced by the 'whiteness strategy' of its principal competitor.

Other companies go on to target hair shampoos towards split ends, anti-dandruff or other benefits. Lastminute.com claims two quite distinctive benefits for its users. First, it aims to offer people bargains that appeal because of price and value. Second, the company has recently been laying more emphasis on the benefit of immediacy. This idea is rather akin to the impulse-buy products placed at checkout tills, which you never thought of buying until you bumped into them on your way out. Whether 10 days on a beach in Goa or a trip to Istanbul are the type of things people 'pop in their baskets' before turning off their computers, only time will tell.

Multi-variant segmentation

This is where more than one variable is used and can give a more precise picture of a market than using just a single factor. One increasingly popular segmentation strategy is one that marries demographic, psychographic, and/or benefit segmentation. BMW, for example, defines its owners as being wealthy, adrenalin-seeking, competitive, driven and looking for the ultimate experience.

Geodemographic segmentation

This technique involves combining geographical and demographic segmentation. We may start by focusing on a particular segment in which to sell a new food product on the basis of regional preferences, or avoid launching a new wine to a country where alcohol is prohibited. Spatial units such as these can be very easy to determine. As the sole basis for market segmentation this is unlikely to be extremely sufficient. The next logical step is to apply standard demographic variables, ie age, sex, income, education, social status, family life-cycle stage, etc. In practice many demographic variables have geographic characteristics. High net worth families are often clustered in particular geographical locations. Geodemographic segmentation thus seeks to combine the two, identifying geographic clusters of potential customers who satisfy specified demographic criteria. For example, an upmarket grocery retailer such as Waitrose is unlikely to choose to open in an area where there is a cluster of high unemployment and low-income families.

Industrial segmentation

This is usually a form of multi-variant segmentation that groups together commercial customers according to a combination of their geographic location, principal business activity, relative size, frequency of product use, buying policies and a range of other factors.

Table 2.4 shows partial market share details for Cisco, the US high technology company. The three segments shown account for between 10 and nearly 30 per cent of the company's turnover and their share of each market ranges from 27 to over 98 per cent. They face varying amounts of competition in each segment. In Switches, a segment they dominate with a 98.43 per cent share only Juniper Networks, Inc competes against them. In Routers, where their market share is 27.17 per cent, they face 10 competitors, including Juniper Networks, Inc. However in this segment once company, Broadcom Corporation has a very similar market share (25 per cent). Cisco's approach to each segment will recognize both the different competitive environment and the specific needs of each industry sector.

Specifiers, users and customers

When analysing market segments it is important to keep in mind that there are at least three major categories of people who have a role to play in the buying decisions and whose behaviour and needs have to be considered in any analysis of a market:

- The 'user', or 'end-customer', will be the recipient of any final benefits associated with the product.
- The 'specifier' will want to be sure that the end-user's needs are met in terms of performance, delivery and any other important parameters. Their 'customer' is both the end-user and the budget holder of the cost centre concerned. There may even be conflict between the two (or more) 'customer' groups. For example, in the case of, say, hotel toiletries, those responsible for marketing the rooms will want high-quality products to enhance their offer, while the hotel manager will have cost concerns close to the top of their concerns and the people responsible for actually putting the product in place will be interested only in any handling and packaging issues.

TABLE 2.4   Cisco's competition by market segment

COMPANY NAME	SEGMENT Service Provider Video	% OF TOT. Company Revenue	MARKET SHARE
CISCO SYSTEMS, INC.		10.63%	28.28%
Broadcom Corporation	Total	100%	43.65%
PMC-Sierra, Inc.	Total	–	2.72%
Broadcom Corporation	Broadband communications	26.78%	11.69%
Motorola Solutions, Inc.	Enterprise	31.78%	13.65%
COMPANY NAME	SEGMENT NAME Routers	OF TOT. REV.	MARKET SHARE
CISCO SYSTEMS, INC.		17.52%	27.17%
Corning Incorporated	Telecommunications	25.92%	5.97%
CIENA CORPORATION	Total	100%	6.45%
JDS Uniphase Corporation	Communications Products	44.21%	2.27%
Juniper Networks, Inc.	Infrastructure	79.6%	11.63%
F5 NETWORKS, INC.	Total	–	4.7%
Broadcom Corporation	Total	100%	25%
PMC-Sierra, Inc.	Total	–	1.59%
Broadcom Corporation	Broadband communications	26.78%	6.82%
Motorola Solutions, Inc.	Enterprise	31.78%	7.96%
COMPANY NAME	SEGMENT NAME Switches	OF TOT. REV.	MARKET SHARE
CISCO SYSTEMS, INC.		29.45%	98.43%
CIENA CORPORATION	Packet Optical Switching	11.3%	1.57%
Juniper Networks, Inc.	Switches	–	–

- The 'non-consuming buyer', who places the order, also has individual needs. Some of their needs are similar to those of a specifier, except that they will have price at or near the top of their needs. A particular category here is those buying gifts. Once again their needs and those of the recipient may be dissimilar. For example, those buying gifts are as concerned with packaging as with content. Watches, pens, perfumes and fine wines are all gifts whose packaging is paramount at the point of purchase. Yet for the user they are often things to be immediately discarded.

Worthwhile criteria for a market segment

These are four useful rules to help decide if a market segment is worth trying to sell into:

1 Measurability: Can you estimate how many customers are in the segment? Are there enough to make it worth offering something 'different'?

2 Accessibility: Can you communicate with these customers, preferably in a way that reaches them on an individual basis? For example, you could reach the over-50s by advertising in a specialist 'older people's' magazine, with reasonable confidence that most young people will not read it. So if you were trying to promote Scrabble with tiles 50 per cent larger, you might prefer that young people did not hear about it. If they did, it might give the product an old-fashioned image.

3 Open to profitable development: The customers must have money to spend on the benefits that you propose to offer.

4 Size: A segment has to be large enough to be worth your exploiting it, but perhaps not so large as to attract larger competitors.

Arriving at the segments

These nine steps will help you arrive at the appropriate market segments for a business.

1 Determine your key marketing objectives in terms of sales, profit and margin growth over your planning horizon.

2 Select the initial basis for segmentation based on your observations of distinct customer groups, for example demographic variables such as age, sex, occupation; education and income and psychographic variables on.

3 Select a set of segment descriptions with hypotheses on the possible link between those and the basis for segmentation. For example with mobile phones differences in usage – voice, video, apps, messaging etc – could be used to arrive at descriptions of different clusters. Taking apps, for example, six clusters have been observed: Application Ignorant, representing 25 per cent of the market, with a very low volume of use. Basic Application Users, also around 25 per cent of the market. Up from this level are Average Application Users (17 per cent), Information Seekers (12 per cent), Application Savvy (10 per cent) and High Utility User (8 per cent).

4 With the above descriptions in mind and certain demographic/psychographic criteria in mind a sample of users can be identified to test out, confirm or suggest as basis for the proposed segments to be modified.

5 Using a survey or some other basis for collecting data, question a sample across the selected segments.

6 Confirm the segments based on the data collected.

7 Establish a clear descriptive profile of the segments and the relative size of each.

8 Develop specific marketing strategies for each target segment. For example for the Application Ignorant segment knowledge tools, special offers and free trials may be appropriate. For the Application Savvy and High Utility segments more sophisticated and expensive Apps with more unique features and a greater emphasis on forums and user groups may prove effective.

9 Confirm that the segments identified and the strategies proposed to exploit them will yield results sufficient to meet your key marketing objectives.

What market segmentation can help a business achieve

Market segmentation can help your organization to achieve a number of valuable benefits that will prove useful when using the marketing mix to develop a marketing strategy. The process will also prove useful in setting marketing budgets and designing the structure of the marketing organization. The main benefits are to:

1 Better understand and define your market. Breaking your market into its component parts will help you develop a more comprehensive appreciation of what matters most to different types of customer, how many customers share those values or needs and how you might become better or different from your competitors in each of those segments.

2 Identify gaps in the market. Segmentation helps to identify customers and potential customers whose needs are not currently being fully met. In the case of Victoria's Secret there is no doubt that men made product purchases before Victoria launched, but their needs were not specifically targeted.

3 Improve matching of customer needs. Customer needs differ so creating separate offers for each segment rather than having a 'one size fits all' approach provides customers with a better solution.

4 Achieve lifetime customer retention. Customers are costly to acquire and the longer you can keep them the more valuable they become. However, customers' circumstances change over time. They grow older, form families, change jobs or get promoted, buy a property, or change their buying patterns in some other way. By marketing products that appeal to customers at different stages of their

purchasing life cycle, a business can retain customers who might otherwise switch to competing products and brands or suppliers.

5 Gain a higher share of the market segment. Having a strong or leading share of a market is an important factor in maximizing profitability. Segmentation and targeting enables a business to achieve competitive operating and marketing costs and become the preferred choice for customers in that segment. Saga, the over-55s' travel business, is not in the biggest market segment for travel and tourism. The 15–54 age group make 55.7 million trips a year in the UK and 23.9 million abroad. The over-55s take just 19.7 and 8.2 million such trips. But as a market segment the over-55s are both valuable and have different needs and buying habits. They tend to travel out of season when airlines and hotels need more volume; they stay in serviced accommodation rather than self-catering, so spend more money; they take longer holidays, so the average transaction cost is lower; and they are less sensitive to economic downturns.

6 Target marketing communications. Taking a broad brush approach to advertising to and communication with your customers can be prohibitively expensive and inefficient. Delivering your marketing message to a relevant customer audience ensures the key customers are not missed and the target customer can be reached more often and at lower cost. Taking the Saga business as an example, advertising in the quality press or other media will probably reach the over-55s. But you will be paying to reach hundreds of thousands of people who have no possibility of becoming customers as they are out of the desired age range. Media charge on audience numbers, so finding media targeting only or mostly the over-55s will cost less and yield fewer wasted contacts.

CASE STUDY   Victoria's Secret

Roy Raymond, an alumnus of Tufts University, took his MBA at Stanford Graduate School of Business. He opened his first Victoria's Secret store in 1977 at the Stanford Shopping Center with an $80,000 loan, half provided by a bank and the remainder borrowed from relatives. It was an immediate success exceeding $500,000 sales in its first trading year. The first UK store opened in August 2012 in London's New Bond Street.

Victoria's Secret is the number one intimate apparel brand in the USA. With around 1,600 shops worldwide and one of the most visited websites dating back to 1998, over 400 million copies of their catalogue are distributed annually. The company is in great shape having ridden out the post 2008 downturn with relative ease. In 2014 in less than great economic conditions sales at Victoria's Secret

Stores & Victoria's Secret Beauty and Victoria's Secret Direct grew 10 per cent and 3 per cent, respectively. Gross profit climbed 5 per cent to $945.3 million, gross margin pushed up 270 basis points to 39.4 per cent. Operating income nudged up 1 per cent to $308.9 million and the operating margin moved up to a healthy 12.9 per cent, a near-best for the sector.

So what's the secret of Victoria's success? The business was founded, so the story goes, out of Raymond's embarrassment at trying to buy lingerie for his wife in the less than comfortable environment of a public shopping floor in a department store. Without men, Raymond reckoned the lingerie business was missing out on half its potential customer base. Men were in fact a major untapped market segment. Men, he reckoned, would be more comfortable if the decor of the stores were along the lines of a Victorian drawing room, complete with Oriental rugs and antique armoires housing lingerie displays. The business's name was inspired by the period of the home that Roy and his wife Gaye were living in at the time. Friendly and inviting staff went out of their way to make purchasing lingerie an un-embarrassing, almost normal event.

In 1982 Raymond sold the Victoria's Secret company together with its six stores and 42-page catalogue, grossing $6 million per year, to Leslie Wexner, founder of The Limited, for $4 million. Wexner who had taken Limited Brands public, listed as LTD on the NYSE, in 1977 was on an acquisition spree. He went on to buy Lane Bryant stores, then in 1985, a single Henri Bendel store was purchased for $10 million, 798 Lerner stores for $297 million and finally in 1988, 25 Abercrombie & Fitch stores were added to the portfolio for $46 million. This represented the high water mark for Wexner's who sold out to the venture capital firm Sun Capital Partners Inc. in stages completing his exit in 2010.

Victoria's Secret was founded on a simple demographic market segmentation criteria; the sex of the buyer, not the user. Victoria's Secret today still segments its market demographically, but in much greater detail. The company knows the age, gender, income and social class of their target market in every area in which they operate and deliver specific messages, refining their strategy along the way.

A case study on the company, prepared by Theodore Durbin, a MBA Fellow at the Center for Digital Strategies at the Tuck School of Business at Dartmouth under the supervision of Adjunct Professor Kathleen L Biro, reviewed how Victoria's Secret went about gathering data to help it segment markets. They developed, Durbin noted 'a sophisticated algorithm called Recency, Frequency, and Monetary Value (RFM), based on the theory that recent shoppers were more responsive to catalogue mailings, as were more frequent shoppers and those with higher recent order sizes' (**http://digitalstrategies.tuck.dartmouth.edu/cds-uploads/case-studies/pdf/6-0014.pdf**).

Postscript

Sadly the future for Roy Raymond, the company's founder, was not as happy as for the company itself. With £650,000 from the sale Raymond started up a new business, My Child's Destiny, a retail outlet selling children's products. The store failed and as Raymond hadn't incorporated the business, he was liable for the debts. Raymond went on to start a children's book store, a mail-order home-repair hardware business and a company that made wigs for women who had lost their hair due to cancer treatment. Raymond and his wife lost two homes and their cars and in 1993 they divorced. As if to twist the knife in further, at the same time Victoria's Secret had become the biggest US lingerie retailer. On 26 August 1993, Raymond, aged 46, leapt to his death off the Golden Gate Bridge.

Sources of help and advice with market segmentation

Decision Analyst. They have some free Statistical Software for Marketing Research and free white papers (research) on market segmentation and related topics at **www.decisionanalyst.com/services/ MarketSegmentation.dai?gclid=CKTFIquj1bgCFeXMtAodOBkA-Q**

The Market Segmentation Company (**www.marketsegmentation.co.uk**). The Market Segmentation Company (tMSC) was established in 1995 by Malcolm McDonald, until 2003 Professor of Marketing and Deputy Director Cranfield University School of Management in the UK, where he is now an Emeritus Professor, and Ian Dunbar, a leading practitioner in customer-focused segmentation. They provide a centre of expertise and a resource pool for companies wanting to conduct market segmentation projects and then position these segments at the heart of their marketing strategy.

Market Segmentation Study Guide (**www.segmentationstudyguide.com/ understanding-market-segmentation/main-tools-use/**). A free study guide for segmentation, targeting and positioning.

Strategic Business Insights (**www.strategicbusinessinsights.com/vals/ ustypes.shtml**). VALS™ segments US adults into eight distinct types – or mindsets – using a specific set of psychological traits and key demographics that drive consumer behaviour.

Online video courses and lectures

Consumer Behavior Review – Professor Myles Bassell, Brooklyn College: **www.youtube.com/watch?v=M9DLFDG314E**

Consumer Behavior, The Decision Making Process. Kim Donahue, Kelley School of Business: **www.youtube.com/watch?v=yKb3j45QTpA**

The Consumer Buying Process: How Consumers Make Product Purchase Decisions, Alanis Business Academy: **www.youtube.com/watch?v=zPFeoNkZYGc**

Positioning, Segmentation and Differentiation, IE Business School: **www.youtube.com/watch?v=_0yFXLA6YW0**

Segmentation and Targeting. Wharton, Knowledge for Action: **www.youtube.com/watch?v=9QKGo5rLdw4**

Social Effects in Buying Behavior, Pedro Gardete, Stanford Graduate School of Business, Yale Consumer Insights Conference 2014: **www.youtube.com/watch?v=yLnTSF_ZtVc**

Online video case studies

BMW and Mercedes Benz. HSC Hub: **www.youtube.com/watch?v=yL8NUI_91zk**

Coca-Cola Life. Using Consumer Psychology to Understand Buyer Behaviour. Westminster Business School – Marketing Management 2014: **www.youtube.com/watch?v=aGfdubLAtY8**

Demandware Case Example: Market Segmentation. Hi (Harvard Innovation Lab): **www.youtube.com/watch?v=dZJGNyAwWxE&list=PLv y2hkfDK8JrKqZumPYVbO-qo5qSMU5Pa**

ICI Fertilizers, Market segmentation: a case study by Malcolm McDonald: **www.youtube.com/watch?v=laTzwz08M94**

Pizza Hut Buyer Behavior Analysis 2014. Westminster Business School: **www.youtube.com/watch?v=ao2CNbfklmU_**

Marketing strategy

3

- Marketing strategy, the main options
- Measuring market share
- Understanding marketing dynamics
- The importance of being third
- Investment in brands
- The marketing mix

Strategy has its origins in the military. Webster's *New World Dictionary* defines strategy as 'the science of planning and directing large-scale military operations, of manoeuvring forces into the most advantageous position prior to actual engagement with the enemy'. The earliest known treatise to discuss strategy was Sun Tzu's *The Art of War*, written in 400 BC. His chapter headings – 'Laying Plans', 'Waging War', 'Attack by Stratagem', 'Tactical Dispositions', 'Energy, Weak Points and Strong, Manoeuvring', 'Variations in Tactics', 'The Army on the March', 'Terrain', 'The Nine Situations', 'The Attack by Fire' and 'The Use of Spies' – transpose well into the business world.

It was not unto the early 1900s that idea of strategy began to seep into the business vocabulary. Until the late 19th century firms had generally been simple affairs carrying out a limited range of functions in a tightly concentrated market. True, there were exceptions. Britain's East India Company was granted a monopoly of all trade with the East Indies and acquired a fleet of ships, an army and a governing structure to enforce its rights. But that was very much the exception. Around that period a new type of business came on the scene, first in the United States and later in Europe and beyond. This was a vertically integrated, multidivisional enterprise with a large shareholder base able to make substantial investments in manufacturing and marketing using management hierarchies to direct and control them.

In the 1930s, Chester Barnard, who briefly studied economics at Harvard University, a top executive with AT&T (then American Telephone and Telegraph Company), maintained that managers should be seriously concerned with 'strategic factors', which depend on 'personal or organizational action' (Barnard, C (1968) *The Functions of the Executive*, Harvard University Press, Cambridge, MA). Alfred Sloan, chief executive of General Motors from 1923 to 1946 and which under his direction became the largest company in the world attributed his success as follows: 'It was that plan, policy or strategy of 1921 – whatever it should be called – which I believe more than other single factor enabled us to move into the rapidly changing market of the 1920s with the confidence that we knew what we were doing commercially and were not merely chasing around in search of a luck star' (Sloan, A (1964) *My Years with General Motors*, Doubleday, New York, NY).

The academic study of strategy can be traced back to 1912 when Harvard Business School offered a core course giving students a broader perspective on the strategic problems faced by corporate executives. By the early 1950s, George Albert Smith Jr and C Roland Christensen, two professors at Harvard, taught students to question whether a firm's strategy matched its competitive environment (Smith, G A Jr and Christensen, C R (1959) *Suggestions to Instructors on Policy Formulation*, Homewood, Chicago, IL). Once having sized up the competitive environment, the student was challenged to determine 'On what basis must any one company compete with the others in this particular industry? At what kinds of things does it have to be especially competent, in order to compete?' (Smith, G A Jr (1951) *Policy Formulation and Administration*, Irwin, Chicago, IL).

Peter Drucker, the 'éminence grise' of business management, argued that 'management is not just passive, adaptive behaviour; it means taking action to make the desired results come to pass'. His book *The Practice of Management* (1954, New York) was published after a two-year secondment to General Motors from his teaching job at New York Graduate School of Business. His later works included introducing the concept of Management by Objectives, with its implication that a business should organize itself to achieve strategic goals. Igor Ansoff, while Professor of Industrial Admin-istration in the Graduate School at Carnegie Mellon University, published his landmark book, *Corporate Strategy* (1965), where he explained a way of categorizing strategies as an aid to understanding the nature of the risks involved, ranging from low risk areas such as market development through to high risk areas – diversification.

By the late 1960s Harvard was using tools such as SWOT (strengths, weaknesses, opportunities and threats) analysis to assist with competitive strategy formulation, a process explained and expanded on in the seminal book *Business Policy, Text and Cases* (1969, Learned *et al*). The book, in its 7th revised edition was still in use in business schools around the globe in the early 1990s.

The 1960s and early 1970s saw the subject of strategic planning dominated by consulting practices including the Boston Consulting Group, Bain &

Company, AT Kearney and McKinsey. Between them they produced numerous tools and concepts to advance the practical aspects of using strategic planning in real business situations.

Marketing strategy is such a key part of MBA programmes that many business schools have their very own dedicated professor of that subject. Hiroshi Tanaka, for example, is Professor of Marketing Strategy at Chuo University, Graduate School of Strategic Management, in Tokyo. His track record includes working on such blue-chip accounts as Nestlé, American Express, Unilever, IBM, SmithKline Beecham, Europe Union, United Airlines and Toyota.

Marketing strategy has three dimensions; the intellectual analytical and thinking aspect used to devise broad strategic direction; the development and shaping of specific marketing actions in pursuit of those strategies; and the implementation of strategy through the execution of marketing and business plans. If an organization gets it wrong in any of these areas the results they are aiming for may not be achieved, they may fall behind others in the market or in the worst case fail altogether. Getting all three areas right can be more of an art than a science, rather like a short-sighted person trying to thread several needles held in parallel by different people in one swift movement.

CASE STUDY

In a LinkedIn post (**www.linkedin.com/pulse/making-rain-4-steps-happy-successful-salesforce-michael-dell?trk=prof-post**) on 16 March 2015, Michael Dell announced that, as usual at the beginning of a new fiscal year, 'it's time to rally and align our global salesforce'. Top of his list of key messages was to celebrate. 'Always take time to recognize the successes of your team members. Dell had a great FY15, so we carved out ample time to celebrate together.' In fact the last few years had been tough. Sales had been flat in 2013/14, profits depressed and much time had been spent in fighting off Carl Icahn, the hostile takeover guru, to take the company private in a $25 billion leveraged buyout deal.

The foundations of the company's new found vigour were set back in 2010 when Michael Dell gazing around his empire had plenty to be pleased about. He had come a long way since founding his business from his dorm at the University of Texas nearly a quarter of a century earlier, aged just 19. He had turned his $1,000 initial stake into a business generating over $60 billion a year in revenues, making nearly 16 per cent of PCs sold globally. It was only in 1980 that he had acquired his first computer, the Apple II, and on founding his company, PC Limited, had as his goal to beat IBM. His first product, the Turbo PC, was supported by a no-quibble returns policy and a unique home-support service. The initial public offering (IPO) in 1988 valued his $1,000 business, founded four years earlier, at $85 million. From the outset Dell had three golden rules: disdain inventory, always listen to the customer and cut out middlemen.

An internet pioneer, the company launched a static online ordering page in 1994, and by 1997 Dell.com claimed to be the first company to record a million dollars in online sales.

Dell since its early beginnings has focused on fundamentally different strategies from its competitors. Unlike Apple it has never tried to design sexy devices or to build a global network of retail outlets. Dell's strategy was to create the leanest possible supply chain direct to the end-user while allowing them to choose the features they wanted. It extended that successful strategy across to related products such as servers, printers and storage devices to build a business shipping 140,000 systems a day worldwide – more than one every second – ranking 34 in the Fortune 500 listing of companies, and had become one of the world's leading brands.

But just as Dell looked to be in an unchallengeable position, the company lost its position as the world's biggest maker of personal computers to Hewlett-Packard (HP), a company founded back in 1939 in a Palo Alto garage. No stranger to setbacks, HP had seen that growth in the PC world had crossed from corporate markets to consumers and from developed economies to emerging markets where people had less access to the internet and were both more wary and less able to shop online. In addition, the competition was hotting up on a new front brought about by past success and galloping innovation with auction sites like eBay and uBid enjoying flourishing growth rates in PC sales. Dell saw that it had to develop new strategies for the new environment. As well as beefing up its website and launching 'IdeaStorm', a blog that has already pulled in 9,000 customer suggestions for improvements, the company's products are now in 10,000 outlets worldwide. It has set up a bulk supply chain alongside its lean customized one and started to design products to hanker after rather than just highly specified black boxes. Dell has also bought up several firms in the IT systems management sector as it sees the shift from product- to service-driven growth as an important factor in the future of its business sector. Dell has had to cut $3 billion of expenses, lay off 8,800 employees and change the mindset of its engineers and designers to reposition it to execute its new strategy.

Devising marketing strategy – the overview

Credit for devising the most succinct and usable way to get a handle on the big picture has to be given to Michael E Porter, who trained as an economist at Princeton, taking an MBA (1971) and PhD (1973) at Harvard Business School, where he is now a professor. His book, *Competitive Strategy: Techniques for Analyzing Industries and Competitors* (1980, Free Press, Old Tappan, New Jersey), which is in its 63rd printing and has been translated into 19 languages, sets out the now accepted methodology for devising strategy. As well as being essential reading in most business schools, courses based on Porter's work are taught in partnership with more than 80 other universities around the world, using curriculum, video content and instructor support developed at Harvard.

The three generic strategies

Porter's first observation was that two factors above all influenced a business's chances of making superior profits. First, there was the attractiveness or otherwise of the industry in which it primarily operated. Second – and in terms of an organization's sphere of influence, more importantly – was how the business positioned itself within that industry. In that respect a business could only have a cost advantage in that it could make a product or deliver a service for less than others. Or it could be different in a way that mattered to consumers, so that its offers would be unique, or at least relatively so. He added a further twist to his prescription. Businesses could follow either a cost-advantage path or a differentiation path industry wide, or they could take a third path – they could concentrate on a narrow specific segment either with cost advantage or differentiation. This he termed 'focus' strategy.

TABLE 3.1 Gaining competitive advantage

Market Scope	Competitive Advantage	
	Low Cost	Unique Product and or Service
Broad Whole Market	**Cost Leadership**	**Differentiation**
Narrow Specific Market Segment(s)	**Focus** Low Cost	Differentiation

Cost leadership

Low cost should not be confused with low price. A business with low costs may or may not pass those savings on to customers. Alternatively it could use that position alongside tight cost controls and low margins to create an effective barrier to others considering either entering or extending their penetration of that market. Low-cost strategies are most likely to be achievable in large markets, requiring large-scale capital investment, where production or service volumes are high and economies of scale can be achieved from long runs.

Low costs are not a lucky accident; they can be achieved through these main activities:

- Operating efficiencies: new processes, methods of working or less costly ways of working. Ryanair and easyJet are examples where analysing every component of the business made it possible to strip out major elements of cost – meals, free baggage and allocated seating, for example – while leaving the essential proposition – 'We will fly you from A to B' – intact.

- Product redesign. This involves rethinking a product or service proposition fundamentally to look for more efficient ways to work or cheaper substitute materials to work with. The motor industry has adopted this approach with 'platform sharing', in which major players including Citroen, Peugeot and Toyota have rethought their entry car models to share major components. This has now become common.

- Product standardization. A wide range of product and service offers claiming to extend customer choice invariably leads to higher costs. The challenge is to be sure that proliferation gives real choice and adds value. In 2008 the UK railway network took a long hard look at its dozens of different fare structures and scores of names, often for identical price structures, that had remained largely unchanged since the 1960s, and reduced them to three basic product propositions. Adopting this and other common standards across the rail network, it estimates, will substantially reduce the currently excessive £0.5 billion transaction cost of selling £5 billion worth of tickets.

- Economies of scale. These can be achieved only by being big or bold. The same head office, warehousing network and distribution chain can support Tesco's 3,263 stores as it could, say, the 997 that Somerfield have. The former will have a lower cost base by virtue of having more outlets to spread its costs over as well as having more purchasing power.

The experience (or learning) curve

The fact that costs declined as the output volume of a product or service increased, though well known earlier, was first developed as a usable accounting process by T P Wright, an American aeronautical engineer, in 1936. His process became known as the cumulative average model or Wright's model. Subsequently models were developed by a team of researchers at Stanford known as the unit time model or Crawford's model, and the Boston Consulting Group (BCG) popularized the process with their experience curve, showing that each time the cumulative volume of doing something – either making a product or delivering a service – doubled, the unit cost dropped by a constant and predictable amount. The reasons for the cost drop include:

- Repetition makes people more familiar with tasks and consequently faster.
- More efficient materials and equipment become available from suppliers themselves as their costs go down through the experience curve effect.
- Organization, management and control procedures improve.
- Engineering and production problems are solved.

BCG was founded in 1963 by Bruce D Henderson, a former Bible salesman and engineering graduate from Vanderbilt University, who left the Harvard Business School 90 days before graduation to work for Westinghouse Corporation. From there he went on to head Arthur D Little's management services unit before joining the Boston Safe Deposit and Trust Company to start a consulting arm for the bank. The experience curve was the strategy tool that put BCG on the path to success and has served it well ever since.

The value of the experience curve as a strategic process is that it helps a business predict future unit costs and gives a signal when costs fail to drop at the historical rate, both vital pieces of information for firms pursuing a cost leadership strategy. Every industry has a different experience curve that varies over time. You can find out more about how to calculate the curve for your industry on the Management and Accounting website (**http://maaw.info/ LearningCurveSummary.htm**). The National Aeronautics and Space Agency

FIGURE 3.1 The experience curve

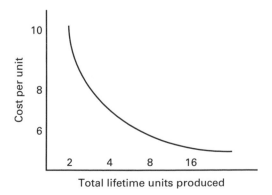

Total lifetime units produced

(**http://fas.org/news/reference/calc/learn.htm**) provides a learning curve calculator.

Differentiation

The key to differentiation is a deep understanding of what customers really want and need and more importantly what they are prepared to pay more for. Apple's opening strategy was based around a 'fun' operating system based on icons, rather than the dull MS-DOS. This belief was based on its understanding that computer users were mostly young and wanted an intuitive command system and the 'graphical user interface' delivered just that. Apple has continued its differentiation strategy, but adds design and fashion to ease of control as the ways in which it delivers extra value. Sony and BMW are also examples of differentiators. Both have distinctive and desirable differences in their products and neither they nor Apple offer the lowest price in their respective industries; customers are willing to pay extra for the idiosyncratic and prized differences embedded in their products.

Differentiation doesn't have to be confined to just the marketing arena, nor does it always lead to success if the subject of that differentiation goes out of fashion without much warning. Northern Rock, the failed bank that had to be nationalized to stay in business, thought its strategy of raising most of the money it lent out in mortgages through the money markets was a sure winner. This allowed the bank to grow faster than its competitors, who placed more reliance on depositors for their funds. As long as interest rates were low and the money market functioned smoothly, it worked. But once the differentiators that fuelled its growth were reversed, its business model failed.

Focus

Focused strategy involves concentrating on serving a particular market or a defined geographic region. IKEA, for example, targets young white-collar workers as its prime customer segment, selling through 235 stores in more than 30 countries. Ingvar Kamprad, an entrepreneur from Småland province in southern Sweden, who founded the business in the late 1940s, offers home furnishing products of good function and design at prices young people can afford. He achieves this by using simple cost-cutting solutions that do not affect the quality of products.

Warren Buffett, the world's richest man, who knows a thing or two about focus, combined with Mars to buy US chewing gum manufacturer Wrigley for $23 billion (£11.6 billion) in May 2008. Chigago-based Wrigley, which launched its Spearmint and Juicy Fruit gums in the 1890s, has specialized in chewing gum ever since and consistently outperformed its more diversified competitors. Wrigley is the only major consumer products company to grow comfortably faster than the population in its markets and above the rate of inflation. Over the past decade or so, for example, other consumer product companies have diversified. Gillette moved into batteries, used to drive many of its products, by acquiring Duracell. Nestlé bought Ralston Purina, Dreyer's, Ice Cream Partners and Chef America. Both have trailed Wrigley's performance.

Businesses often lose their focus over time and periodically have to rediscover their core strategic purpose. Procter & Gamble (P&G) is an example of a business that had to refocus to cure weak growth. In 2000, the company was losing share in seven of its top nine categories, and had lowered earnings expectations four times in two quarters. This prompted the company to restructure and refocus on its core business: big brands, big customers and big countries. They sold off non-core businesses, establishing five global business units with a closely focused product portfolio.

First-to-market fallacy

'Gaining first-mover advantage' are words used like a mantra to justify high expenditure and a headlong rush into new strategic areas. This concept is one of the most enduring in business theory and practice. Entrepreneurs and established giants are always in a race to be first. Research from the 1980s that shows that market pioneers have enduring advantages in distribution, product-line breadth, product quality and, especially, market share underscores this principle.

Beguiling though the theory of first-mover advantage is, it is probably wrong. Gerard Tellis, of the University of Southern California, and Peter Golder, of New York University's Stern business school, argued in their book *Will and Vision: How latecomers grow to dominate markets* (2001, McGraw-Hill) and subsequent research that previous studies on the subject were deeply flawed. In the first instance earlier studies were based on surveys of surviving companies and brands, excluding all the pioneers that failed. This helps some companies look as though they were first to market even when they were not. P&G boasts that it created America's disposable nappy (diaper) business. In fact, a company called Chux launched its product a quarter of a century before P&G entered the market in 1961.

Also, the questions used to gather much of the data in earlier research were at best ambiguous, and perhaps dangerously so. For example the term, 'one of the pioneers in first developing such products or services', was used as a proxy for 'first to market'. The authors emphasize their point by listing popular misconceptions of who were the real pioneers across the 66 markets they analysed; online book sales: Amazon (wrong), Books.com (right); copiers: Xerox (wrong), IBM (right); PCs: IBM/Apple (both wrong) – Micro Instrumentation Telemetry Systems (MITS) introduced its PC, the Altair, a $400 kit, in 1974, followed by Tandy Corporation (Radio Shack) in 1977.

In fact, the most compelling evidence from all the research was that nearly half of all firms pursuing a first-to-market strategy were fated to fail, while those following fairly close behind were three times as likely to succeed. Tellis and Golder claim the best strategy is to enter the market 19 years after pioneers, learn from their mistakes, benefit from their product and market development, and be more certain about customer preferences.

Industry analysis

Aside from articulating the generic approach to business strategy, Porter's other major contribution to the field was what has become known as the Five Forces theory of industry structure. Porter postulated that the five forces that drive competition in an industry have to be understood as part of process of choosing which of the three generic strategies to pursue. The forces he identified are:

1 Threat of substitution. Can customers buy something else instead of your product? For example, Apple and to a lesser extent Sony, have laptop computers that are distinctive enough to make substitution difficult. Dell, on the other hand, faces intense competition from dozens of other suppliers with near-identical products competing mostly on price alone.

2 Threat of new entrants. If it is easy to enter your market, start-up costs are low and there are no barriers to entry such as intellectual property protection, then the threat is high.

3 Supplier power. The fewer the suppliers, usually the more powerful they are. Oil is a classic example, where fewer than a dozen countries supply the whole market and consequently can set prices.

FIGURE 3.2   Five Forces theory of industry analysis (after Porter)

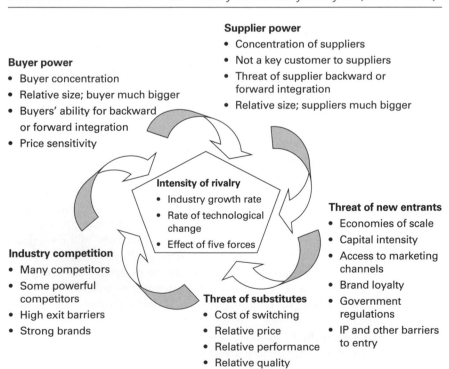

Supplier power
- Concentration of suppliers
- Not a key customer to suppliers
- Threat of supplier backward or forward integration
- Relative size; suppliers much bigger

Buyer power
- Buyer concentration
- Relative size; buyer much bigger
- Buyers' ability for backward or forward integration
- Price sensitivity

Intensity of rivalry
- Industry growth rate
- Rate of technological change
- Effect of five forces

Threat of new entrants
- Economies of scale
- Capital intensity
- Access to marketing channels
- Brand loyalty
- Government regulations
- IP and other barriers to entry

Industry competition
- Many competitors
- Some powerful competitors
- High exit barriers
- Strong brands

Threat of substitutes
- Cost of switching
- Relative price
- Relative performance
- Relative quality

4 Buyer power. In the food market, for example, with just a few powerful supermarket buyers being supplied by thousands of much smaller businesses, these buyers are often able to dictate terms.

5 Industry competition. The number and capability of competitors are one determinant of a business's power. Few competitors with relatively less attractive products or services lower the intensity of rivalry in a sector. Often these sectors slip into oligopolistic behaviour (see also Chapter 7), preferring to collude rather than compete.

You can see a video clip of Professor Porter discussing the Five Forces model on the Harvard Business School website or at: **http://www.youtube.com/watch?v=mYF2_FBCvXw**.

PEST analysis

This is a framework predating Porter's Five Forces approach that categorizes the external factors that influence strategy under the headings of political, economic, social and technological forces. Often two additional factors, environmental and legal, are added, changing the acronym to PESTEL.

FIGURE 3.3   PESTEL analysis framework

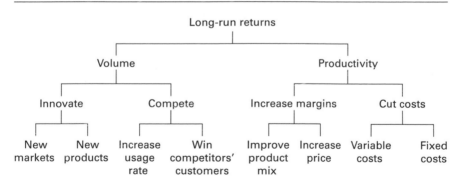

Examples of PEST events that have had a major effect on marketing strategy include:

● Pendragon, Britain's biggest car dealer (Stratstone, selling luxury brands, Mercedes, BMW and Jaguar, and Evans Halshaw, selling volume cars such as Ford and Vauxhall), made a loss of £194 million in 2008 and was close to collapse. Its shares were trading at less than 2p each, valuing it at £10 million, when a year earlier it had bought out rival Reg Varly for £500 million in a hotly contested takeover battle. Yet by February 2010 the business was back in the black and its shares were up 3,000 per cent from their low point 18 months earlier. The miracle marketing cure that delivered this result was the used car scrappage scheme pressed onto a sceptical Labour government by the motor industry in 2009 to save it from total collapse. The scheme put £2,000 of taxpayer's money on the table when any car over six years old was traded in.

- GlaxoSmithKline responded to a UK government scheme known as the 'patent box', that in effect cuts tax on patents developed in the UK to just 10 per cent, by planning to create 1,000 new jobs. This change, one that already operates in Switzerland, Belgium and the Netherlands, makes it more attractive to develop new pharmaceutical products in the UK than was previously the case.

Getting the measure of markets

The starting point in marketing strategy is definition of the scope of the market you are in or are aiming for. This comes from the business objectives, mission and vision that form the heart of the strategy of the enterprise. These are topics covered in the strategy section of Chapter 12. For most MBA graduates for most of the time these will be a 'given' and as such will not inhibit your ability to apply the marketing concepts explored in this chapter. So, for example, if you are working in, say, The Body Shop, McDonald's, IBM, a hospital trust or the Prison Service, the broad market thrust of your current business will be self-evident. Later you may want or need to change strategic direction, but effective marketing is concerned fundamentally with dealing with a defined product/service and market scope. These concepts apply to any marketing activity, but you will find that understanding them is made easier by applying them to the business you are in, or have some appreciation of.

Assessing the relevant market

Much of marketing is concerned with achieving goals such as selling a specific quantity of a product or service or capturing market share. MBAs are frequently set the challenging task of measuring the size of the market. In principle this is not too difficult. Desk research (see the discussion of market research later in this chapter) will yield a sizeable harvest of statistics of varying degrees of reliability. You will be able to discover that the consumption of bread in Europe is £10 billion a year. But first you need a definition of bread. The industry-wide definition of bakery includes sliced and unsliced bread, rolls, bakery snacks and speciality breads. It covers both plant-baked products (those that are baked by in-store bakers) and products sold through craft bakers.

Assessing the relevant market, then, involves refining global statistics down to provide the real scope of your market. If your business only operates in the UK, the market is worth over £2.7 billion, equivalent to 12 million loaves a day, one of the largest sectors in food.

If you are only operating in the craft bakery segment, then the relevant market shrinks down to £13.5 million; this contracts down still further to £9.7 million if you are only operating within the radius of the M25.

The importance of market share

The relevant market will be shared by various competing businesses in different proportions. Typically there will be a market leader, a couple of market followers and a host of businesses trailing in their wake. The portion each competitor has of a market is its market share. You will find that marketing people are fixated on market share, perhaps even more so than on absolute sales. That may appear little more than a rational desire to beat the 'enemy' and appear higher in rankings, but it has a much more deep-seated and profound logic.

Back in the 1960s a firm of American management consultants observed a consistent relationship between the cost of producing an item (or delivering a service) and the total quantity produced over the life of the product concerned. They noticed that total unit costs (labour and materials) fell by between 20 per cent and 30 per cent for every doubling of the cumulative quantity produced (see earlier in this chapter for more on the experience curve effect).

Figure 3.4 demonstrates the advantage of market share even where the shares are relatively small and the businesses are already operating successfully. Nairn's larger market share gives it an eighth more profit per percentage point of market share than its smaller rival. Natural Balance Foods, the brand behind Nakd and Trek bars was started in Oxfordshire by Californian-born brothers Jamie and Greg Combs in 2005. Securing a contract to supply the British Athletic Association boosted its credibility. The need to grow market share explained, in part at least, why in March 2015 the company hired advisors at industry specialist Stamford Partners to find new investors to fund growth.

Competitive position

It follows that if market share and relative size are important marketing goals, you need to assess your products and services positions relative to the competition in your market. The techniques most used to carry out this analysis are SWOT analysis and perceptual mapping.

FIGURE 3.4   Market share of UK Gluten Free segment of the food market

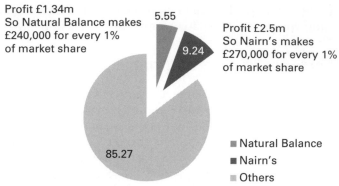

Market Share

Profit £1.34m
So Natural Balance makes
£240,000 for every 1%
of market share

5.55

Profit £2.5m
So Nairn's makes
£270,000 for every 1%
of market share

9.24

85.27

■ Natural Balance
■ Nairn's
■ Others

Strengths, weaknesses, opportunities and threats (SWOT)

This is a general-purpose tool developed in the late 1960s at Harvard by Learned, Christensen, Andrews and Guth, and published in their seminal book, *Business Policy, Text and Cases* (1969, Richard D Irwin). The SWOT framework consists of a cross with space in each quadrant to summarize your observations, as in Figure 3.5.

FIGURE 3.5   Example SWOT chart for a hypothetical Cobra Beer competitor

Strengths	*Weaknesses*
1. Beginning to get brand recognition 2. Established strongly in Indian restaurants	1. Don't have own production 2. Need more equity finance to be able to advertise more strongly
Opportunities	*Threats*
1. We could capitalize more on our relationships in Indian restaurants 2. We are only in the UK – so have the world to go for	1. We are vulnerable to a big player targeting our niche 2. Our sector looks like being the target of major tax rises which could reduce overall demand

In this example the SWOT analysis is restricted to a handful of areas, though in practice the list might run to a dozen or more areas within each of the four quadrants. The purpose of the SWOT analysis is to suggest possible ways to improve competitive position and hence market share while minimizing the dangers of perceived threats. A strategy that this SWOT would suggest as being worth pursuing could be to launch a low-alcohol product (and sidestep the tax threat) that would appeal to all restaurants, rather than just Indian (widen the market). The company could also start selling in India, using the international cachet of being a UK brand. That would open up the market still further and limit the damage that larger UK competitors could inflict.

SWOT is also used as a tool in strategic analysis and indeed it was so used by General Electric in the 1980s. While it is a useful way of pulling together a large amount of information in a way that is easy for managers to assimilate, it can be most effective when used in individual market segments, as a strength in one segment could be a weakness in another. For example, giving a product features that would enhance its appeal to the retiree market might reduce its appeal to other market segments.

CASE STUDY TomTom

In February 2015 TomTom's Chief Executive Officer Harold Goddijn stated that the company was well on track to fully replacing their map-making system with a transaction-based platform that will enable near real-time maps in the second half of 2015. The preceding year saw TomTom claim to have 52 per cent of the European market for PNDs (Portable Navigation Devices), a market the company assessed as nearly 7 million units a year. With revenue approaching £1 billion per year, the company has come a long way since 1991, when TomTom was founded and began a journey that would change the way people drive forever.

Harold Goddijn and Corinne Vigreux, married for more than two decades, are the co-founders of the satellite navigation device that has come to define the sector. Vigreux studied at a Paris business school starting out at a French games firm before moving to the UK to Psion, then a FTSE 100 technology company famed for its handheld PDA (Personal Digital Assistant). Goddijn read economics at Amsterdam University and whilst working for a venture capital firm came across some of Psion's handheld computers and organizers and was impressed. He approached Psion suggesting a joint distribution venture selling the company's products in the Netherlands. Vigreux was sent to the Netherlands to negotiate with Goddijn, the first time the pair had met. They married in 1991 and Vigreux resigned from Psion and moved to Amsterdam.

A brief spell working for a Dutch dairy cooperative saw Vigreux suffering from technology withdrawal symptoms. With software wizards Peter-Frans Pauwels and Pieter Geelen, she started Palmtop Software, later to become TomTom, designing software such as dictionaries, accounting packages and diet books that could be loaded on to Palm Pilots and Pocket PCs. In late 1998 Goddijn and Vigreux saw a navigation system built for a computer and gradually the idea took shape. Three years and €4 million later the quartet had created the TomTom, launching it at €799. Even at this price it was far cheaper than existing products and superior in that it featured a touch screen, a first for the sector.

The year after launch the company floated, selling 50 per cent of the business to fund the growth and acquisition. But 2008 saw them hit turbulence. The credit crunch, market saturation, a high level of debt, and Google starting to offer maps for free represented more serious problems in a single year than many face in a lifetime. The company restructured, reduced debt and now generate half their revenue from selling licences to their maps, constructing in-built systems for the car industry, and telematics. TomTom Telematics is now recognized as a leading provider of telematics solutions with over 350,000 subscriptions worldwide. In 2013 TomTom launched its own branded GPS sport watches to help runners, cyclists and swimmers keep moving towards their fitness goals, by providing essential performance information at a glance. The company now employs 3,600 people and is a globally recognized brand.

Perceptual mapping

Perceptual or positioning maps are much used by marketing executives to position products and services relative to competitors on two dimensions. In Figure 3.6 the positions of companies competing in a particular industry are compared on price and quality, on a spectrum from low to high.

Similar maps can be produced for any combination of variables that are of importance to customers – availability, product range, after-sales support, market image and so on. The technique is used in a variety of ways including highlighting possible market gaps when one quadrant is devoid of players, suggesting areas to be built on or extended, or where a USP (see below) is required to create a competitive edge.

Brands

A brand is a distinguishing trademark, logo, name, term, sentence or a combination of these items that distinguishes a company's product or service

FIGURE 3.6   Perceptual mapping

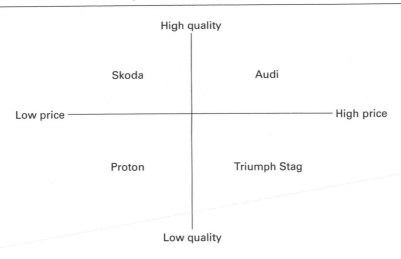

from others in the market, so creating a positive reaction among its target audience, who become loyal consumers. The term is derived from the Old Norse 'brandr', meaning 'to burn', and refers to the custom of owners burning their mark (or brand) onto their goods, usually though not always, cattle. From the 1950s the concept of branding moved into the mainstream of marketing. Consumer packaged goods companies like Procter & Gamble, Unilever and Heinz developed the discipline of appointing a manager to oversee a product or group of products, ensuring that they would outsell their competitors. These appointees soon became known as brand managers and they became responsible for giving a product an identity that allowed it to stand out from competitors offering very much the same product. One bar of soap does pretty much what every other bar of soap on the market does.

The brand manager's task was to understand their target consumer so that they could create a value proposition over and above the purely functional value of the product. This emotional value was reinforced over time by heavy promotional spend and over time, the emotional value came to protect the brand from competitors who could only offer the same functionality. A strong brand was seen in the eyes of the consumer as offering superior value to its competitors so allowing the company to charge a premium for its products. If the value of the premium was greater than the cost of building a brand, the company created a sum that became known as the brand value.

Building a brand

This is considered the holy grail of the product/service aspect of the marketing mix. A brand encompasses not just what a product is or does but all the elements such as logo, symbols, image, reputation and associations. McDonald's arches represent its brand as a welcoming beacon, drawing customers in. Branding is an intangible way of differentiating a product in a way that captures and retains markets through loyalty to that brand.

To some people, Coca-Cola might taste little different from a supermarket brand, but the promotion that supports the brand confers on the consumer the chance to share the attractive lifestyle of those 'cool' people in the adverts. Apple's iPod is differentiated from just any old MP3 player in much the same way. Intel and Audi are examples of branding designed to reassure consumers in unfamiliar territory that a product will deliver. Body Shop International exudes ethics and concern for the environment, where other cosmetics concentrate on how they will make the wearer look beautiful.

Building a brand takes time and a considerable advertising budget. But by creating brand value – that is, the price premium commanded by that product over its unbranded or less appealing competitors – a business can end up with a valuable asset.

Branding on the internet has been less successful to date. When they work, brands provide benefits for both consumers and suppliers. Customers like brands because it saves them spending time finding out about the features and benefits of all the products and services they buy. A familiar brand reassures the customer that the product or service has certain qualities. The theory then is that the customer is willing to pay a premium for this reassurance. That then is the benefit that a supplier could expect.

Unfortunately, the theory of brands is proving harder to transpose to the internet than many hoped. The problem is that 'service' brands, which are really what you will be trying to establish via the internet, are for the most part invisible. This in turn makes it hard for an internet brand to deliver one other major benefit consumers hope to get from a brand: the admiration and perhaps even the envy of their peers. The logo on a T-shirt or pair of trainers, clearly marked for all to see, is, for some consumers, the most important value of the transaction. But all the internet firm may do is deliver a service that no one else can see. Even where a tangible product is delivered, such as a book or record, it will not be obvious to the onlooker who your internet supplier was. A further problem for the e-business is that information on a competitor's offer is only a click away, making customers even more fickle than ever, and much more likely to compare prices each time they make a purchase.

What branding can do for a business

The share prices of the top 100 brands as identified in the BrandZ study have outperformed the S&P 500 by over 40 per cent over the period 2008–15. In fact whilst companies in the S&P 500 lost 11.5 per cent in value, those of the top 100 brands gained 18.5 per cent. The reasons for this out-performance in hard times seem to be:

- A brand generates trust, a fact that appears to transcend business sectors. Consumers are as loyal to Coca-Cola, Procter & Gamble and

WalMart as business users are to Cisco, HSBC and Goldman Sachs for a company, for its products, and for its services. According to BrandZ consideration of brand in the purchase decision has risen by 20 percentage points since 2005 so in uncertain economic conditions people turn to something they can trust – an established brand.

- Brands are established in almost every corner of the globe. In China, India and Russia brands are as prevalent as in France, the UK or the United States. Today over a dozen emerging market economies now have world-class brands, where there were none at all in 2000. This global dimension allows businesses with top brands to keep growing across economic cycles. So while the Western economies shrank between 2008 and 2010, China, India, Brazil and much of South America were powering ahead.

- The population of top brands is relatively stable, and that in turn allows them the luxury of formulating and implementing long-term strategy, rather than being buffeted by turbulence. Seven of the same brands are present in both the 2007 and the 2013 BrandZ rankings. True, some positions have changed with Google now number 1 brand up from 7th in 2006 and IBM in the second slot up from 8th. This resilience means that firms such as Starbucks, Samsung, Toyota and Exxon had the ability to recover from difficulties relatively quickly. Exxon, for example, a virtual pariah after the Valdez oil spill disaster in 1989, was back in the top rankings in under a decade, coming in at 39th in the world, ahead of Disney, Orange and Colgate. It remains to be seen if BP is as fortunate.

Branding pitfalls

Brands have global visibility and as a consequence problems can appear to be on some distant horizon yet suddenly become amplified and virtually omnipresent with unfortunate consequences. Nowhere has this capacity to suffer global reputation for local or narrow specific problems been more in evidence than the fall from grace in 2010 of two of the world's most successful brands, BP ranked 34th and Toyota ranked 26th in the top 100 brands of 2009/10. Both brands suffered catastrophic, though perhaps not terminal, blows to their reputations for quality, integrity and honesty.

Whilst BP tussled with leaking oil in the Gulf of Mexico, it received four times as many mentions in the world press as it did two years earlier on 29 July 2008 when it announced record profits of £3.5 billion ($5.53 billion) for a single quarter. Though the brand may survive on the international arena a survey running on a local Gulf website puts 48 per cent in favour of adopting Amoco for US gas stations, a brand it abandoned when that company was acquired by BP. Toyota and its near-invisible chairman Akio Toyoda, also found themselves the centre of a storm of unwelcome public visibility when the company had to recall a few million cars for a variety of reasons – ranging from sticking accelerator peddles to steering lock defects.

Sources of information on branding

BrandZ (**www.brandz.com**), a research company that studies global brands, has asked over 1.5 million consumers and professionals across 31 countries to compare over 50,000 brands each year since 2005. They rank the top 100 brands each year.

Superbrands (**www.superbrands.com**) has a listing of the top brands by country, often with a case study supporting the top brands in any country.

Marketing mix

Marketing mix refers to the mix of ingredients with which marketing strategy can be developed and implemented. The ingredients, originally referred to as the 4 Ps, are: price, product (or/and service), promotion and place. This is now extended to 7Ps, people, process and physical evidence, to accommodate the increasing emphasis on customer focus in business. Just as with cooking, taking the same or similar ingredients in different proportions can result in very different 'products'. The ingredients in the marketing mix represent only the elements that are largely, though not entirely, within a firm's control. Uncontrollable ingredients include the state of the economy, changes in legislation, new and powerful market entrants and rapid changes in technology.

Origins

The term 'marketing mix' has a pedigree going back to the late 1940s when marketing managers referred to mixing ingredients to create strategies. James W Coulton, a Harvard Business School professor, made the earliest recorded reference to the term 'mix' in this context in an article, *The Management of Marketing Costs* (Division of Research, Graduate School of Business Administration, Harvard University, 1948). In this study of manufacturers' marketing costs Coulton described the business executive as a 'decider, an artist – a mixer of ingredients, who sometimes follows a recipe prepared by others, sometimes prepares his own recipe as he goes along, sometimes adapts a recipe to the ingredients immediately available, and sometimes experiments with or invents ingredients no one else has tried'.

A Harvard colleague of Coulton, Neil Borden liked his idea of calling a marketing executive a 'mixer of ingredients', one who is constantly engaged in fashioning creatively a mix of marketing procedures and policies in his efforts to produce a profitable enterprise. He introduced the term 'marketing mix' into his 1953 American Marketing Association Presidential Address, and went on to summarize his ideas on how to use the concept in 1964 in his paper, The Concept of the Marketing Mix (*Journal of Advertising Research*, 4 (2), pp 2–7).

By the time Borden's work was published a rash of academics had arrived on the scene. P J Verdoorn's Marketing from the Producer's Point of View (*Journal of Marketing*, 20 January 1956, pp 221–35) and Albert W Frey's *The Effective Marketing Mix: Programming for Optimum Results* (1956) The Amos Tuck School, Dartmouth College, Hanover, NH) were just two of the many influential works on the subject.

Early proponents of the marketing mix advanced a variety of checklists of decision variables, given a variety of different forms. It was down to a relative latecomer, E Jerome McCarthy, a marketing professor at Michigan State University to coin the expression, the 4 Ps: product, price, place and promotion – which became the most popular. In his 1960 book, *Basic Marketing: A Managerial Approach* (Irwin, Homewood, IL), McCarthy suggested that 'it is useful to reduce the number of variables in the marketing mix to four basic ones – Product, Place, Promotion, Price'.

Mary Jo Bitner (Arizona State University) and Bernard H Booms (Washington State University) in a 1981 paper Marketing Strategies and Organization Structures for Service Firms (in Donnelly, J H and George, W R (eds), *Marketing of Services*, American Marketing Association, Chicago) modified and expanded the traditional marketing mix elements from 4 Ps to become 7 Ps by adding three new Ps – people, process and physical evidence. The authors had in mind the unique problems in marketing intangible services, however as almost every 'product' has a major service element, the 7 Ps have been adopted in mainstream marketing mix analysis.

Using the marketing mix

A change in the way the elements in the marketing mix are put together can produce an offering tailored to meet the needs of a specific market segment. For example, a hardback book is barely more expensive to produce than a paperback. However, with a bit of clever publicity, bringing a hardback out a few weeks before the paperback edition, and a hefty price hike, an air of exclusivity can be created which satisfies a particular group of customers. A similar effect can be achieved by carefully timing the launch of an e-version (Kindle *et al*), shortly after the paper version.

In the e-business world the same rules apply. You can take almost any business proposition and change the ingredients in the marketing mix to appeal more specifically to one of the target **market segments** you have identified as being worth pursuing. Take an online share dealing business, for example. Their key market segments may include such diverse groups of clients as day traders, novice share clubs and sophisticated private investors. The company's core 'product', which consists of providing information to enable investors to make choices and so place orders, can be altered along with other elements of the marketing mix, to appeal more to a certain segment.

Using the marketing mix successfully in your organization can help your organization to:

- Get a better fit between your product service offer and your customer segments requirements. Often organizations spend more time looking in than out. As a consequence much of what they do is to meet their needs rather than those of the customers. Using the elements of the marketing mix to produce a product or service that delivers more value at the same or a lower cost is a key benefit that arises from analysing your marketing.

- Make more profit. It follows that if you are better at meeting a particular customer segments needs through changing elements in the marketing mix you should be able to command a better price or capture a larger market share.

- Improve the efficiency of your marketing efforts. Analysing the elements of the marketing mix and the extent to which they matter to your customers will help improve the way you deal with your customers. If your customers want a price quote faster than you currently provide, then that is the element of 'price' you need to examine. If certain important customer segments want products in a different size, as with all liquid containers destined for cabin luggage on flights post 9/11 then there is an opportunity to produce toiletries in containers smaller than 100 ml.

- Provide new product opportunities. British American Tobacco (BAT), the world's second biggest tobacco company, saw its sales slump to 332 billion cigarettes in the first half of 2013, against 344 billion in the first half of 2012, as mature markets proved less lucrative. The company, which owns Lucky Strike, Dunhill, Kent and Pall Mall, revealed revenues of £7.57 billion in the first half of 2013, up 2 per cent on the previous year and pre-tax profits were up slightly too. Smokers were paying on average 7 per cent more for cigarettes than the year before, due in part to price increases and to consumers upgrading to premium brands. BAT decided on an aggressive expansion of its nascent electronic cigarettes business in an effort to counter declining sales. BAT is using some of its profits from conventional cigarette sales. In August 2013 BAT started selling its Vype e-cigarette brand over the internet in Britain with a roll out to other European countries and the US scheduled to follow soon after. Kingsley Wheaton, BAT's director of corporate affairs announced it to be their 'declared intent to be the leading player in that business. The market is currently small and fragmented but showing movement, creating a buzz.'

- Develop specific product features. The iPhone 4S is a case in point. Launched in October 2011 and sandwiched between the 4 that came on stream in June 2010 and the 5 that arrived in September 2012. The iPhone 3 was introduced in 2008 so the 4S represented a minor product adjustment to the marketing mix, launched the day before Steve Jobs, Apple's co-founder and the inspiration behind Apple's iPhone and a host of other iDevices, died. The new feature introduced in the 4S was a new voice-activated assistant, called 'Siri'.

- Introduce new service options. Service can be one of the quickest and cheapest elements of the marketing mix to change. Live traffic avoidance systems offered by brands such as TomTom (HD Traffic) and Garmin (3D Traffic Live) on their mid-range and high-end sat-navs are examples of how the market leaders keep a healthy distance between themselves and their less nimble competitors.

- Build an optimal distribution strategy. The classic route to market with the birth of the internet was to move from 'bricks to clicks', taking a physical presence and putting the offer online. Amazon and Ocado are relative oddities in going the other way. Another group that are going from online beginnings to a physical presence in their efforts to build the best route to market is Connections Academy. Launched in 2001 with 400 students, they offered a complete, full-time education online for kindergarten through 12th grade students. Their target market was those who for reasons of work, health or ability wanted or needed to learn at home rather than in a school setting. However, Connection's Executive Vice President Steven Guttentag, recognized that though a life saver for some students, this was always going to be a 'drop in the bucket'. Connections had 30,000 of the country's 50 million potential students and could see a total market of two million. Blended learning with online material delivered from a physical premises where students could have PE, lunch and contact time with teachers on school campus was the key to tapping into a much larger market. In 2005 they set up their first school, in 2009 they partnered with an all-boys school in Texas and are now setting up their own blended or hybrid schools, and applying for a hybrid charter.

- Optimize product pricing. Price is the easiest element of the marketing mix to change quickly and can deliver some stunning results in terms of increased sales volume and profit. Booking.com, the hotel booking website, changed its flat commission pricing model to one of bidding for a place on the first page of a destination. Priceline, Bookings.com parent company saw revenues explode from $3,084 million in 2010 to $5,261 million in 2012.

CASE STUDY   Match.com

From a seedy corner of the internet on the fringes of pornography, online dating is now a mainstream business with global reach. Those in search of friendship and more have extended their reach from local classified adverts to stretch out to the furthest continents. People from New York and Boston can hook up with those from Saigon and Manila with as little effort as a stroll to their local newsagent. According to the US Census, some 40 million of the 90 million singles in the US have tried online dating. YouGov statistics show that one in five relationships in the UK now begins online, and meeting via the internet is the third most popular way to find a date behind 'through friends' or making acquaintance at a pub or bar. Today Match.com generates over $400 million a year in revenue and has 1.8 million paying users.

Gary Kremen, Match.com's founder, started out in a very different field of business. In 1989, the year he completed his MBA at Stanford, he co-founded, Los Altos Technologies (**www.lat.com**), a company that cleaned sensitive data off hard drives for the military and other businesses. Sold to an employee in late 1992, the company is still in business. At LAT, Kremen noticed an important demographic change. New systems such as IBM's Lotus Note enabled administrative staff to send electronic purchase orders without resorting to the assistance of IT staff. That in turn meant an increasing number of women were using these tools to go online for the first time. A user himself of telephone-based dating agencies, he saw a parallel potential in the small but growing presence of women online.

With Electric Classifieds founded in 1993, Kremen developed the idea to do classified ads but make it electric, as a test for his idea of doing something similar in the dating market. He saw the mouth-watering revenues that print media made from classified advertising. The Los Angeles Times made 40 per cent of their overall revenue from classifieds. A quarter of that was from personal ads. Two years later, the test proving successful, he unveiled Match.com. Backed with €200,000 of venture finance the company was one of the first sites to use the internet to smooth the progress of dating. The company was among the first to charge money for this service, which in turn put a tremendous pressure on delivering value. In 1995 few people were online and even fewer were women looking for men. Kremen started out by designing the site with women in mind. 'You have to design the whole system for women, not men,' he said. 'Who cares what men think? So things like security and anonymity were important. And little things, like talking about body types, not pounds. Never ask a woman her weight.' But still Match.com struggled to get the numbers to sign up. And online dating is very much a numbers game. Kremen got everyone he knew to sign as well as getting his employees to create profiles. He and his girlfriend signed up, too, with an unforeseen and unwelcome outcome. Kremen's girlfriend met another man through Match and left him. On the upside at least he had proof positive that the site worked.

Codenamed 'Synapse', Match developed an algorithm that, while taking into account a user's stated preferences, such as desired age range, hair colour and body type, it also learns from their actions on the site. So, if a man says he doesn't want to date anyone older than 30, but often looks at profiles of forty-some-things, Match deduces that he is in fact open to meeting older women. Synapse also uses 'triangulation', looking at the behaviour of similar users and factors in that information, too. Match uses its customer knowledge to operate a readily varied pricing strategy. Match.com operates in a highly competitive and fragmented market, with a low barrier for competition to enter the market. Online dating software is inexpensive; website creation is simple and the market huge. Though their largest age group is between 30 and 49 years old, some 15 per cent of members are 50 years and older, an age group likely to grow fast given high divorce rates and the large number of baby boomers. Nevertheless with an estimated 8,000 competitors worldwide and 1,000 new online dating services opening, every year price is a sensitive issue.

Match spends over $70 million in television, radio, and fees to online search engines and distribution partners. That draws people to the website, but pricing strategy is used to pull them in. Match.com's tiered pricing menu reflects price discrimination strategy known in the trade as 'goldilocks'. By offering three price options, potential clients are in effect offered a Good-Better-Best choice. People who are unsure what they want will usually buy the middle, or 'Better' choice out of Good-Better-Best, so providing a middle choice is key to having an acceptable enquiry to conversion ratio. Match.com also uses an à la carte pricing strategy. In addition to the monthly subscription fee, subscribers are offered additional routes of communicating with other prospective dates, through video, voice mail, and text messaging. Once members join as a basic subscriber, Match.com increases revenue by offering premium or supplemental services. Seasonal offers are also made, capitalizing, for example, on the post-Christmas slump as the time to find romance. The period between Boxing Day and the turn of the year is the busiest for online dating sites with some websites reporting a treble-digit increase in traffic. In that week alone Match.com has over three million e-mail messages sent by hopeful site users.

Kremen and his board had a number of disagreements resulting in the company being sold in 1998 for $7m to Cendant, a Connecticut consumer-services business. A year later, Cendant sold it to IAC, trading as Ticketmaster, for $50m. Kremen got little from the initial sale; barely $50,000 and a lifetime account on the website, which proved of little value as he met and married his wife in a very low tech way; through a mutual friend. Kremen's fortune came from a different sort of sex. In 2001 he was awarded $65 million in a dispute over the domain name sex.com, which he registered in the '90s. Then, in 2004, after Electric Classifieds went out of business, Kremen bought the company for $20,000 in order to retrieve its valuable patent selling it on almost immediately for $1.7 million.

The next five chapters that follow essentially expand on these elements of the mix explaining their fit in the overall strategic marketing process.

Sources of help and advice with the marketing mix

Analytics Partners: They have a neat free Marketing Mix Modelling tool that lets you 'Leveraging Marketing MixSimulations for Business Planning' (**www.analyticpartners.com/services/marketing-mix-modeling**)

How to achieve an effective marketing mix. The Chartered Institute of Marketing: Here you can find this tool to help you find the optimum marketing mix in your business (**www.cim.co.uk/files/marketingmix.pdf**)

Online video courses and lectures

Business strategy. Professor Carlo Alberto Carnevale Maffe of SDA Bocconi School of Management, Milan: **www.youtube.com/watch?v=a_1O-3xhKm4**

Evolution of Marketing Mix Models and Optimization. CommNexus is a non-profit technology industry association whose webcast can be see here: **http://vimeo.com/68570749**

The Five Competitive Forces That Shape Strategy, Professor Michael Porter, interviewed for the Harvard Business Review: **www.youtube.com/watch?v=mYF2_FBCvXw**

Generic Strategies. Professor David Kryscynski of Goizueta Business School, Emory University, Atlanta, Georgia: **www.youtube.com/watch?v=V14kuqYEsxE**

Good Strategy/Bad Strategy: the difference and why it matters, Professor Richard Rumelt at the LSE: **www.youtube.com/watch?v=UZrTl16hZdk**

How to Build a Strategy for 'the Long Game'. Paul Schoemaker, research director for Wharton's Mack Institute for Innovation Management: **http://knowledge.wharton.upenn.edu/article/how-to-build-a-strategy-for-the-long-game**

How to Complete a SWOT Analysis: Alanis Business Academy: **www.youtube.com/watch?v=0D2fT6obqdg**

How to Cut Costs – Strategically. Cesare Mainardi, Managing Director Booz & Company, Harvard Business Publishing: **http://freevideolectures.com/Course/2526/Strategy**

The Importance of urgency. Professor John Kotter, Harvard Business: **http://freevideolectures.com/Course/2526/Strategy/7**

Introduction to Strategic Management, by Professor David Kryscynski of Goizueta Business School, Emory University, Atlanta, Georgia: **www.youtube.com/watch?v=rJ2tmqRkiCM**

Reinventing Your Business Model. Professor Clayton M Christensen, Harvard Business School, talks to the Harvard Business Review: **https://hbr.org/2008/12/reinventing-your-business-model**

The reinvention of brands and marketers – Mark Zablan, President of Adobe: **http://tv.adobe.com/watch/adobe-summit-2014-emea/ the-reinvention-of-brands-and-marketers-mark-zablan/**

Transforming Giants. Professor Rosabeth MossKanter, Harvard Business: **http://freevideolectures.com/Course/2526/Strategy/8**

Online video case studies

Airbnb. Nathan Blecharczyk – CTO and co-founder talks about their strategy to reach customers located in 192 different countries: **www.akamai.com/html/customers/testimonials/airbnb.html**

Costa Coffee: Project Marlow 'Saving the World from Mediocre Coffee'. Jim Slater (Managing Director, Costa Enterprises), presents a case study from Costa Coffee at the London Business School's Deloitte Institute of Innovation and Entrepreneurship: **www.youtube.com/ watch?v=0wLjM9BYUYs**

Facebook Strategy Revealed: Move Fast And Break Things! Business Insider: **www.businessinsider.com/henry-blodget-innovation-highlights-2010-2?IR=T**

Grace Vineyard, China. Judy Leissner, CEO speaks to INSEAD about the strategy used to make their Reserve Merlot/Cabernet 'the finest wine so far made in the country that is already the world's sixth most important grower of grapevines': **www.youtube.com/watch?v=y20iOjyNDE4**

The Intel 80386 Business Case: Under the leadership of Andy Grove and Gordon Moore, the personal computer market changed in October 1985 with the launch of the Intel 80386 microprocessor. Harvard Business School Professor Richard S Tedlow presents and reviews Intel's business strategy: **www.youtube.com/watch?v=XFgFWdxHlLc**

Just-Eat. MD of the Irish company, Amanda Roche-Kelly, discusses with Silicon Republic, the group strategy and how Ireland became their fastest-growing market. Their Irish website attracts more than 6m visitors a year: **www.siliconrepublic.com/new-media/item/ 37593-the-interview-just-eat-ie**

LinkedIn. CEO Jeff Weiner and LinkedIn's SVP of Global Solutions Mike Gamson discuss people strategies: **www.youtube.com/ watch?v=oU8BoQmgTp8**

Southwest Airlines: Strategy Genius or Common Sense? (**https://www.youtube.com/watch?v=Szn-TbvEL2I**) and Colleen Barrett, Southwest Airlines president at the Wharton Leadership Conference on how the airline has posted profits for 35 consecutive years: **www.youtube.com/watch?v=6TgR95vnM0c**

Suki Group. Founder and COO Kelvin Ong speaks to NUS Business School about strategy and challenges for SMEs in Singapore's highly competitive food business: **www.youtube.com/watch?v=SH7yavzxCyM**

Virgin. Richard Branson at the TED conference in 2012: **www.youtube.com/watch?v=ufPweb-mO70**

Walmart Case Study – Strategic Marketing. Rod McNealy, Johnson & Johnson Marketing Executive, Wharton Lecturer, presenting the Walmart Case Study on Strategic Marketing to Princeton audience: **www.youtube.com/watch?v=cFhfOj36s4I**

Products and services

4

- Grasping the product bundle
- Product categories
- Life-cycle strategies
- Range – depth vs breadth
- Quality matters
- Process

Philip Kotler, Kellogg Graduate School of Management's distinguished Professor of International Marketing, defines a product as anything offered to a market for acquisition, attention, use or consumption that might satisfy a need or a want.

When the term 'marketing mix' was first coined, the bulk of valuable trade was concerned with physical goods. Certainly services existed, but these were mostly supplied by professions such as law, accountancy, insurance and finance, where the concept of marketing was in any event taboo. Today a product is generally accepted as the whole bundle of 'satisfactions' either tangible, such as a physical product, or intangible, such as warranties, guarantees or customer support that support that product. Generally the terms 'product' and 'service' will be used synonymously in this part of this chapter.

The bundle that makes up a successful product includes the following physical and service elements:

- Colour, flavour, odour, touch. These are the sensory elements, which for cosmetics are vital, but even more prosaic products such as computers can be endowed with additional value by the judicious use of colour.
- Payment terms. The use of credit can prove a vital element in a product's 'availability'. Motor vehicle sales slumped during and immediately after the credit crunch due first to the lack of credit finance and later because of its excessive cost.

- Specification and functionality. These describe the functionality of your product. For example, you could not offer a computer for sale without providing details of its memory, processor speeds and so forth. An internet recruitment business would include details on how it sources candidates, how it interviews and evaluates them and then matches them to job opportunities in the 'specification' of its offer.

- Features and benefits. The product or service is what people use but what they buy are the underlying benefits it confers on them. Business people usually define their products in terms of features. Customers, on the other hand, are only interested in what it does for them. Compare a Bic with a Parker pen. Basically they perform identical functions when it comes to writing. The Parker, however, confers intangible benefits such as status on its user. It is for those that people pay the majority of the price difference, not the relative writing qualities.

- Design. This is the element of the product that is the hardest to describe, yet in many ways it is the most tangible to its intended target market. The Apple Mac, for example, promotes both its funky design and its advanced graphics capability. Apple sees its product as appealing particularly to creative people who would see value in having something other than a plain PC box on their desk. So they make their product visually distinctive as a way of emphasizing its difference as a product. You need to consider what your product should look like visually and the chances are your website will be the first and main opportunity to do so. We will look at website construction later.

- Branding. Usually aligned with design, this involves giving the product or service a distinct identity. This subject was covered in the previous chapter, but the Toyota case study revisits the subject, in particular in respect to its relationship with quality.

- Quality is another complex area and one that is usually seen as one that can be traded off against price. While that may be true to a certain extent, everything you do within a product range, needs to be of similar quality, otherwise your brand will become devalued. Mercedes have small and less expensive cars on the market, but they come up to the same finish quality as the largest cars in their range. Quality on the internet is as much about the visual elements of your website as its functionality and the way you deal with customer support. A slow response to complaints or cries for help tend to tarnish the image of quality. However, don't be misled into believing everything has to be high quality. It simply has to be the quality that's right for the market segment you are aiming for, and the quality of the competitor's products.

- Packaging is the wrap around your product. It can be thought of as whatever the customer opens first to get at what they have bought. So again you can see, for many internet businesses, the website performs the function that packaging usually does for a tangible product. Software sold on the internet but delivered to your door needs packaging that protects, informs and gives a sense of value. Computer software packaging is bulky and usually comes with a bulky manual that is less useful than the help facilities in the software itself. The reasoning behind this approach is that customers might feel disappointed receiving little more than a letter-sized package for the substantial sum they may have paid.

- Guarantee. This is what gives people comfort that in ordering over the internet they will get their product and get it on time, that it will do what it says it will do, and if it doesn't perform they will get their money back. Customers also want to feel secure in making their financial transaction online. Buying offline, customers have fewer concerns. Often they can see the product or even try it out. They can go round to the place they bought from and either get help or exchange or return the product.

- After-sales service. The whole area of customer support has become one of the most important aspects of any product offering. The virtual nature of the internet makes customer support an even greater issue for people buying online. By helping your customers get their questions answered quickly and their problems resolved, you can build customer loyalty and competitive advantage. As well as having a good online support service of your own, you can pool the expertise and experiences of your other customers. A Frequently Asked Questions (FAQ) site can help with the most common problems people might face in using your product, as can discussion notice boards. You could also make your site an indispensable resource, full of useful hyperlinks and other information that can help customers make even better use of your product.

- Performance and reliability. These cover the whole field of the product's or service's ability to sustain its functionality. Failure or usage rates, for example, are a standard feature of many product propositions. Motor tyres are usually affixed with a mileage duration stating how far you can expect to travel on them.

- Safety. Customers want to be reassured that the product or service has no harmful side effects – pharmaceutical products are a case in point. But many less sophisticated products come with some safety assurance. Food products come with details of fat content, for example.

- Availability. For some products, lack of availability is a plus. Mercedes, Morgan and other luxury or specialist motor brands often invite you to 'queue' for a delivery date and perhaps visit the factory and see your car being made. All part of the brand mystique. But generally customers for, say, chewing gum, cigarettes or wine will expect the products to be on the shelf.

- Delivery. This covers how the product or service will reach the customer. Many customers, especially those whose entire family is out or working during the day, are irritated by those firms who indicate that a delivery will be made only between 8 am and 6 pm, or at best a half day within that period. If you are not in at the time, the product delivery has to be rescheduled at best or at worst collected from an often inaccessible office.

The principal tools that marketing managers use to manage product issues are as follows.

Generic product categories

The two broad categories of product or service are consumer products/services and industrial products/services.

Consumer products and services

Consumer products can be defined as products for which the buyer and consumer are either the same or closely associated and the entire value proposition in the acquisition process rests with them. Consumer products can be further subdivided into:

- Convenience products are mostly frequent purchases bought on a regular basis, where availability and price are more important than most other factors. Most food and basic clothing fit into this category.
- Loss leaders and special purchases are products that purport to offer exceptional value and are only available for a limited period of time. Their goal is to tempt customers into a store or onto a website. Sellers need to be sure that they can keep such products distant from their more conventional products so as not to destroy their value.
- Shopping products are those that a customer buys less frequently, pays more attention to brand values and carries out some research at the minimum to ensure products meet their specification, are reliable and good value for money. Clothing, furniture, computers, hi-fi equipment are all products that fit into this category. Shopping services include such items as insurance or a holiday.
- Speciality products are usually higher-priced goods such as designer clothing, branded watches, motor cars, furniture and white goods such as TVs, washing machines, dishwashers and medical or legal services. Consumers will carry out lots of research to ensure they get the product or service that meets their needs and they will demand strong after-sales support.

Industrial products and services

Industrial or business products are those that are usually bought as part of a process to add value for some future end-consumer. They include:

- Capital items such as equipment, machinery and buildings required as part of a production process. Capital services include specialist tax advice, corporate finance assistance in raising capital or an acquisition, and help with securing intellectual property. These are relatively infrequent purchases made usually by a board of directors with specialist staff support, typically those with MBA-type training.

- Materials, supplies and parts. These are the raw ingredients of the production process, are consumed over relatively short periods of time and as such are a frequent purchase.

- Supplies, services and utilities. These don't usually end up as part of the finished product, though they play a key part in the process. Nothing much could be made and sold, for example, without telephone services or stationery. Internet service providers (ISPs), office cleaners, advertising agencies and business consultants are all providers of such supply services.

Product/service life cycle

The idea that business products and services have a life cycle much as any living being does was first seen in management literature as far back as 1922, when researchers looking back over the growth of the US automobile industry observed a bell-shaped pattern for the sales of individual cars. Over the following four decades various practitioners and researchers added to, substituted and renamed the stages in the life cycle, arriving at the five steps in Figure 4.1. The length of a product's life cycle can be centuries, as with say Oxo, or just weeks or months in the case of fads such as the hula hoop or Rubik's cube.

Stages in the product life cycle

Products typically go through distinct stages over their life from birth to death, or relaunch if that proves to be a viable marketing strategy:

- Research and development. This stage is typified by cash outlays only and can last decades in the case of medical products or down to a few months or even weeks to launch a simple consumer product.

- Introduction. Here the product is brought to market, perhaps just to one initial segment, and it may comprise little more than a test marketing activity. Once again costs are high; advertising and selling costs have to be borne up-front and sales revenues will be minimal.

- Growth. This stage sees the product sold across the whole range of a company's market segments, gaining market acceptance and becoming profitable.

- Maturity and saturation. Sales peak as the limit of customers' capacity to consume is reached and competitors or substitute products enter the market. Profit starts to tail off as prices drop and advertising is stepped up to beat off competitors.

- Decline. Sales and profits fall away as competition becomes heavy and better and more competitive or technologically advanced products come into the market.

The usefulness of the product life cycle as a marketing tool is as an aid to deciding on the appropriate strategy to adopt. For example, at the introduction stage the goal for advertising and promotion may be to inform and educate, during the growth stage differences need to be stressed to keep competitors at bay, during maturity customers need to be reminded you are still around and it's time to buy again. During decline it's probable that advertising budgets could be cut and prices lowered. As all major costs associated with the product will have been covered by now, this should still be a profitable stage.

These of course are only examples of possible strategies rather than rules to be followed. For example, many products are successfully relaunched during the decline stage by changing an element of the marketing mix or being repositioned into a different marketplace. Cigarette manufacturers are responding to declining markets in the developed economies by targeting markets such as Africa and China, even setting up production there and buying up local brands to extend their range of products.

The dotted curves in Figure 4.1 indicate where sales would naturally decline without some marketing intervention.

Unique positioning proposition

This used to be known as the unique selling proposition (USP) and still is in the sales field. For marketers the term is synonymous with the idea of a slogan or strap line that captures the value of the product in the mind of the user. It should position your product against competitors in a manner that is hard to emulate or dislodge. John Lewis, for example, uses 'Never knowingly undersold' as its powerful message to consumers that they can safely set price considerations to one side when they come to making their choice.

Another strategy is to set out to own a word and turn it into a verb. Hoover with vacuum cleaners and FedEx with overnight delivery are examples of this approach.

FIGURE 4.1   Product market strategy and the product life cycle

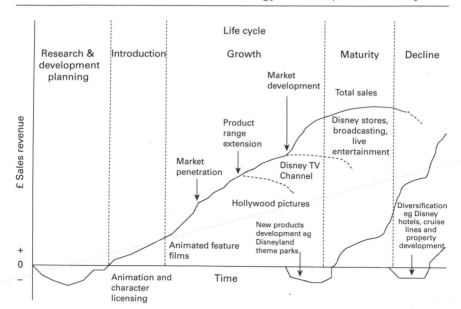

Product range

Being a single-product business is generally considered too dangerous a position except for very small or start-up businesses. The two options to consider are:

- Depth of line. This is the situation when a company has many products within a particular category. Washing powders and breakfast cereals are classic examples of businesses that offer scores of products into the same marketplace. The benefits to the company are the same channels of distribution and buyers are being used. The weakness is that all these products are subject to similar threats and dangers. However 'deep' your beers and spirits range, for example, you will always face the threat of higher taxes or the opprobrium of those who think you are damaging people's health.

- Breadth of line. This is where a company has a variety of products of different types, such as Marlboro with cigarettes and fashion clothing, or 3M with its extensive variety of adhesives and adhesive-related products such as Post-it® notes.

Product/service adoption cycle – who will buy first?

Customers do not sit and wait for a new business to open its doors. Word spreads slowly as the message is diffused throughout the various customer groups. Even then it is noticeable that generally it is the more adventurous types who first buy from a new business. Only after these people have given their seal of approval do the 'followers' come along. Research shows that this adoption process, as it is known, moves through five distinct customer characteristics, from Innovators to Laggards, with the overall population being different for each group.

The product/service adoption cycle is as follows:

Innovators: 2.5 per cent of the overall market;

Early adopters: 13.5 per cent of the overall market;

Early majority: 34.0 per cent of the overall market;

Late majority: 34.0 per cent of the overall market;

Laggards: 16.0 per cent of the overall market;

Total market: 100 per cent.

Let's suppose you have identified the market for your internet gift service. Initially your market has been constrained to affluent professionals within five miles of your home, to keep delivery costs low. So if market research shows that there are 100,000 people that meet the profile of your ideal customer and they have regular access to the internet, the market open for exploitation at the outset may be as low as 2,500, which is the 2.5 per cent of innovators.

This adoption process, from the 2.5 per cent of innovators who make up a new business's first customers, through to the laggards who won't buy from anyone until they have been in business for 20 years, is most noticeable with truly innovative and relatively costly goods and services, but the general trend is true for all businesses. Until you have sold to the innovators, significant sales cannot be achieved. So an important first task is to identify these customers. The moral is: the more you know about your potential customers at the outset, the better your chances of success.

One further issue to keep in mind when shaping your marketing strategy is that Innovators, Early Adopters and all the other sub-segments don't necessarily use the same media, websites, magazines and newspapers or respond to the same images and messages. So they need to be marketed to in very different ways.

CASE STUDY   Intuit, Inc

By 2010 Intuit, Inc was in its third decade and still creating a range of 'Right for Me' customer-driven products and services to help manage small businesses. Its software is on construction sites, in retail stores, in real estate, at Fortune 500 companies and in accounting offices, helping manage projects and accounts, track sales and monitor inventories. Net sales revenue was over $3 billion, with profits in excess of $540 million and headcount around 8,000.

Founded in 1983 by Scott Cook, still chairman of the executive committee, and Tom Proulx, Intuit embarked on a quest to revolutionize the way individuals and small businesses manage their finances.

Quicken®, the company's first product, introduced in 1984, struck a chord with consumers and has since become synonymous with personal finance. Quicken's success fuelled the creation of Intuit's other businesses, beginning with QuickBooks® small business accounting software in 1992 and continuing with TurboTax® personal tax software (through acquisition of ChipSoft in 1993). To enhance the value of these products, Intuit created a financial supplies business selling paper checks, forms and envelopes to software customers. In 1995, the company pioneered the notion of e-finance by adding online banking and bill payment to Quicken.

However, Intuit's entry onto the web nearly didn't happen – at least not in 1996. In late 1995, Intuit entered a 'period of reflection' to reconsider 'who we were and what we were about'. It had just had a bruising experience after the collapse of the proposed merger with Microsoft and needed to take stock of its direction.

One of Intuit's strengths was to take customer research very seriously indeed. They asked customers what they wanted and tried to supply it. In 1996, following the period of reflection, Intuit's management decided to explore the web. They asked their customers if they would put their personal financial information on a website.

The answer was a resounding no. No ifs or buts – just no. Yet today the website has several million personal financial portfolios on it, using Intuit's competitively priced software, QuickBooks Online Basic ($9.95 a month) and QuickBooks Online Plus ($34.95 a month).

So did market research fail Intuit? Probably not. It looks as though its customer base had a fairly normal new product adopter base. If only 2.5 per cent (the Innovators) said, 'Yes, we'll put our finances on the web', the remaining 97.5 per cent probably said no, in various ways. Yet introducing new web products quickly caught on and once the Innovators bought in, the Early Adopters, Early Majority and even some Laggards are doing their books online.

Intuit overcame initial market resistance by making QuickBooks Online a VeriSign Secured™ product using the same data-encryption technology that banks rely on to ensure their data is secure. Because the accounting function and data are online it can be run from any computer anywhere, making it easy to outsource business function. Also, being online, data is automatically backed up and can't be lost.

Quality

As well as using efficient marketing operation and control procedures, an organization has to deliver a quality product or service. Quality in marketing does not carry quite the same meaning as it does in, say, production, where it signifies something of a high standard. In marketing, quality means that something meets a customer's needs and performs as expected. In other words, promises are made and kept. But quality is also part of the efficiency equation. Quality below standard can lead to high waste, disrupted schedules and lost orders, all factors that directly impact on the marketing side of the enterprise.

The product/quality/price proposition

There are nine strategic marketing options when it comes to positioning a product or service in relation to its quality and price. Any strategy pursued here has to be consistent with the rest of the marketing mix and the individual elements of the product construction. For example, a premium product would be expected to have premium packaging and strong after-sales support. But sometimes companies try to set a high price for a relatively low-quality product; some brands of watches, for example, attempt to occupy this space. They attempt to compensate with excessive and high-quality packaging, but rarely does this achieve either satisfaction or the all-important customer referrals.

Inspection

Frederick W Taylor in his book, *The Principles of Scientific Management*, stated that one of the clearly defined tasks of management was to ensure that no faulty product left the factory or workshop. This led to a focus on the detection of problems in the product, testing every item to ensure that it

FIGURE 4.2 The product/quality/price proposition

complied with product specifications. The task was carried out at the end of the production process, using specially trained inspectors. The 'big idea' emerging from this approach was defect prevention as the means to ensure quality. Inspection still plays a part in modern quality practices, but less as an answer and more as one tool in the toolkit.

The philosophy behind quality

W Edwards Deming (**www.deming.org**), an American statistician and member of the faculty at the New York University Graduate School of Business and Columbia University, where he taught until 10 days before his death in 1993, is considered the founder of modern quality management. He took the inspection aspect of quality control a stage further with the introduction of statistical probability techniques. His view was that quality should be designed into products and processes and that mass inspection was redundant as statistical sampling using control charts will signal when a process is out of control.

Deming is remembered most for his 14-point 'System of Profound Knowledge'. In this he explains that becoming a quality-driven organization requires everyone, starting with top management, 'to fully embrace a new way of thinking that involves seeking the greater good for everyone involved and implementing continuous improvement'. He wanted slogans, targets and numerical targets removed, instead emphasizing to all employees in the company that if change is to be made and processes are to be continuously improved, it's down to them to achieve it. Deming's ideas were adopted enthusiastically by the Japanese, whose economy, crippled by the Second World War, was ready to embrace radical change. It was not until the

Japanese motor industry was cutting deep into the US market that US industry woke up to Deming's message on quality. Total Quality Management, Quality Circles and Six Sigma have become buzzwords for variations and extensions of Deming's and other pioneers' work on quality. 'Sigma' was in use in the 1920s where mathematicians used it as symbol for a unit of measurement in product quality variation. But it was not until the mid-1980s that engineers in US company Motorola used 'Six Sigma' first as an informal name and later as a brand name for their initiative aimed at reducing defects in production processes. The name was chosen because mathematically it represents 3.4 parts – or defects – per million, an extremely high level of quality.

CASE STUDY   Toyota

In February 2015 Toyota said it expected to post an operating profit of ¥2.7 trillion ($23 billion) in the fiscal year ending in March, up 17.8 per cent from a year earlier. True volume had not grown but as the *Financial Times* quoted Toyota managing officer Takuo Sasaki: 'We made efforts during the strong-yen era to firmly cut costs and improve per-vehicle profitability and as a result, we have built a leaner structure that does not rely on sales increase and the currency.' (*Financial Times*, 4 February 2015).

This was a far cry from January 2010, when Toyota announced a recall of up to 1.8 million cars across Europe, including about 220,000 in the UK, following an accelerator problem. At the same time the US Transportation Department opened an investigation into brake problems in a number of Toyota vehicle ranges. Company share price sagged by $25 billion (£15.9 billion) when the news broke. There was nothing especially new in vehicle recalls. GM had recalled nearly 6 million of its cars back in 1981 due a defective bolt in the front suspension and Ford had pulled in nearly 8 million vehicles in 1996 due to a faulty ignition switch that could catch fire. Ford also recalled 4.5 million cars in 2009; this time it was the cruise control that could potentially overheat and catch fire.

What hit Toyota so badly was that its heritage, strategy and brand value proposition were linked inexorably to product quality. Since 1890, when Sakichi Toyoda invented a wooden handloom to which he gave his name, the company has been in the reliability business. In the decades that followed, Toyoda added a number of related innovations including the non-stop shuttle-change-type automatic loom. In 1929 while on a trip to Europe and the USA, Toyoda transferred the patent rights to his automated loom to the British company Platt Brothers and began his investigations into the latest product to hit the headlines in the world of mass production, the automobile. By 1933 an automobile department had been established in Toyoda Automatic Loom Works Ltd and in 1935 Hinode Motors (currently Aichi Toyota) started operations. Vehicles were initially sold under the family name Toyoda, and in September 1936 the company ran a competition to design a new logo. Out of nearly 30,000 entries, the three Japanese *katakana* letters for 'Toyoda', in a circle, were chosen. However, Risaburō Toyoda, an adopted son of the founder, preferred a runner up, 'Toyota', because it took eight brush strokes (a fortuitous number) to write in Japanese and was visually simpler. 'Toyota' also helped distance the company from its past association with old-fashioned industries such as farming – 'Toyoda' literally means 'fertile rice paddies'. The new name was trademarked, the company was registered in August 1937 as the 'Toyota Motor Company', and it began operations in a dedicated facility, the Koromo Plant (currently Honsha Plant).

Toyota Motor Corporation introduced TQC (Total Quality Control) in 1961, and in 1965 were awarded the Deming Application Prize, named after the American quality guru whose teachings had inspired the company.

The Toyota route to product quality is enshrined in their five principles:

Challenge;

Kaizen (improvement);

Genchi Genbutsu (go and see);

Respect;

Teamwork.

Toyota was also an early adopter of lean manufacturing and just-in-time production, both aids to delivering value products of superior quality.

The company's quality problems have, according to Akio Toyoda, the company's current president, been caused by its growth outstripping the speed with which it could develop appropriate technical expertise. He went on to say that the company's priorities, traditionally ranked as safety, quality and volume, had become confused, with the last moving to a higher position.

In February 2010, when the latest ranking of the world's most valuable brands was published, Toyota was still ranked as the top motor brand and 10th overall in the top 500 companies across all industries. Mercedes and BMW were ranked 3rd and 2nd respectively in motor brands. The question now is: will the Toyota brand survive the crisis?

Process

This element of the marketing mix is concerned with the customer's experience in its dealings with a supplier. Essentially this is bringing the service element of company's offer into sharper relief. Process can spread across every aspect of the customer/supplier relationship. For example a recent Nespresso offer, the £25 Club Reward on a Nespresso Machine from March 2015, was made somewhat less attractive by the *process* of redeeming the reward:

How to participate in this offer:

1 *Purchase a Nespresso coffee machine.* Purchase any Nespresso coffee machine from **www.nespresso.com** and register with the Nespresso Club, where you will receive a Nespresso Club Member Account Number.

2 *Receive your machine and apply for your £25 Nespresso Club Reward.* Once you have received your machine you must apply for your Nespresso Club Credit online at **www.nespresso.com/ UKpromotion**. You will be required to upload a copy of your proof of purchase and input the 19-digit serial number of your machine. Alternatively you can download an application form from **www.nespresso.com/UKpromotion**, attach a photocopy of your proof of purchase and return to us at the address found on the application form by the stated closing date.

Websites and mobile apps are another source of potential customer dissatisfaction with a firm's process. Google has introduced 'Mobile-Friendly Test' that will analyse a URL and report if the page has a mobile-friendly design. Visit **www.google.co.uk/webmasters/tools/mobile-friendly.**

By way of an incentive, Google favours mobile-friendly websites in its page ranking criteria.

With a myriad of rating services and the National Cross-Industry Benchmarks of Customer Satisfaction for the United States and the UK (**www.theacsi.org**) measuring the satisfaction of household consumers with the quality of products and services offered by both foreign and domestic firm's business products, services and processes are being put under the spotlight as never before. The Industry Benchmarks annual studies involve roughly 70,000 customers in the US and 30,000 in the UK being surveyed about the products and services they use the most. The survey data benchmarks customer satisfaction with more than 300 companies in 43 industries and 10 economic sectors, as well as various services of national and local government agencies.

Online video courses and lectures

The Difference Between Goods & Services: Alanis Business Academy: **www.youtube.com/watch?v=AyyvFASW6Nw**

How to Develop Breakthrough Products and Services. Professor Eric von Hippel of MIT in a series of four lectures with accompanying notes: **http://ocw.mit.edu/courses/sloan-school-of-management/15-356-how-to-develop-breakthrough-products-and-services-spring-2012/**

Introduction to Marketing: The Product Mix from Alanis Business Academy: **www.youtube.com/watch?v=KhRd0MSmgfQ**

Product. Professor Noah Gans at Knowledge Wharton: **http://kwhs.wharton.upenn.edu/term/product/**

Product Category. Professor Reibstein David at Knowledge Wharton: **http://kwhs.wharton.upenn.edu/term/product-category/**

Product Life Cycle. Professor Mogilner Cassie at Knowledge Wharton: **http://kwhs.wharton.upenn.edu/term/product-lifecycle/**

Product Loyalty. Professor Reed Americus at Knowledge Wharton: **http://kwhs.wharton.upenn.edu/term/product-loyalty/**

Online video case studies

Amazon. Jeff Bezos Starts Amazon: **www.biography.com/people/jeff-bezos-9542209/videos/jeff-bezos-starts-amazon-40696899865**

Coca-Cola. The company's work towards achieving zero waste through life-cycle studies, packaging considerations about functionality, light-weighting, and transportation. Scott Vitters, director of sustainable packaging, talks at The Plastics Industry Trade Association: **www.youtube.com/watch?v=ldwHSismGHA**

Evolution of the iPod, iPhone, and iPad. Biographer Walter Isaacson, author of 'Steve Jobs', discusses Steve Jobs' return to Apple, and his focus on consumer products that were simple and intuitive: **www.biography.com/people/steve-jobs-9354805/videos/steve-jobs-evolution-of-the-ipod-iphone-and-ipad-34379057**

How P&G tripled its product innovation, Harvard Business Review: **https://hbr.org/2011/06/how-pg-tripled-its-innovation-success-rate**

Kalashnikov launches fashion line. The Age: **http://media.theage.com.au/news/world-news/kalashnikov-launches-fashion-line-6060738.html**

5　Advertising and promotion

- Advertising philosophy
- The medium and the message
- Measuring results
- The power of PR
- Using the internet
- Selling
- Social media strategies

Advertising is to some extent an intangible activity, although the bills for it are certainly not. It is, as Lord Bell, formerly of Saatchi & Saatchi, has described it, 'essentially an expensive way for one person to talk to another'.

Advertising and promotion, A&P for short, have been around in a form that would be easily recognizable by today's marketers for nearly four centuries. In 1631 *La Gazette*, a French paper, printed the first classified advertisements, and just under 80 years later the world's first magazine, *Tatler*, was launched. A&P were mainstream enough by 1841 for Volney B Palmer, the first ad agency, to open its doors in Philadelphia. By 1892 Sears, the US mail order giant, had launched its first direct marketing campaign, sending out 8,000 handwritten postcards, getting over 2,000 orders for its pains. In 1905 Fatty Arbuckle, a silent movie star, became the first recorded celebrity endorsement, supporting Murad, a cigarette brand, claiming it to be 'the natural preference of cultivated men'.

The business school world was quick to recognize the subject as an important subdivision of marketing, and professors of the subject quickly sprang up. CEIBS (China Europe International Business School) recruited Robert F Lauterborn to a visiting chair. He is the James L Knight Chair Professor of Advertising at the University of North Carolina, backed by a million-dollar grant from the Knight Foundation 'to improve the teaching of advertising'. Columbia, Tennessee, Michigan and Ball State universities all have designated professors in adverting or related fields such as consumer psychology.

A leading French business school, Reims Management School, has gone one step further and appointed a professor to research the promotion of champagne. Major champagne houses, including Moët & Chandon, Veuve Clicquot, Ruinart and Krug (all owned by LVMH), Laurent Perrier, Nicolas Feuillatte and Pommery, have clubbed together to fund the chair.

The media used by A&P professionals have expanded exponentially and their relative importance is constantly being influenced by changes in technology.

Research by Group M (**www.groupm.com**), the media buying arm of WPP, one of the biggest advertising, marketing and communication companies, forecast that world advertising budgets would continue their upward trend in 2016 growing by 3.9 per cent. The surprise was that TV would hold its share and that digital media would become the largest sector so rapidly. In the UK 50.1 per cent of all promotional spend would be on digital media, the largest share of any country followed in size by Sweden (47 per cent of total ad spend will be digital), Denmark (43 per cent), Australia (42 per cent) and Norway (40 per cent).

The most profound change in the advertising world is the way media is viewed. In 2013 Smart Phones and Tablets overtook PCs and Desktops as viewing platforms and by 2015 those new devices had over twice as large a share of the market. The rate of mobile adoption is unprecedented. It took nearly four decades for radio to reach 50 million users in the United States; Facebook took 3 years to reach the same level of saturation whilst Instagram got there in 180 days. Credible market forecasts predict that Mobile will account for 75 per cent of US Digital Ad spend by 2020.

The rules of advertising

Whilst the media delivery world is in transformation, the basic rules of advertising endure. An MBA with responsibilities in the marketing area is unlikely, except in the smallest of businesses, to be directly involved in designing or delivering promotional material. They will need a sound overview of the underlying principles and key areas – above and below the line, push pull and so forth as well as a rudimentary grasp of the mechanics. The answers to these five questions underpin all advertising and promotional strategies:

1 What do you want to happen?
2 If that happens, how much is it worth?
3 What message will make it happen?
4 What media will work best?
5 How will you measure the effectiveness of your effort and expense?

What do you want to happen?

Do you want prospective customers to visit your website, phone, write or e-mail you, return a card or send an order in the post? Do you expect them to have an immediate need to which you want them to respond now, or is it that you want them to remember you at some future date when they have a need for whatever it is you are selling?

The more you are able to identify a specific response in terms of orders, visits, phone calls or requests for literature, the better your promotional effort will be tailored to achieve your objective, and the more clearly you will be able to assess the effectiveness of your promotion and its cost versus its yield.

How much is that worth to you?

Once you know what you want a particular promotional activity to achieve, it becomes a little easier to estimate its cost. Suppose a £1,000 advertisement is expected to generate 100 enquiries for your product. If experience tells you that on average 10 per cent of enquiries result in orders, and your profit margin is £200 per product, then you can expect an extra £2,000 profit. That 'benefit' is much greater than the £1,000 cost of the advertisement, so it seems a worthwhile investment. Then with your target in mind decide how much to spend on advertising each month, revising that figure in the light of experience.

Deciding the message

Your promotional message must be built around facts about the company and about the product. The stress here is on the word 'fact', and while there may be many types of fact surrounding you and your products, your customers are only interested in two: the facts that influence their buying decisions, and the ways in which your business and its products stand out from the competition.

These facts must be translated into benefits. There is an assumption sometimes that everyone buys for obvious, logical reasons only, when we all know of innumerable examples showing this is not so. Do people only buy new clothes when the old ones are worn out? Do bosses have desks that are bigger than their subordinates' because they have more papers to put on them?

The message should follow the AIDA formula: get Attention, capture Interest, create Desire and encourage Action. Looking at each in turn:

- Getting attention requires a hook. Colour, humour, design are tools used to focus people on your offer and away from the masses of distracting clutter that occupies minds.

- Interest is achieved by involving people in some aspect of the product, perhaps by posing a question such as one diet company does with its challenge 'Would you like to lose 2 kgs in 2 weeks?'

- Desire is about showing people the end result they could achieve by having or using your product. Every speedboat advertisement has a beautiful bikini-clad girl posing on the bow, the inference being if you owned the boat you would be sure to get the girl too.

- Action means provoking a painless way for people to start the buying process. Free trial, money-back guarantee, offer only lasts this week and so forth are examples of the strategies used to achieve this result.

'UACCA – Unawareness, Awareness, Comprehension, Conviction, Action' is another acronym used in this context.

Choosing the media

Your market research (see Chapter 3) should produce a clear understanding of who your potential customer group is, which in turn will provide pointers as to how to reach it. But even when you know who you want to reach with your advertising message, it's not always plain sailing. *Fishing Times*, for example, will be effective at reaching fishermen but less so at reaching their partners who might be persuaded to buy them fishing tackle for Christmas or birthdays. Also, *Fishing Times* will be jam-packed with competitors. It might just be worth considering a web ad on a page giving tide tables to avoid going head to head with competitors, or getting into a gift catalogue to grab that market's attention.

If a consumer already knows what they want to buy and are just looking for a supplier, then, according to statistics, around 60 per cent will turn to print – Yellow Pages (or similar); 12 per cent will use a search engine; 11 per cent will use telephone directory enquiries; and 7 per cent online Yellow Pages. Only 3 per cent will turn to a friend. But if you are trying to persuade consumers to think about buying a product or service at a particular time, then a leaflet or flyer may be a better option. Once again it's back to your objectives in advertising. The more explicit they are, the easier it will be to choose media.

Above or below the line

Advertising media are usually clustered under two headings, above the line and below the line. It has to be said that the line is becoming increasingly indistinct but it is still a term that is part of the lexicon in setting the advertising budget.

Above the line   Above the line (ATL) involves using conventional impersonal mass media to promote products and services, talking at the consumer. Major above-the-line techniques include:

- TV, cinema and radio advertising. The vast array of local newspapers, TV channels and digital radio stations can make this a more targeted advertising strategy than has been the case.

- Print advertising in newspapers, magazines, directories and classified ads. Print of all forms has the merit of having a long life, so it can be used for handling more complex messages than radio or TV.

- Internet banner ads act as a point of entry for a more detailed advert.

- Search engines. Search engine advertising comes in two main forms. Pay per click (PPC) is where you buy options on certain key words so that someone searching for a product will see your 'advertisement' to the side of the natural search results. Google, for example, offers a deal where you only pay when someone clicks on your ad and you can set a daily budget stating how much you are prepared to spend, with $5 a day as the starting price.

- Podcasts in which internet users can download sound and video free are now an important part of the e-advertising armoury.

- Posters and billboards.

Below the line   Below the line (BTL) talks to the consumer in a more personal way, using such media as:

- Direct mail – leaflets, flyers, brochures. Response rates are notoriously low, often less than 1 per cent resulting in sales, but this medium has the merit of being a proven method of reaching specific targeted market segments.

- Direct e-mail and viral marketing. The latter is the process of creating something so hot that recipients will pass it on to friends and colleagues, creating extra demand as it rolls out. Jokes, games, pictures, quizzes and surveys are examples.

- Sales promotions, including point-of-sales material. Activities carried out in this area include free samples, try before you buy, discounts, coupons, incentives and rebates, contests and special events such as fairs and exhibitions.

- Public relations (PR). This is about presenting yourself and your business in a favourable light to your various 'publics' – at little or no cost. It is also a more influential method of communication than general advertising, because people believe editorials. There may also be times when you have to deal with the press – anything from when you are trying to get attention for a new product, to handling an adverse situation, say if your product has to be recalled for quality reasons or worse. See 'Creating favourable publicity', below.

- Letterheads, stationery and business cards are often overlooked in the battle for customer attention, but are in fact often the first and perhaps only way in which a business's image is projected.

- Blogs, in which the opinions and experiences of particular groups of people are shared using online communities such as MySpace, are an extension of this idea. Over 3 billion community sites are viewed every month in the UK alone.

Push or pull   Like above and below the line, push and pull are different advertising strategies used for achieving different results. Pull advertising is geared to draw visitors into your net if they are actively looking for your type of product or service. Search engines, listings in on- and offline directories, Yellow Pages and shopping portals are examples here.

Push advertising tries to get the word out to groups of potential customers in the hope that some of them will be considering making a purchase at about that time. Magazines, newspapers, TV, banner ads and direct mail both on- and offline are examples here.

As with above and below the line, the distinctions are fast becoming blurred, but the message used in your advertising will be different. With pull there is the assumption that people want to buy; they just need convincing they should buy from you. Push calls for a different message, convincing them of their need and desire in the first place.

Measuring results

A glance at the advertising analysis in Table 5.1 will show how to tackle the problem. It shows the advertising results for a small business course run in London. At first glance the Sunday paper produced the most enquiries. Although it cost the most, £3,400, the cost per enquiry was only slightly more than for the other media used. But the objective of this advertising was not simply to create interest; it was intended to sell places on the course. In fact, only 10 of the 75 enquiries were converted into orders – an advertising cost of £340 per head. On this basis the Sunday paper was between 2.5 and 3.5 times more expensive than any other medium.

Judy Lever, co-founder of Blooming Marvellous, the upmarket maternity wear company, believes strongly not only in evaluating the results of advertising, but in monitoring a particular medium's capacity to reach her customers: 'We start off with one-sixteenth-page ads in the specialist press,' says Judy, 'then once the medium has proved itself we progress gradually to half a page, which experience shows to be our optimum size. On average there are 700,000 pregnancies a year, but the circulation of specialist magazines is only around the 300,000 mark. We have yet to discover a way of reaching all our potential customers at the right time – in other words, early on in their pregnancies.'

Creating favourable publicity

This is about presenting yourself and your business in a favourable light to your various 'publics' – at little or no cost. It is also a more influential method

TABLE 5.1 Measuring advertising effectiveness

Media used	Cost per advert £	Number of enquiries	Cost per enquiry £	Number of customers	Advertising cost per customer £
Sunday paper	3,400	75	45	10	340
Daily paper	2,340	55	43	17	138
Posters	1,250	30	42	10	125
Local weekly paper	400	10	40	4	100

of communication than general advertising – people believe editorials. This is a particularly important communications strategy in times of crisis when you need to reassure your customers or investors. The classic business school case study on this subject is that of Perrier, whose fizzy mineral water was found to be contaminated with benzene some 20 years ago. While the company recalled all its bottles it fluffed its PR message badly, changing tack several times. The brand was sold to Nestlé, but never recovered.

CASE STUDY Rococo

Chantal Coady, the Harrods-trained chocolatier who founded Rococo, was 22 when she wrote the business plan that secured her £25,000 start-up capital. The cornerstone of her strategy to reach an early break-even point lay in a carefully developed public relations campaign. By injecting fashion into chocolates and their packaging, she opened up the avenue to press coverage in such magazines as *Vogue, Harpers & Queen* and the colour supplements. She managed to get over £40,000 worth of column inches of space for the cost of a few postage stamps. This not only ensured a sound launch for her venture but eventually led to a contract from Jasper Conran to provide boxes of chocolates to coordinate with his spring collection.

Writing a press release

To be successful, a press release needs to get attention immediately and be quick and easy to digest. Studying and copying the style of the particular paper, magazine or website you want your press release to appear in can make publication more likely:

- Layout. The press release should be typed on a single sheet of A4. Use double spacing and wide margins to make the text both more readable and easy to edit. Head it boldly 'Press Release' or 'News Release' and date it.
- Headline. This must persuade the editor to read on. If it doesn't attract interest, it will be quickly 'spiked'. Editors are looking for topicality, originality, personality and, sometimes, humour.
- Introductory paragraph. This should be interesting and succinct and should summarize the whole story; it could be in the form of a quote and it might be the only piece published. Don't include sales-orientated blurb as this will 'offend' the journalist's sense of integrity.

- Subsequent paragraphs. These should expand and colour the details in the opening paragraph. Most stories can be told in a maximum of three or four paragraphs. Editors are always looking for fillers, so short releases have the best chance of getting published.

- Contact. List at the end of the release your name, mobile and other telephone numbers and e-mail address as the contact for further information.

- Style. Use simple language, short sentences and avoid technical jargon (except for very specialized technical magazines).

- Photographs. While you can send a standard photograph of yourself, your product or anything else relevant to the story being pitched, you should also give the journalist concerned the option of having a digital version e-mailed.

- Follow-up. Sometimes a follow-up phone call or e-mail to see if editors intend to use the release can be useful but you must use your judgement on how often to do so.

Targeting your media

Find out the name of the editor or relevant writer/reporter and address the envelope or e-mail to him or her personally. Remember that the target audience for your press release is the professional editor; it is he or she who decides what to print. So the press release is not a 'sales message' but a factual account designed to attract the editor's attention. Too many small companies, in their enthusiasm for their products, overlook this difference between the sales leaflet and PR release, which explains why a recent survey showed that only 6 per cent of press releases are printed and 94 per cent are not. With UK editors receiving an average of 80–90 press releases per week, make sure that you are making your latest newsworthy item public, but make sure it is free of puffery and jargon.

Websites and effective internet presence

Many businesses have poor and ineffective websites, largely because the site is static and in effect an online brochure; or because it is designed to be visually exciting and commissioned by managers with a limited grasp of how internet visibility works. This is an area that the MBA should be able to have an impact on quickly and senior managers will expect them to at least have a better grasp of the subject than them. Good website design is essential if your internet presence is to be fully effective. Short loading time (use graphics, not photographs), short and sweet legible text and an attractive layout are important features of a user-friendly website. Research indicates that 'within three clicks, visitors must be captivated or they will leave'. So clear signposting is necessary, including a menu on every page so that visitors can return to the home page or move to other sections in just one click.

Promote your website by acquiring links on other commercial websites, using key words to ensure you can be found and by promoting outside the internet – feature your website address on all products and publications. Fill your home page with regularly updated 'success stories', give discounts to first-time buyers, ask customers to 'bookmark' your site or add it to their list of 'favourites' on their browser. You could also try partnering with manufacturers and distributors in related business fields.

Dos and don'ts in website design

Do

1 Think about design. Create a consistent visual theme, grouping elements together so that your reader can follow the information you are presenting easily.

2 Prepare your content. It should be focused on the needs of your target audience and be credible, original, current and varied.

3 Plan your site navigation. Your pages need to be organized intuitively so they are easy to navigate.

4 Consider usability and accessibility. Use graphics sparingly as not everyone has super access speeds. Optimize your HTML, especially on your home page, to minimize file size and download time by removing excess spaces, comments, tags and commentary.

5 Optimize for searching. Build in key words and tags and markers so your site will be found easily.

Don't

1 Have long pages. Content beyond the first 1.5 to 2 page lengths is typically ignored.

2 Have pointless animation. Many are distracting, poorly designed in terms of colour and fonts, and add unnecessarily to file size, slowing down your reader's search.

3 Use the wrong colours. Colour choice is crucial; black text on a white background is the easiest to read while other colours such as reds and greens are harder to read. Check out Visibone's website (**www.visibone.com/colorblind**) for a simulation of the web designer's colour palette of browser-safe colours.

4   Have stale information anywhere, especially on your home page. Nothing turns readers off so much as seeing information that relates to events long gone: recipes for Christmas pudding at Easter, for example.

5   Waste your readers' time. Making readers register on your site may be useful to you, but unless you have some compelling value to offer, don't. If you absolutely must, keep registration details to a couple of lines of information.

To get some idea of what to include in and exclude from your website, check your competitors' websites and those of any other small business that you rate highly.

Getting seen

Nine out of 10 visitors reach internet sites via a search engine or equivalent, so you need to fill the first page with 'key terms' that search engines can latch on to.

This process is known as SEO (search engine optimization), where your website is 'optimized' so that it improves its position in search engine rankings. It also helps if you know a little about how search engines work.

If you want to be sure of getting seen by a search engine, first make a list of the words that you think a searcher is most likely to use when looking for your products or services. For example, a repair garage in Penzance could include key words such as car, repair, cheap, quick, reliable, insurance, crash and Penzance in the home page to pull in searchers looking for a competitive price and a quick repair. As a rule of thumb, for every 300 words you need a key word or phrase to appear between 10 and 15 times. Search engines thrive on content, so the more relevant the content the better. You can use products such as that provided by strategy studio Keyword (**www.goodkeyword.com**), which has a free Windows software programme to help you find words and phrases relevant to your business and provides statistics as how frequently those are used. There is a 'try before you buy' facility.

Tracking website traffic

There is a wealth of information available on who visits your website, where they come from in terms of geography, search engine, search term used, and where they entered your website (home page, FAQs, product specifications, price list, order page) and how long they spent in various parts of your website; that's aside from the basic information you will automatically receive on orders placed, enquiries made or e-mail contacts.

This data can then be used to tweak your website and content to improve user experience and so achieve your goals for the website. For example, you may find that lots of visitors are entering your website via a link found on a search engine that takes them to an inappropriate section of your site, say the price list, when you want them to start with the benefits of your product or success stories. By changing the key words on which your website is optimized, or by putting more visible links through the site, you can drive traffic along your chosen path.

Measuring advertising effectiveness on the internet

Seeing the value from internet advertising can be a difficult proposition. The first difficulty is seeing exactly what you are getting for your money. With press advertising you get a certain amount of space, on TV and radio you get airtime. But on the internet there are at least three new ways to measure viewer value, aside from the largely discredited 'hits', used only because there was no other technique available. (Hits measured every activity on the web page, so every graphic on a page as well as the page itself counts as a hit.)

These new methods are:

- Unique visitors. This is more or less what it says – new visitors to a website. What they do there and how long they stay are not taken into account, so it's a bit like tracking the number of people passing a billboard. Could be useful, but perhaps they just stumbled across the site by accident. Also, if users clear their cookies and clean up their hard drive, there is no way to identify new and old visitors.

- Time spent. Clearly if visitors stay on a website for a few minutes they are more likely to be interested or at least informed about your products and services than if they were there for a second or two.

- Page views. Much as in hard-copy world, a page on the web can now be recognized and the number of viewers counted.

Nielsen, a market-leading audience and market research measurement company, suggests that 'time spent' is the best way to measure advertising effectiveness, other, of course, than actual sales if you can trace them back to their source. The order of the worldwide top websites is changed radically using this measure. For example, in January 2008 Google ranked first for unique visitors and page views, but only third for time spent.

Internet and blogs

Your website is an obvious place to advertise, but the millions of other websites and search engines provide plenty of opportunities to get your message in front of your market. The normal rules of advertising apply in cyberspace as in any other medium. The main options are:

- Search engine advertising, which comes in the forms described earlier.
- E-mail marketing is just like conventional direct mail sent by post, except e-mail is the medium and you target e-mail databases.
- Display advertising, like advertising in newsprint, takes the form of words and images of varying sizes on websites that people looking for your product are likely to come across. The Audit Bureau of Circulations Electronic (**www.abce.org.uk**) audits website traffic.
- Viral marketing, as described earlier, is when recipients pass web material on to friends and colleagues, creating extra demand.
- Blogs are online spaces where the opinions and experiences of particular groups of people are shared.
- Podcasts, where internet users can download sound and video free, are now an important part of the e-advertising armoury.
- White papers are sales and marketing documents used to persuade potential customers to learn more about a particular product, service, technology, procedure and to help establish you as an authority and source of reliable information in a particular area. TechRepublic, for example, goes one further here and has on its website a 'Resource Library' claiming to be 'the web's largest directory of free vendor-supplied technical content'. A neat way of high-jacking content and using that to draw traffic your way (**www.techrepublic.com/ resource-library/whitepapers**).
- Videos embedded in your web pages. Industry experts reckon that by 2017, video will account for 69 per cent of all promotional internet traffic (Cisco) with 64 per cent of marketers expecting video to dominate their strategies in the near future (Nielsen). YouTube already receives more than one billion unique visitors every month – that's more than any other channel, apart from Facebook. The old advertising adage that says a picture paints a thousand words has been updated to read one minute of video is worth 1.8 million (Forrester's Research).

The Internet Advertising Bureau (**www.iabuk.net**) has a wealth of further information on internet advertising strategies as well as a directory of agencies that can help with some or all of these methods of promoting your business. Nielsen NetRatings (**www.nielsen-netratings.com**>Resources>Free Data and Rankings) provides some free data on internet advertising metrics.

Social media strategy

The Oxford Dictionary has a suitably pithy definition of social media – 'websites and applications that enable users to create and share content or to participate in social networking'. Social media can be seen as a collection of online communications channels dedicated to community-based input, interaction, content-sharing and collaboration. Social media was in its infancy when the first edition of *The 30 Day MBA* was being written in 2008, but in just a few short years has become prolific, influential and now occupies half the promotional world space. The notion that using social media for business has become a mainstream activity is evident in the fact that the options are numerous and expanding fast. Aside from the usual suspects – Facebook, LinkedIn and Twitter – hundreds of sector-specific sites exist. Pinterest, for example, is a tool for collecting and organizing pictures of things that inspire you. YouTube provides a forum for people to inform billions of people around the world by distributing videos for free. eHarmony, Match.com and 6,000 other dating sites aim to help the lonely find love. Social bookmarking sites, including Digg, Delicious, Newsvine, and Reddit allow users to recommend online news stories, music and videos. Then you have word-of-mouth forums including blogs, company-sponsored discussion boards and chat rooms, and consumer product or service ratings websites and forums like Skytrax airlines rating, TripAdvisor and local-business review site Yelp. Social media sites make up at least half of the top 20 websites in most regions of the world.

Today even the smallest of businesses can incorporate social media into their promotional plan, and it is essential for the prospective MBA marketer to have a reasonable grasp of the basics of the subject and the benefits that knowledge can bring to his or her organization. Stanford's 'Social Media Use Among Directors and Senior Managers' report suggests that this is fertile ground for an MBA to sow the seeds of fast-tracked career progression. Whilst 80 per cent of senior managers had a LinkedIn account, only half used it regularly. Forty per cent had a Twitter account but less than 10 per cent actually used it. Around a fifth of those they surveyed – typically in their mid-50s – across a broad set of industries — manufacturing, utilities, banking, and services – and from fairly large companies ($500 million in revenue), didn't access social media (**www.gsb.stanford.edu/sites/default/files/13SocialMedia.pdf**).

Different social media reach different audiences. Facebook, for example, dominates in the B2C space (67 per cent of marketers select it as their number one choice). However, in B2B, LinkedIn and Facebook are in joint first place at 29 per cent each. Blogging and Twitter play a much more important role for B2B marketers – 19 per cent and 16 per cent respectively, whilst for B2C the shares are 11 per cent and 10 per cent. Companies such as Ning (**www.ning.com**) and engagor (**http://engagor.com**) will let you create and cultivate your own custom social network as well as being able to measure, monitor and manage all your social media activity. Both these sites offer a free trial.

Key uses of social media include:

Improve market intelligence

Social media has fundamentally transformed the way people exchange information. Today people with similar interests band together in different online communities sharing information and exchanging views on blogs and forums, both excellent sources of continuous information on industry issues, customers and competitors. Bloggers are no longer inhibited if they are not a recognized expert in the field. Anyone and everyone can and does express their comments and views through blogs and forums. The quality of information can be variable and there are often many blogs, sometimes hundreds, on any topic. Alternatively you can create a blog or forum on your own website. You can use information on blogs to arrive at a crowd forecast, that is one which relies on the 'wisdom of the crowd' effect to get a feel for what people are feeling. The term refers to the phenomenon that the average of estimates provided by a group of individuals is more accurate than most of the individual estimates. The idea that the combination of many forecasts usually performs better than the forecast of a single person, however expert was spread by the lead story in James Surowiecki's 2005 book, *The Wisdom of Crowds* (Abacus; New Ed edition). The story tells of a 1906 contest to guess the weight of an Ox. The analysis of the 787 usable entries found that the sample average of 1,197 pounds was extraordinarily close the actual weight of 1,198 pounds. Crowd forecasting allows you to balance expert perspectives with that of a wider audience for a more representative view of where a trend is heading.

Enhance company profile

Most company websites are used as marketing tools used to draw in more prospective customers or to maintain relationships with current buyers. The corporate image is developed by public relations by way of press releases announcing expansion, new strategic partnership and new products and services; and by journalists reading, analysing and commenting on company financial results. Two social media routes are open to help cultivate a particular type of image, over which a company has some editorial control:

- Wikipedia. This site now gets 600 million visitors a month, putting it up alongside Google. Companies can have their own Wikipedia page created putting their own slant on the information. Information on their site must be verifiable and fair comment can be made by anyone, which is a risk. For example Kerry Group, a Food Ingredients and Flavours business quoted on the Dublin and London stock markets, devotes a substantial portion of its page to its acquisition history. A clear indication that they are in the market for businesses for sale (**http://en.wikipedia.org/wiki/Kerry_Group**).

- LinkedIn. This is the social media site of choice in the corporate world. There is virtually no editorial control over this site so almost anything legal can be published. Once again you can put your own spin on the facts. Kerry Group's LinkedIn profile again emphasizes is acquisitive nature. 'The Group has grown organically and through a series of strategic acquisitions in its relatively short history,' is the second sentence on the page. An advantage of LinkedIn is that you can alert your followers (in Kerry Group's case 32,624 of them) to anything you feel useful. On 24 February 2015 they let them know that their latest interim accounts were available. LinkedIn can also be used for precision B2B targeting of messages by job title and function, by industry and company size, by seniority and geography.

CASE STUDY   Caterpillar

You couldn't get a more conservative company than Caterpillar. Started in 1925 the company has grown to become the world's leading manufacturer of construction and mining equipment, diesel and natural engines and industrial gas turbines. In 2015 their worldwide sales exceeded US$ 56 billion. It is a name associated with yellow bulldozers and building sites. Caterpillar recognizes the power of the big three social media platforms – Facebook, Twitter, and YouTube – but are also exploring other platforms that are used in specific areas of the world as well as social media tools such as Foursquare, Facebook Places and Gowalla.

The company even has a dedicated Digital Marketing Manager, Kevin G Espinosa, and a social media strategy based on what they describe as their four pillars: social listening, customer support, promotion and thought leadership. All of their social media activities fall under these pillars. For thought leadership, Espinosa states they 'want to provide our customers the information they need to become better in their job and be seen as an industry leader when it comes to construction equipment, and we have a lot of knowledge to share'. They are using social listening 'to understand what people are saying about our products, the issues they have, where they are saying it, and who the key influencers are'.

Caterpillar is an active participant in social media channels, seeing them as powerful tools that allow them to connect with their customers, investors, potential employees and fans.

The Social Media section of their website (**www.caterpillar.com/en/news/social-media.html**) lists their areas of interest such as Cat Auction Services, a partnership of Cat Dealers, providing both buyers and sellers with a better heavy equipment auction experience and Caterpillar Safety Services advising on the right Personal Protective Equipment. With these separate areas the company has 23 different Facebook sites for different aspects of their business, five blogs and Google + sites as well as dedicated links to YouTube ,Instagram ,Vimeo, SoundCloud and Pinterest.

These are some of the services that are used to track website activity.

Google Analytics. The basic version is free and will deliver most of what you need to get a strategic view of what is happening on your website. This is rated the most comprehensive of website tracking tools. It helps you paint a complete picture of your audience and their needs, wherever they are along the path to purchase, from just viewing a page to shortlisting options or comparing prices. Traffic Sources and Visitor Flow, two of the Analytics tools, help you track the routes people take to reach you, and the devices they use to get there – PC, tablet or smartphone. In-Page Analytics, another tool in the service, lets you make a visual assessment of how visitors interact with your pages and what they're looking for and what they seem most interested in about your proposition based on viewing time. Mobile App Analytics covers all the same ground letting you know who uses your apps, on what devices, and where they come from. Custom reports can be set up to track specific advertising campaigns. Visit **www.google.com/analytics**.

SiteMeter. This service delivers 'the Who, What, When and Where' of your online traffic. They can't tell you specifically who is visiting your site, but are able to record a list of visitors with general geographic location information for each visitor. So you could establish that 'x' per cent of visitors to your site come from Athens, Berlin or Sofia, for example and using the 'Referring URL' report you could see a large number of these visitors have an '**.edu**' or '**.a.c.uk**' extension, indication an occupation in the education sector. SiteMeter can provide you with a list of your sites most visited pages, what times of the day are your busiest and any season trends or patterns. Site Meter Basic provides all the essential data, statistics, and reports needed to know who is visiting your site, how many pages have been viewed, and detailed information about each individual visitor. Site Meter Premium, at a modest monthly cost of around £7, offers additional statistics including ranked reports, more historical data and the ability to export data on recent visitors. Visit **www.sitemeter.com**.

AWStats. This log analyser shows you all possible information your log contains, in few graphical web pages covering information such as:

- Authenticated users, and last authenticated visits;
- Days of week and rush hours (pages, hits, KB for each hour and day of week);
- Domains/countries of hosts visitors (pages, hits etc);
- Hosts list, last visits and unresolved IP addresses list;
- HTTP errors (Page Not Found with last referrer, etc);
- Most viewed, entry and exit pages;
- Number of visits, and number of unique visitors;
- Search engines, keyphrases and keywords used to find your site from the 115 most prominent search engines;
- Visits duration and last visits;

- Visits of robots (319 robots detected);
- Worms attacks (5 worm's families).

AWStats is free, but if you want to support future development you can make a donation. Visit **www.awstats.org**.

StatCounter: This is a free service that lets you drill down into the data about visitors to your website to see what are your most popular pages, which sites people reach you from, the pages visitors enter and exit your site, visitor, paths, length of time at each stage, keyword analysis and recent key word used. Visit **http://statcounter.com/features**.

Selling

Marketing is the thinking process behind selling; in other words, finding the right people to buy your product or service and making them aware that you are able to meet their needs at a competitive price. But just because customers know you are in the market is not in itself sufficient to make them buy from you. Even if you have a superior product at a competitive price they can escape your net.

Getting customers to sign on the dotted line almost invariably involves selling. This is a process that business people have to use in many situations other than in persuading customers to buy. MBAs have to 'sell' the bank manager the idea that lending their business money is worthwhile, that shareholders should invest, that employees by working for them are making a good career move or that their boss should back one of their proposals.

Though essential, selling on its own is an inefficient method of getting potential customers to the point of buying. Understanding the 'ascending ladder of influence', as marketers call it, puts the salesperson's role in perspective. This is a method to rank the 'warm bodies' a customer will encounter in the selling process in the order most likely to favourably influence your customers. At the top of the scale is the personal recommendation of someone whose opinion is trusted and who is known to be unbiased. An example here is the endorsement of an industry expert who is not on the payroll, such as an existing user of the goods or services, who is in the same line of business as the prospective customer. While highly effective, this method is hard to achieve and can be expensive and time-consuming.

Further down the scale is an approach by you in your role as a salesperson. While you may be seen to be knowledgeable, you clearly stand to gain if a sale is made. So you can hardly be unbiased. Sales calls, however they are made, are an expensive way to reach customers, especially if their orders are likely to be small and infrequent.

How selling works

There is an erroneous view that salespeople, like artists and musicians, are born, not made. Selling can be learnt, improved and enhanced just like any other business activity. First, you need to understand selling's three elements:

- Selling is a process moving through certain stages if the best results are to be achieved. First, you need to listen to the customers to learn what they want to achieve from buying your product or service; then you should demonstrate how you can meet their needs. The next stage is handling questions and objections – a good sign as they show that the customer is sufficiently interested to engage. Finally comes 'closing the sale'. This is little more than asking for the order with a degree of subtlety.

- Selling requires planning in that you need to keep records and information on customers and potential customers so you know when they might be ready to buy or reorder.

- Selling is a skill that can be learnt and enhanced by training and practice, as shown in the case study below.

CASE STUDY

When Sumir Karayi started up in business in the spare room of his flat in West Ealing, London, he wanted his business to be distinctive. He was a technical expert at Microsoft and with two colleagues he set up 1E (**www.1e.com**) as a commune aiming to be the top technical experts in their field. The business name comes from the message that appears on your screen when your computer has crashed. Within a year of starting up, the team had learnt two important lessons: businesses need leaders, not communes, if they are to grow fast and prosper; and they need someone to sell.

On the recommendation of an advisor, Karayi went on a selling course and within months had won the first of what became a string of blue-chip clients. The company is now one of the 10 fastest-growing companies in the Thames Valley with annual turnover approaching £15 million, profits of 30 per cent and partners and reseller partners worldwide.

Negotiating

Like selling, negotiating, of which it usually forms a part, is as much a science as an art. There are a few immutable rules – easily understood but invariably difficult to execute:

- Aim high at the outset. Unless you can find the point of resistance you can't find the outer limits of your negotiating range.

- You must be prepared to walk away from a deal and make that evident if you are to have any negotiating leverage. To achieve this you must have prepared plans B and C ready to execute if the terms you want can't be achieved. For example, when negotiating to buy out a competitor, have other businesses in the frame too; or have plans to enter that market without the company you are trying to acquire.

- Search out a range of variables to negotiate on other than price. Delivery date, payment terms, quantities, currencies, shared future profits, know-how swaps – these are just a handful of areas rich in negotiating possibilities.

- Never give a concession away. Anything given for nothing is seen as being worth nothing. Instead, trade concessions and always put the highest value possible on the concession. 'We will pay 30 per cent up-front rather than the 20 per cent you're asking for (a gain for the seller) if you bring the price down to £1.2 million rather than the £1.3 million you're asking' (a gain for the buyer) is the place to start if you hope to hit a £1.25 million final price.

- Talk as little as possible. The less you say, the less you can give away.

- Once you have put a proposition on the table, shut up. The first to blink is the loser.

Online video courses and lectures

Advertising, Professor Kim Donahue, Kelley School of Business: **www.youtube.com/watch?v=NroY4SSrjL8**

Introduction to Marketing: This course covers topics including branding strategies (eg, brand positioning, brand communications) and customer-centric marketing strategy. Wharton Online Learning: **http://online.wharton.upenn.edu/**

Personal Selling: Professor Kim Donahue, Kelley School of Business: **www.youtube.com/watch?v=cOkycHYyz5k**

SEO at Harvard Business School. Andrew Masanto, one of the Founders of Higher Click SEO Company, talks at Harvard: **www.youtube.com/watch?v=Op28m1wnqu0**

Social Media, Search-Engine Optimization. Ohio Wesleyan University: **www.youtube.com/watch?v=yWkQIIrQjIA**

Online video case studies

Apple Think Different ad (1997) (**www.youtube.com/ watch?v=nmwXdGm89Tk**) and Steve Jobs talking about how the advertising campaign was developed at an internal meeting the same year (**www.youtube.com/watch?v=9GMQhOm-Dqo**).

Coca-Cola Content 2020: Jonathan Mildenhall, Vice-President, Global Advertising Strategy and Creative Excellence at The Coca-Cola Company explains how Coke will leverage the opportunities in the new media landscape: **www.youtube.com/watch?v=LerdMmWjU_E**

Comcast: A day in the life of a sales person: **www.youtube.com/ watch?v=Jm5u6_xoc0Q**

Eyemotion: Their primary objective is to help create a dynamic website that enhances the doctor–patient relationship and improve profitability. Case study at the Reel Summit: **www.youtube.com/watch?v=I5jKP609Qyc**

Heinz. The first television commercial in 1955 reminded frugal post-war housewives of the beans' value for money: **www.youtube.com/ watch?v=QtlWq7GtjU8**

Place and distribution

6

- Assessing distribution routes
- Understanding channel structures
- Logistics and routes to market
- Outsourcing the supply chain

'**P**lace' is the third 'P' in the marketing mix. This aspect of marketing strategy is about how products and services are actually got into customers' hands. In the online world this is sometimes known as 'the last mile', originally used to describe the final leg of delivering connectivity from a communications provider to a customer, but now used more generally. The whole chain from seller to consumer is itself dynamic and changes to reflect market conditions and a firm's strategy. A case in point is Amazon, which until 2010 had confined its distribution to some 30 state-of-the-art giant fulfilment and warehousing operations stretching from Arizona to Beijing, passing through Ontario, Bedford (UK), Orléans (France) and Leipzig (Germany) en route. At $50 million a pop these represent a colossal strategic commitment to a particular route to market. In February 2015 Amazon opened its first staffed pick-up and drop-off location that is a shop in all but name at Perdue University in the US. They are expected to follow this by opening university shops across America starting in California and Massachusetts. They are rumoured to be looking for a brick and mortar chain to buy to jump-start their strategy to set up pick-up and drop-off points everywhere. In March 2015 Google got in on the retail act too and opened its first ever bricks and mortar store, inside a Currys PC World on London's Tottenham Court Road. It follows the Apple Store model with products on wooden tables and staff on hand to guide users through their hardware and software letting them try before they buy. This is only following a strategy adopted by Argos, which claims that nearly a fifth of products bought online are actually collected in-store by customers who are either too impatient to wait or who don't want the hassle of waiting at home to sign for deliveries.

On the academic front, Martin Christopher, Emeritus Professor of Marketing and Logistics at Cranfield School of Management, is the leading light in the field of logistics and supply chain management. In the USA the Supply Chain and Logistics Institute (SCL) at Georgia Tech provides global leadership for research and education in supply chain management, which it defines as 'the application of scientific principles to optimize the design and integration of supply chain processes, infrastructure, technology and strategy'.

Channel structures

A marketing channel is a set of businesses that are involved in making a product or service available for use or consumption by a business or another end-user. Such businesses may be independent, owned by others in the channel, they may coexist, compete or collaborate in a wide variety of ways.

The members of a channel carry out some or all of these functions:

- promotion and contact including advertising, creating awareness and providing contact resources;
- information on the product or service;
- matching the product or service to specific customer requirements;
- risk sharing in elements of the transaction;
- negotiation in setting the terms of trade and price;
- financing the cost of the transaction, eg by providing credit;
- physical distribution of the product or execution of the service.

There are four main types of channel, as described below.

Conventional

This is when each link in the chain is independent of the other and in effect competes for a slice of the value in getting the end product to the end-consumer or user. There are usually four links in the chain (see Figure 6.1). However, on occasions one link will leapfrog over the other.

Horizontal marketing systems (HMS)

These occur where two or more non-competing businesses at one level in the chain combine together to market an existing product or create a new channel to market. This may be because they lack physical or capital resources or an established brand name, or to secure economies of scale. The music partnership started by Apple and Starbucks in 2007 is one such example. The aim

FIGURE 6.1   Marketing channels

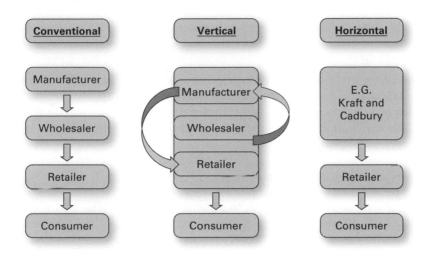

was to allow Starbucks' customers to wirelessly browse, preview, buy and download music from iTunes Music Store onto anything running iTunes. Apple's brand leadership in digital music combined with Starbucks' loyal customer base was expected to create a win–win situation for both parties. Apple hoped to sell a million songs in the first six months but passed that threshold in six days. Starbucks benefited from higher sales and even stronger customer loyalty.

This strategy works particularly well in global distribution strategies. For example, one goal of US giant Kraft in making its bid for British firm Cadbury's in January 2010 was that becoming a part of Kraft meant that Cadbury's products would go through a far bigger global distribution network. Products such as Creme Eggs and Fruit and Nut will be introduced to two of the superpowers of the 21st century – Russia and China – where, as an independent company, Cadbury's has made little impact while Kraft has a strong presence. Kraft in return expected increased penetration in Western Europe.

Vertical marketing systems (VMS)

This strategy integrates producer, wholesalers and retailers working in one unified system. The goal of vertical marketing is to eliminate unnecessary competition between chain participants as occurs, say, when producers and retailers slug it out to get better prices from each other. VMS give all those involved control but not necessarily ownership. Marks & Spencer, for example, provides considerable technical assistance to its suppliers, as well as providing detailed sales and stock forecasts, but does not own the suppliers.

Vertical integration is a strategy that is best pursued at the mature stage of the product life cycle (see Chapter 4) as at earlier stages each part of the chain will have a more distinct role to perform.

VMS comes in three forms: corporate, contractual and administered.

Corporate

This arises when one member of the chain owns some or all of other elements – for example, in forward integration, which arises where a supplier such as Apple owns its own retail outlets. Backward integration arises when a retailer owns its own suppliers. Spanish clothing chain Zara outflanks its competitors such as Gap and Benetton by having control over almost every element of the supply chain from design and production (it makes nearly half of all the fabrics it uses) through to worldwide distribution and retailing. Zara can get a new line to market in just one month, some nine times faster than the industry average, which gives it a significant market edge in a fashion-dominated industry.

Contractual

This is where independent firms at different levels of the distribution chain agree to cooperate in return for specific advantages. Retail cooperatives are one example, where independent retailers band together to increase their buying power, improve their operating systems or to create distinctive brands. The International Co-operative Alliance, the trade body representing this sector, has 230 member organizations from 92 countries active in all sectors of the economy. Japan is home to the number one ranked cooperative, Zen-Noh, a national federation of agriculture and food cooperatives with revenue of over $60 billion.

Franchising   Franchising is the most prevalent form of contractual VMS, operating in hundreds of business sectors, both those providing services such as advertising, accounting and web design, as well as products – Ziebart in car protection and the near-ubiquitous McDonald's. The International Franchise Association Educational Foundation's report, Franchise Business Economic Outlook for 2015 confirms that there are just short of 800,000 franchise outlets in the United States alone, employing 9 million people generating $890 billion in sales (**http://emarket.franchise.org/ FranchiseBizOutlook2015.pdf**).

The franchisor supplies the product or teaches the service to the franchisee, who in turn sells it to the public. In return for this, the franchisee pays a fee and a continuing royalty, based usually on turnover. Franchisees may also be required to buy materials or ingredients from the franchisor, giving the latter an additional income stream. The advantage to the franchisee is a relatively safe and quick way of getting into business but with the support and advice of an experienced organization close at hand.

The franchisor can expand its distribution with the minimum strain on its own capital and have the services of a highly motivated team of owner-managers.

Administered

Administered VMS are those where one or at most a few members dominate the distribution chain and use that position to coordinate the other members' activities. Any part of the chain can dominate. Big retailers such as Wal-Mart, Sainsbury's, Toys R Us and Carrefour can leverage their strength on manufacturers to such an extent they can make them bid for shelf space. Giant consumer firms with strong brands – P&G, Kraft, Coca-Cola, for example – can exert a similar pressure on retailers. Firms away from the fast-moving consumer sector such as Sony and Samsung also exert power over the distribution chain. Samsung achieved its strong position by ditcing its dozen or so subsidiary brands – Wiseview, Tantus and Yepp, none of which meant much to consumers – to put all its resources behind the Samsung name.

Multiple channels

Major companies almost invariably use several channels to market, most noticcably clicks and bricks (see Amazon above for example). There are significant benefits to using more than one route to market if they deliver superior benefits to a particular market segment and don't erode the brand value. Dorling Kindersley, prior to its acquisition by Pearson plc, part of the Penguin Group, had a party plan operation promoting its books along the lines of Avon and other multilevel marketing companies. Pearson, however, cut out this channel immediately post acquisition as it did not correspond with the image of its high street branding.

Channels of distribution

If you are a retailer, restaurant or hotel chain, for example, then your customers will come to you. Your physical location will most probably be the key to success. For businesses in the manufacturing field it is more likely that you will go out to 'find' customers. In this case it will be your channels of distribution that are the vital link. For many businesses delivering a service, the internet will be both the ordering and fulfilment vehicle.

If your customers don't come to you, then you have the following options in getting your product or service to them:

- Retail stores. This general name covers the great range of outlets from the corner shop to Harrods. Some offer speciality goods such as hi-fi equipment, where the customer expects professional help from the staff. Others, such as Marks & Spencer and Tesco, are mostly self-service, with customers making up their own mind on choice of product. The retail experience comes in all shapes and sizes, from the city-centre mini branches of Tesco, Sainsbury's and Marks & Spencer, through speciality discounters – Pound Stretcher *et al* – to hypermarkets and shopping malls and factory outlets selling seconds and last season's fashions in a manner that won't harm brand value.

- Wholesalers and distributors. The pattern of wholesale distribution has changed out of all recognition over the past two decades. It is still an extremely important channel where physical distribution, stock holding, finance and breaking bulk are still profitable functions.

- Cash and carry. This slightly confusing route has replaced the traditional wholesaler as a source of supply for smaller retailers. In return for your paying cash and picking up the goods yourself, the 'wholesaler' shares part of its profit margin with you. The attraction for the wholesaler is improved cash flow and for the retailer a bigger margin and a wide product range. Hypermarkets and discount stores also fit somewhere between the manufacturer and the marketplace.

- Mail order. This specialized technique provides a direct channel to the customer, and is an increasingly popular route for new small businesses.

- Door-to-door selling. Traditionally used by vacuum cleaner distributors and encyclopedia companies, this is now used by insurance companies, cavity-wall insulation firms, double-glazing firms and others. Many use hard-sell techniques, giving door-to-door selling a bad name. However, companies such as Avon Cosmetics have managed to sell successfully door to door without attracting the stigma of unethical selling practices.

- Party plan selling. This is a variation on door-to-door selling that is on the increase, with new party plan ideas arriving from the United States. Agents enrolled by the company invite their friends to a get-together where the products are demonstrated and orders are invited. The agent gets a commission. Party plan has worked very well for Avon and other firms that sell this way.

- Internet. Revenue generation via the internet is big business and getting bigger. For some sectors – advertising, books, music and video – it has become the dominant route to market. There is no longer any serious argument about whether 'bricks' or 'clicks' are the way forward, or if service businesses work better on the web than physical products. Almost every sector has a major part to play and it is increasingly likely that any serious 'bricks' business will either have or be building an internet trading platform. Dixon's, a major electrical retailer, has shifted emphasis from the high street to the web and Tesco has built a £1 billion-plus home delivery business on the back of its store structure. Amazon, the sector's pioneer, now has in effect the first online department store, with a neat sideline in selling second-hand items once the customer has finished with the product.

Selecting distribution channels

These are the factors you should consider when choosing channels of distribution for your particular business:

1 Does it meet your customers' needs? You have to find out how your customers expect their product or service to be delivered to them and why they need that particular route.

2 Will the product itself survive? Fresh vegetables, for example, need to be moved quickly from where they are grown to where they are consumed.

3 Is it compatible with your image? If you are selling a luxury product, then door-to-door selling may spoil the impression you are trying to create in the rest of your marketing effort.

4 How do your competitors distribute? If they have been around for a while and are obviously successful, it is well worth looking at how your competitors distribute and using that knowledge to your advantage.

5 Will the channel be cost-effective? A small manufacturer may not find it cost-effective to sell to retailers over a certain distance because the direct 'drop' size – that is, the load per order – is too small to be worthwhile.

6 Will the mark-up be enough? If your product cannot bear at least a 100 per cent mark-up, then it is unlikely that you will be able to sell it through department stores. Your distribution channel has to be able to make a profit from selling your product too.

7 Push–pull. Moving a product through a distribution channel calls for two sorts of selling activity. 'Push' is the name given to selling your product in, for example, a shop. 'Pull' is the effort that you carry out on the shop's behalf to help it to sell your product out of that shop. That pull may be caused by your national advertising, a merchandising activity or the uniqueness of your product. You need to know how much push and pull are needed for the channel you are considering. If you are not geared up to help retailers to sell your product, and they need that help, then this could be a poor channel.

8 Physical distribution. The way in which you have to move your product to your end-customer is also an important factor to weigh up when choosing a channel. As well as such factors as the cost of carriage, you will also have to decide about packaging materials, warehousing and storage. As a rough rule of thumb, the more stages in the distribution channel, the more robust and expensive your packaging will have to be.

9 Cash flow. Not all channels of distribution settle their bills promptly. Mail-order customers, for example, will pay in advance, but retailers can take up to 90 days or more. You need to take account of this settlement period in your cash flow forecast.

CASE STUDY   Ocado – cutting channels and adding value

In the spring of 2015 Ocado made a £7.2 million pre-tax profit in the year to November 30, 2014, its first ever annual profit and a significant improvement on the £12.5 million loss recorded in the preceding year. Founded in 2000, with its first pilot operation getting underway the following year, the company has lost money steadily throughout its short history.

Nor was it especially surprising that it hadn't turned in a profit in any year since start-up. PeaPod Inc, an Illinois-based company, had tried to make a similar business profitable and failed over the 12 years from its start-up to August 2001, when Royal Ahold, operator of American chains Stop & Shop and Giant Food, bought out the entire company.

Ocado launched a partnership with Waitrose in January 2002 and its service is now available to over 13.5 million households across the South East, the Midlands, the North West and the South Coast of Britain. In February 2014 Ocado launched an online distribution service for Morrisons, a major UK supermarket chain. The deal gave Ocado £170 million upfront as part of a 25 year deal to help the supermarket catch up with major competitors who already had home delivery services with online order processing. Ocado was established with a clear vision: to offer busy people an alternative to going to the supermarket every week. As well as adding value to the customer's buying experience, Ocado would be cutting out one layer of cost in the distribution chain. By fulfilling orders from a dedicated warehouse, Ocado aims to show a virtually live inventory on its webshop, enabling customers to choose from a range of groceries that are actually in stock. Ocado claims to have 20 per cent of Britain's online grocery sales, putting it third behind Tesco and Sainsbury's.

Ocado's founders all have impressive track records in the investment banking field, a definite asset when it comes to pumping up value and raising cash. Tim Steiner, CEO, Jason Gissing now in charge of marketing and external communications and formerly Chief Financial Officer, and Neill Abrams, the third member of the start-up trio, all cut their teeth at Goldman Sachs.

Logistics

The goal of a marketing logistics system is to manage the whole process of getting products to customers in an efficient and cost-effective manner to meet marketing goals, and to get faulty or unwanted products back. This interfaces with a host of related areas of business including physical transportation, warehousing, relationships with suppliers, and inventory and stock management. Some important considerations in logistics include:

- Just in time (JIT) aims to reduce the need for warehousing through accurate sales forecasting. All parties in the distribution channel carry minimum stock and share information on demand levels.

- Vendor-managed inventory (VMT) and continuous inventory replenishment systems (CIRS) require customers to share real-time data on sales demand and inventory levels with suppliers.

Both suppliers and customers, while benefiting from cooperation, have mutually conflicting goals in that they want to shift costs onto the other party. Their capacity for doing so depends on their relative strengths. For example, giant retailers such as Tesco and Marks & Spencer have been very successful in getting their suppliers to carry a major part of the cost of stockholding.

Inventory management

High inventory levels are popular with marketing departments as having them makes satisfying customers an easier task; they are less popular with production departments who may have to carry inventory costs in their budgets. Finance departments insist on having the lowest possible stock levels, as high stock pushes working capital levels up and return on investment down. (See Chapter 12 for information on financial ratios, to see how this works.) This tussle between departments is a strategic issue that has to be resolved by top management. The birth of Waterstone's, the bookshop business founded by Tim Waterstone – fortuitously a marketing visionary, qualified accountant and the company's managing director – provides an interesting illustration of the dimension of the stock control issue. Up until the advent of Waterstone's, the convention had been to store books spine out on shelves, in alphabetical order, under major subject headings – Computing, Sport, Travel. This had the added advantage of making it easy to see what books needed reordering, and stock counts were a simple process. Waterstone, however, knew that 'browsers', the majority (60 per cent, according to his research) of people who go into bookshops to look around, had no idea what book they wanted, so didn't know where to start looking. His differentiating strategy was that as well as following the conventional model of having books on shelves, he scattered the books in piles around the store, using a variety of methods: new books in one pile, special offers in another.

Sales and profits soared sufficient to more than compensate for the near doubling of book stock.

Inventory categories

There are three different categories of inventory that a business needs to have and keep track of:

- Finished goods. These are products ready to ship out to customers. For Apple these would be computers, iPods and so forth, for General Motors vehicles, and for a baker loaves of bread.
- Work in progress (WIP). These are products in the process of being completed. They have used up some raw materials and had workers paid to start the manufacturing process, so the cost will reflect those inputs. For General Motors WIP would include vehicles awaiting paint or a pre-delivery inspection.
- Raw materials. These are the basic materials from which the end product is made. For General Motors this would include metal and paint, but it could also include complete bought-in engines for the vehicles in which it uses third-party power units.

Economic order quantity (EOQ)

Businesses have to carry a certain minimum amount of stock to ensure that the production pipeline works efficiently and likely demand can be met. Ordering large quantities infrequently reduces the order cost but increases the cost of holding stock. This has to be balanced with placing frequent orders, so pushing the costs in placing orders up, but reducing stock holding costs. EOQ is basically an accounting formula that calculates the point at which the combination of order costs and inventory carrying costs are at their least and so arriving at the most cost-effective quantity to order.

The formula for EOQ is:

$$\text{Economic order quantity} = \frac{\sqrt{(2 \times R \times O)}}{C}$$

where R = annual demand in units, O = cost of placing an order, C = cost of carrying a unit of inventory for the year.

InventoryOps.com, a website created and run by Dave Piasecki to support his book *Inventory Accuracy: People, Processes, and Technology* (2003, Ops Publishing) provides a useful starting point in your quest for information on all aspects of Inventory Management and Warehouse Operations. You will find a full explanation of how to use EOQ at: **www.inventoryops.com/economic _order_quantity.htm**.

Outsourcing

Outsourcing is the activity of contracting out the elements that are not considered core or central to the business. It is an important logistics and distribution strategy open to a business that will help it to lower costs and hence be more competitive and to move elements of production or service delivery to a more effective point in the value chain. There are obvious advantages to outsourcing: the best people can do what they are best at. But the approach can get out of hand if left unmanaged. In 2008 IBM completed a major overhaul of its value chain and for the first time in its century-long history created an integrated supply chain (ISC) – a centralized worldwide approach to deciding what to do itself, what to buy in and where to buy in from. Suppliers were halved from 66,000 to 33,000; support locations were reduced from 300 to three global centres, Bangalore, Budapest and Shanghai; manufacturing sites were reduced from 15 to nine, all 'globally enabled' in that they can make almost any of its products at each plant and deliver them anywhere in the world. In the process IBM has lowered operating costs by more than $4 billion a year,

CASE STUDY

No manufacturing. No salesmen. No research and development. Jill Brown grew her business from a standing start to a turnover of £2 million a year in just five years as much by deciding what not to do as by what it actually does. The business she founded, Brown Electronics, supplies switches for computer equipment, the kind of gadget that, for example, allows half a dozen personal computers to use one printer between them.

She says: 'I didn't want to get into manufacturing myself. I save myself the headaches. Why should I start manufacturing as long as I've got my bottom line right? Turnover is vanity, profit is sanity. I have worked for other people who wanted to grow big just for the kudos.'

Instead, Jill contracts out to other people's factories. She feels she still has control over quality, since any item that is not up to standard can be sent back. She also has the ultimate threat of taking away trade, which would leave the manufacturers she uses with a large void to fill. 'We would do so if quality was not good enough. Many manufacturers have underutilized capacity.'

Jill uses freelance salesmen on a commission basis. She explains: 'I didn't want a huge sales force. Most sales managers sit in their cars at the side of the road filling in swindle sheets. Research and development are another area where expenses would be terrific. We have freelance design teams working on specific products. We give them a brief and they quote a price. The cost still works out at twice what you expected, but at least you have a measure of control. I could not afford to employ R&D staff full-time and I would not need them full-time. My system minimizes the risks and gives us a quality we could not afford as a small business.'

Indirectly, Jill provides work for about 380 people, while still being able to operate out a space not much larger than a two-bedroom flat.

Pros and cons of outsourcing

Outsourcing has many benefits for a new business – and for an established one, for that matter. But there are also some inherent dangers. In summary:

Pros

- Access to expertise. It can be almost impossible for a small firm, especially in the start-up phase, to have a team on board with the latest expertise. It is easier for larger, established firms to attract the best staff and to have the latest equipment. That in turn means you as a new entrant can have access to state-of-the-art products and services from the outset.

- Greater scalability. It just isn't cost-effective to have production resources on hand from the outset to meet possible future demand. By outsourcing to one or more suppliers you can have, in effect, any level of output you want, all at a variable cost rather than a fixed cost. (See Chapter 7 for more on fixed and variable costs.)

- More predictable costs. While outside suppliers and manufacturers can sometimes provide products and services at a lower cost than doing it yourself, the main financial reason for choosing an outsourcing solution is to make costs more predictable and establish a smoother cash flow.

- Free up your time. Turning over non-core functions leaves you and your team free to concentrate on strategic development and core business functions.

- Economies of scale. An outsource supplier has a higher volume of throughput than you, or any of their other customers, is likely to have. That means better negotiating leverage, lower material prices and better equipment utilization. So their fixed costs are spread over more than one client and part of that benefit can come to you in lower prices.

Cons

- Confidentiality of data. This is a fundamental concern for any business and if the activity concerned involves giving another business access to such information it may not be a good area to outsource. If you do outsource anything involving company secrets, ensure that basic contractual provisions, including intellectual property rights (see Chapter 10) and non-disclosure agreements, are established to protect confidential information.

- Quality control. This is a strategic issue when it comes to outsourcing, and an emerging danger with the arrival of the 'socially minded customer' is that people are looking more closely at companies and their products before buying from them. Getting garments made cheaply by child labour is very much an issue on consumers' radar. So while outsourcing plays a vital role in operations it still has to be managed and conform with corporate ethical standards. There are a number of well-regarded quality standards that may help you monitor and control your quality. The BS EN ISO 9000 series are perhaps the best-known standards. They can ensure that your operating procedure delivers a consistent and acceptable standard of products or services. If you are supplying to large firms they may insist on your meeting one of these quality standards, or on auditing your premises to satisfy themselves. The British Standards Institute (**www.bsi-global.com**) can provide details of these standards.

- Loss of control. Although you can change outsource suppliers, as long as an activity is bought in you will never have full control over the area. You will also find it difficult to develop the skills needed to keep abreast of changes in the field.

Setting the boundaries

The starting point in outsourcing is to decide what you are good at, then consider outsourcing everything else. Focus your company on your core competency, and stick to the knitting. There are some things that are central to your business that you should probably not outsource at the outset. You need to keep an eye on them until you have them fully under control. These include cash-flow management and most aspects of customer relations. Later on you may consider, for example, outsourcing collecting cash from customers to an invoice discounter or factoring service who may have better processes in place than you could afford to handle larger volumes of invoices.

Some tasks make sense to outsource initially and bring in house later. If you plan to offer a product or service that you're not expert at, it makes sense to contract out the core function, at least until you gain confidence and expertise.

CASE STUDY   Death in China

In March 2015 Tian Fulei, 26, a worker at a factory owned by Pegatron, a Chinese hardware supplier, died suddenly, according to his parents, from working excessive overtime hours. As a Chinese person takes their own life every two minutes, some 287,000 in total each year, this event could reasonably been expected to sink without trace. That might well have been true had it not been for the fact that Pegatron is one of Apple's Chinese outsourced suppliers. That fact along with a history of similar problems – in January 2012 some 150 Chinese workers at Foxconn, another factory used by Apple, Sony, Nintendo and HP, among many others, threatened to commit suicide by leaping from their factory roof in protest at their working conditions – made the story headline news.

Apple's problems with outsourcing in the region stretches back to 2009 when a worker at Foxconn sent a message before jumping from his apartment building, complaining that he had been 'chastised' very seriously for losing an iPhone prototype. Though Apple and other Western companies using Asian outsources have confirmed their serious concern, as only Foxconn and two rivals are capable of mass manufacturing Apple products, the power in this outsourcing relationship does not appear to rest with Apple.

Physical evidence

This 'P' of the marketing mix is concerned with ensuring that any premises used by a business is seen as appropriate and supportive of a business's position in the marketplace. So, for example Lidl's approach to merchandising, where products are typically stacked on or close to the ground on removable pallets for easy re-stocking, would not support a brand such as Whole Foods Market where the emphasis is on quality and range – their bakeries turn out dozens of goodies such as Bavarian pretzels, cranberry scones, oatmeal cream pies, all on display in a visually exciting manner.

Online video courses and lectures

7Ps of Marketing: Physical Evidence. Once a day marketing:
    www.youtube.com/watch?v=zbW4GGf8JU0

Distribution and Logistics Management: London School of Business and Finance: **http://freevideolectures.com/Course/2749/Marketing-Management/4**

The Future of Logistics and Trade – Scott Davis, CEO UPS talks on MIT Global Leadership Lecture: **www.youtube.com/watch?v=wQrltY2K6bs**

Marketing Channels & Their Functions. Professor Kim Donahue, Kelley School of Business: **www.youtube.com/watch?v=fifM5-qBH5E**

Supply Chain Management Masterclass – Dr Sinéad Roden, Cass Business School: **www.youtube.com/watch?v=nmO-y0q8sdI**

Supply Chain Disruptions and Humanitarian Logistics – Professor Yossi Sheffi. MIT: **www.youtube.com/watch?v=ky_h4YB_O4U**

Online case studies

Amazon's Seventh Generation Fulfilment: CBS 60 Minutes: **www.cbsnews.com/news/amazons-jeff-bezos-looks-to-the-future/**

Desigual Fashion, Warehouse Logistics and Distribution: Desigual operates 157 stores worldwide and annually provides 10 million garments: **www.youtube.com/watch?v=9I6HPpDUR-s**

Ford Motor Company's European Supply Chain Case Study: Penske Logistics: **www.youtube.com/watch?v=KWABT48wTFw**

Ocado:

Paul Clarke, Director of Technology at Ocado, talks about how technology is driving their business, outlining why long-term value creation for shareholders comes before anything else: **www.youtube.com/watch?v=GP4T6tMqWcI**

Waitrose and Ocado, Distribution and Logistics Management. London School of Business and Finance: **http://freevideolectures.com/Course/2749/Marketing-Management/2**

Watch this February 2014 video clip explaining why loss-making Ocado was still worth £3bn: **www.telegraph.co.uk/finance/personalfinance/investing/10616950/Why-is-loss-making-Ocado-worth-3bn.html**

P & G: Supply Network Operations (Logistics) at Procter & Gamble, Graeme Carter, Associate Director, Supply Network Operations: **www.youtube.com/watch?v=GEceq7MOSs0**

Wal-Mart Supply Chain: Uni Global Union's video takes a look at Wal-Mart's history of worker mistreatment – including below federal poverty level wages, intimidation and poor health and safety standards: **www.youtube.com/watch?v=yZC4neLax5o**

7

Pricing

- Understanding the economics of demand
- Assessing market structures
- Recognizing the components of cost
- Break-even analysis
- Strategic pricing options
- Identifying unprofitable products and services

Business schools, as you might expect, take the subject of pricing very seriously; their elevated fee structures confirm this. None more so than at the Wharton School, University of Pennsylvania, where Jagmohan S Raju, a leading authority on competitive pricing strategy, resides as Joseph J Aresty Professor. Here students spend the equivalent of four full days systematically studying pricing strategies designed to capture maximum value, under all types of market conditions. These include complex situations such as pricing new products, products with short life cycles, dynamic pricing, and where products and services are bundled together into a single proposition. Professor Raju contrasts the systematic approach he and professors at other business schools take with the ad hoc or trial-and-error approach to pricing taken by most businesses, which his research shows can significantly reduce a firm's bottom line.

For the MBA student, pricing straddles a number of academic disciplines. Economics provides the big picture, a macro, external overview of factors that affect demand, including the nature of the market and competitive structure the firm faces. Accountancy provides the micro framework for understanding the characteristics of a firm's cost structure, how that changes with changes in volume and consequently how to set target prices to achieve desired profit goals. Marketing strategy is used to provide frameworks for determining pricing policies and procedures. Finally, a blend of all these disciplines can be used to eliminate products and services that are unlikely to achieve price levels that will meet profit goals.

Economic theory and pricing strategy

The main economic concept that underpins almost the whole subject of pricing is that of price elasticity of demand. The concept itself is simple enough: the higher the price of a good or service, the less of it you are likely to sell. Obviously it's not quite that simple in practice: the number of buyers, their expectations, preference and ability to pay, the availability of substitute products. Figure 7.1 is that of a theoretical demand curve.

FIGURE 7.1   Demand curve

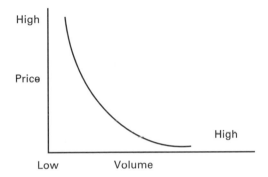

The figure shows how the volume of sales of a particular good or service will change with changes in price. The elasticity of demand is a measure of the degree to which consumers are sensitive to price. This is calculated by dividing the percentage change in demand by the percentage change in price. If a price is reduced by 50 per cent (eg from £100 to £50) and the quantity demanded increased by 100 per cent (eg from 1,000 to 2,000), the elasticity of demand coefficient is 2 (100 ÷ 50). Here the quantity demanded changes by a bigger percentage than the price change, so demand is considered to be elastic. Were the demand in this case to rise by only 25 per cent, then the elasticity of demand coefficient would be 0.25 (25 ÷ 100). Here the demand is described as being 'inelastic', as the percentage demand change is smaller than that of the price change.

Having a feel for elasticity is important in developing a business's marketing strategy, but there is no perfect scientific way to work out what the demand coefficient is; it has to be assessed by 'feel'. Unfortunately the price elasticity changes at different price levels. For example, reducing the price of a bottle of vodka by half might double sales, but halving it again may not have such a dramatic effect. In fact, it could encourage one group of buyers, those giving it as a present, for example, to feel that giving something that cheap is rather insulting.

Market structures

The whole of the subject of economics as practised in advanced economies is predicated on the belief that market forces are allowed a large degree of freedom. New firms can set up in business, charging the price they see fit, and if their strategy is flawed they will be allowed to fail. Price is allowed to send the important signals throughout the economy, apportioning demand and resources accordingly. But perfect competition where price is allowed such freedom is only one of four prevailing market structures; although market economies are dominated by near-perfect competition, that is not maintained without a struggle.

There are four market structures at work in different industries and the one prevailing in your sector will profoundly influence the degree of freedom you have over setting prices.

Monopoly

Monopolies exist where a single supplier dominates the market and so renders normal competitive forces largely redundant. Price, quality and innovation are compromised, so delivering less value to end-consumers than they might otherwise expect. Microsoft has a near-monopolistic grip on the PC operating system market; Pfizer, the pharmaceutical giant, exercises similar domination through its patent on the drug Viagra; British Airports Authority (BAA), which runs Heathrow, Gatwick and Stansted, has a similar hold on London air traffic.

Monopolies claim that without being allowed to dominate their market it would be impossible to get sufficient economies of scale to reinvest. That was the argument of the early railway companies and it was BAA's argument in 2008 in defending itself against the prospects of a government-enforced break-up.

In countries where monopolies are seen as being detrimental, bodies exist to regulate the market to prevent them becoming too powerful. The UK has the Competition and Market Authority (**www.gov.uk/government/organisations/competition-and-markets-authority**), the United States the Federal Trade Commission (**www.ftc.gov**) and EU countries the European Commission (**http://ec.europa.eu/competition/index_en.html**), all keeping monopolies in check.

A duopoly is, as the name would suggest, a particular form of monopoly, with only two firms in the market.

Oligopoly

This is where between three and 20 large firms dominate a market, or where four or five firms share more than 40 per cent of the market. The danger for consumers and suppliers alike is that these dominant firms can control the market to their disadvantage. Supermarket chains in the UK, airlines, oil exploration and refining businesses the world over operate as virtual oligopolies. Frequently the temptation to act in a cartel to fix prices is too great to resist. BA colluded with Virgin Atlantic on at least six occasions between August 2004 and January 2006. In that period the two companies, the dominant players on the route from London to US cities, colluded with each other to fix the price of fuel surcharges, which rose from £5 to £60 per ticket. British Airways had to set aside £350 million to deal with fines in the UK and USA.

Perfect competition

This is a utopian environment in which there are many suppliers of identical products or services, with equal access to all the necessary resources such as money, materials, technology and people. There are no barriers to entry, so businesses can enter or leave the market at will and consumers have perfect information on every aspect of the alternative goods on offer.

Competitive markets

Sometimes referred to confusingly as monopolistic competition, this rests between oligopoly and, but closer to, perfect competition. Here a large number of relatively small competitors, each with small market shares, compete with differentiated products satisfying diverse consumer wants and needs.

CASE STUDY   HourlyNerd

Rob Biederman, Peter Maglathlin and Patrick Petitti co-founded HourlyNerd in 2013 whilst finishing off their MBA programme at the Harvard Business School.

The limiting factor in demand from top consultancy practices such as Bain, McKinsey and the Boston Consulting Group is the exorbitant fee structure. Only the biggest organizations with the most serious of issues to address are willing and able to fork out for advice from serious consulting firms. HourlyNerd, set up by three Harvard MBAs aims to disrupt this marketplace and change the price/demand curve radically. Essentially, HourlyNerd runs a 'marriage bureau', matching up MBA students from the top 20 business schools with small businesses in need of some consulting. Quality is assured as these 'consultants' have all been in effect vetted by the universities through their rigorous admissions standards.

The average pay has been $35 an hour, for projects requiring 10 to 15 hours of work. In the first six months more than 500 MBA students and 45 small businesses with projects in mind have registered on the site. HourlyNerd holds the client's money, only paying the student when the project is completed to the small-business person's satisfaction.

Projects include a small Spanish manufacturer whose objective is to enter the US market and needs pricing information and primary research for construction bricks, glazed bricks, klinker bricks and facing bricks. They are paying $2,500 for this work. A small private equity firm has budgeted $5,000 to fully research and collect data in order to write a business plan. An online e-commerce portal for attracting digital content from elite contributors and selling the same to elite niche target audience has set $20,000 aside for this project.

The company has raised $750,000 in a first round of seed capital finance, over half from a business owner who is on record as saying that getting an MBA is 'an absolute waste of time'.

Pricing decisions and their relationship with costs, volume and ultimately profits

Working out the cost of making a product or delivering a service and consequently how much to charge doesn't seem too complicated. At first glance the problem is simple. You just add up all the costs and charge a bit more. The more you charge above your costs, provided the customers will keep on buying, the more profit you make. Unfortunately as soon as you start to do the sums the problem gets a little more complex. For a start, not all costs have the same characteristics. Some costs, for example, do not change however much you sell. If you are running a shop, the rent and rates are relatively constant figures, completely independent of the volume of your sales. On the other hand, the cost of the products sold from the shop is completely dependent on volume. The more you sell, the more it costs you to buy in stock:

$$\text{Cost of rent and rates for shop} = 2,500$$
$$\text{Cost of 1,000 units of volume of product} = 1,000$$
$$\text{Total costs} = 3,500$$

You can't really add up those two types of costs until you have made an assumption about volume – how much you plan to sell. Look again at the simple example above. Until we decide to buy and, we hope, sell 1,000 units of our product, we cannot total the costs. With the volume hypothesized we can arrive at a cost per unit of product of:

$$\text{Total costs} \div \text{number of units} = 3,500 \div 1,000 = 3.50$$

Now, provided we sell out all the above at 3.50 each, we will always be profitable. But will we? Suppose we do not sell all the 1,000 units, what then? With a selling price of 4.50 we could, in theory, make a profit of 1,000 if we sell all 1,000 units. That is total sales revenue of 4,500, minus total costs of 3,500. But if we only sell 500 units, our total revenue drops to 2,250 and we actually lose 1,250 (total revenue 2,250 – total costs 3,500). So at one level of sales a selling price of 4.50 is satisfactory, and at another it is a disaster. This very simple example shows that all those decisions are intertwined. Costs, sales volume, selling prices and profits are all linked together. A decision taken in any one of these areas has an impact on the other areas. To understand the relationship between these factors, we need a picture or model of how they link up. Before we can build this model, we need some more information on each of the component parts of cost.

The components of cost

Understanding the behaviour of costs as the trading patterns in a business change is an area of vital importance to decision makers. It is this 'dynamic' nature in every business that makes good costing decisions the key to survival and provides the MBA with a wealth of opportunities to demonstrate his or her skill and knowledge.

The last example showed that if the situation was static and predictable, a profit was certain, but if any one component in the equation was not a certainty (in that example it was volume), then the situation was quite different. To see how costs behave under changing conditions we first have to identify the different types of cost.

Fixed costs

Fixed costs are costs that happen, by and large, whatever the level of activity. For example, the cost of buying a car is the same whether it is driven 100 miles a year or 20,000 miles. The same is also true of the road tax, the insurance and any extras, such as a stereo system or satellite navigation system.

In a business, as well as the cost of buying cars, there are other fixed costs such as plant, equipment, computers, desks and answering machines. But certain less tangible items can also be fixed costs – for example, rent, rates, insurance, etc, which are usually set quite independently of how successful or otherwise a business is.

Costs such as most of those mentioned above are fixed irrespective of the timescale under consideration. Other costs, such as those of employing people, while theoretically variable in the short term, in practice are fixed. In other words, if sales demand goes down and a business needs fewer people, the costs cannot be shed for several weeks (notice, holiday pay, redundancy, etc). Also, if the people involved are highly skilled or expensive to recruit and train (or in some other way particularly valuable) and the downturn looks a short one, it may not be cost-effective to reduce those short-run costs in line with falling demand. So viewed over a period of weeks and months, labour is a fixed cost. Over a longer period it may not be fixed.

We could draw a simple chart showing how fixed costs behave as the 'dynamic' volume changes. The first phase of our cost model is shown in

Figure 7.2. This shows a static level of fixed costs over a particular range of output. To return to our previous example, this could show the fixed cost, rent and rates for a shop to be constant over a wide range of sales levels. Once the shop owner has reached a satisfactory sales and profit level in one shop, he or she may decide to rent another one, in which case the fixed costs will step up. This can be shown in the variation on the fixed cost model in Figure 7.3.

FIGURE 7.2   Cost model 1: showing fixed costs

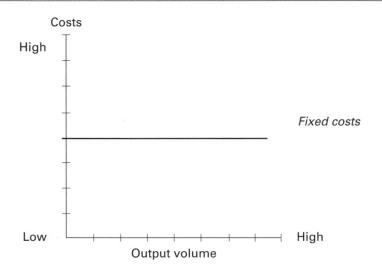

FIGURE 7.3   Variation on cost model 1: showing a step up in fixed costs

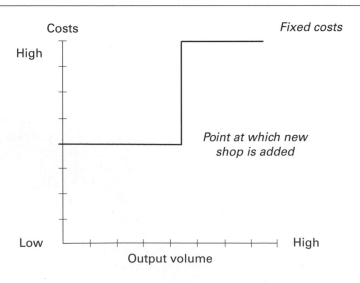

Variable costs

These are costs that change in line with output. Raw materials for production, packaging materials, bonuses, piece rates, sales commission and postage are some examples. The important characteristic of a variable cost is that it rises or falls in direct proportion to any growth or decline in output volumes. We can now draw a chart showing how variable costs behave as volume changes. The second phase of our cost model will look like Figure 7.4.

FIGURE 7.4   Cost model 2: showing behaviour of variable costs as volume changes

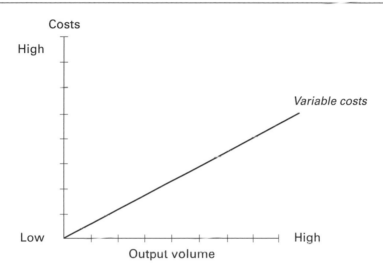

There is a popular misconception that defines fixed costs as those costs that are predictable, and variable costs as those that are subject to change at any moment. The definitions already given are the only valid ones for costing purposes.

Semi-variable costs

The relevant market will be shared by various competing businesses in different proportions. Typically there will be a market leader, a couple of market followers and a host of businesses trailing in their wake. Unfortunately, not all costs fit easily into either the fixed or variable category. Some costs have both a fixed and a variable element. For example, a mobile phone has a monthly rental cost, which is fixed, and a cost per unit consumed over and above a set usage rate, which is variable. In this particular example low consumers can be seriously penalized. If only a few calls are made each month, the total cost per call (fixed rental + cost per unit ÷ number of calls) can be several pounds.

Other examples of this dual-component cost effect are photocopier rentals, electricity and gas.

These semi-variable costs must be split into their fixed and variable elements. For most small businesses this will be a fairly simple process; nevertheless, it is essential to do it accurately or else much of the purpose and benefits of this method of cost analysis will be wasted.

Break-even analysis

Bringing both fixed and variable costs together we can build a costing model that shows how total costs behave for different levels of output (Figure 7.5).

FIGURE 7.5   Cost model showing total costs and fixed costs

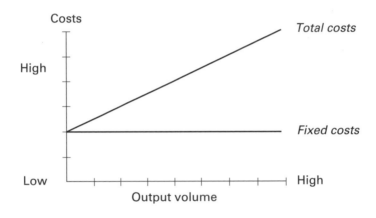

So any company capturing a sizeable market share will have an implied cost advantage over any competitor with a smaller market share. That cost advantage can then be used to make more profit, lower prices and compete for an even greater share of the market or invest in making the product better and so steal a march on competitors. By starting the variable costs from the plateau of the fixed costs, we can produce a line showing the total costs. Taking vertical and horizontal lines from any point in the total cost line will give the total costs for any chosen output volume. This is an essential feature of the costing model that lets us see how costs change with different output volumes: in other words, accommodating the dynamic nature of a business.

It is to be hoped that we are not simply producing things and creating costs. We are also selling things and creating income. So a further line can be added to the model to show sales revenue as it comes in. To help bring the model to life, let's add some figures, for illustration purposes only.

Figure 7.6 shows the break-even point (BEP). Perhaps the most important single calculation in the whole costing exercise is to find the point at which real profits start to be made. The point where the sales revenue line crosses

FIGURE 7.6   Cost model showing break-even point

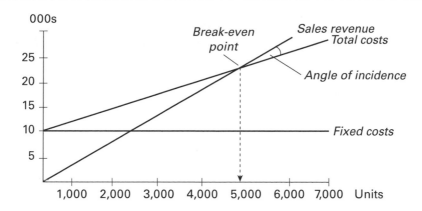

the total costs line is the break-even point. It is only after that point has been reached that a business can start to make a profit. We can work this out by drawing a graph, such as the example in Figure 7.6, or by using a simple formula. The advantage of using the formula as well is that you can experiment by changing the values of some of the elements in the model quickly.

The equation for the BEP is:

BEP = Fixed costs ÷ (unit selling price – variable costs per unit)

This is quite logical. Before you can reach profits you must pay for the variable costs. This is done by deducting those costs from the unit selling price. What is left (usually called the unit contribution) is available to meet the fixed costs. Once enough units have been sold to meet these fixed costs, the BEP has been reached. Let's try the sum out, given the following information shown on the break-even chart:

$$
\begin{aligned}
\text{Fixed costs} &= 10{,}000 \\
\text{Selling price} &= 5 \text{ per unit} \\
\text{Variable cost} &= 3 \text{ per unit} \\
\text{So BEP} = 10{,}000 \div (5 - 3) &= 10{,}000 \div 2 = 5{,}000 \text{ units}
\end{aligned}
$$

Now we can see that 5,000 units must be sold at 5 each before we can start to make a profit. We can also see that if 7,000 is our maximum output we have only 2,000 units available to make our required profit target. Obviously, the more units we have available for sale (ie the maximum output that can realistically be sold) after our break-even point, the better. The relationship between total sales and the break-even point is called the margin of safety.

Margin of safety

This is usually expressed as a percentage and can be calculated as shown in Table 7.1. Clearly, the lower this percentage, the lower the business's capacity

TABLE 7.1   Calculating a margin of safety

Total sales	35,000	(7,000 units × £5 selling price)
Minus break-even point	25,000	(5,000 units × £5 selling price)
Margin of safety	10,000	
Margin of safety as a percentage of sales	29%	(10,000 ÷ 35,000)

for generating profits. A low margin of safety might signal the need to rethink fixed costs, selling price or the maximum output of the business. The angle formed at the BEP between the sales revenue line and the total costs line is called the angle of incidence. The size of the angle shows the rate at which profit is made after the break-even point. A large angle means a high rate of profit per unit sold after the BEP.

Meeting profit objectives

By adding in the final element, desired profits, we can have a comprehensive model to help us with costing and pricing decisions. Supposing in the previous example we knew that we had to make 10,000 profit to achieve a satisfactory return on the capital invested in the business, we could amend our BEP formula to take account of this objective:

BEPP (break-even profit point) = (Fixed costs + profit objective) ÷
(unit selling price − variable costs per unit)

Putting some figures from our last example into this equation, and choosing 10,000 as our profit objective, we can see how it works. Unfortunately, without further investment in fixed costs, the maximum output in our example is only 7,000 units, so unless we change something the profit objective will not be met.

BEPP = (10,000 + 10,000) ÷ (5 − 3) = 20,000 ÷ 2 = 10,000 units

The great strength of this model is that each element can be changed in turn, on an experimental basis, to arrive at a satisfactory and achievable result. Let us return to this example. We could start our experimenting by seeing what the selling price would have to be to meet our profit objective. In this case we leave the selling price as the unknown, but we have to decide the BEP in advance (you cannot solve a single equation with more than one unknown). It would not be unreasonable to say that we would be prepared to sell our total output to meet the profit objective. So the equation now works out as follows:

7,000 = 20,000 ÷ (unit selling price − 3)

Moving the unknown over to the left-hand side of the equation we get:

$$\text{Unit selling price} = 3 + (20{,}000 \div 7{,}000) = 3 + 2.86 = 5.86$$

We now know that with a maximum capacity of 7,000 units and a profit objective of 10,000, we have to sell at 5.86 per unit. Now if the market will stand that price, then this is a satisfactory result. If it will not, then we are back to experimenting with the other variables. We must find ways of decreasing the fixed or variable costs, or increasing the output of the plant, by an amount sufficient to meet our profit objective.

Negotiating special deals

Managers are frequently laid open to the temptation of taking a particularly big order at a 'cut-throat' price and it is the MBA's role to make sure that however attractive the proposition may look at first glance, certain conditions must be met before the order can be safely accepted. Let us look at an example – a slight variation on the last one. Your company has a maximum output of 10,000 units, without any major investment in fixed costs. At present you are just not prepared to invest more money until the business has proved itself. The background information is:

Maximum output	=	10,000 units
Output to meet profit objective	=	7,000 units
Selling price	=	5.86
Fixed costs	=	10,000
Unit variable cost	=	3.00
Profitability objective	=	10,000

The break-even chart will look like Figure 7.7.

The managers you are advising are fairly confident that they can sell 7,000 units at 5.86 each, but that still leaves 3,000 units unsold – should they decide to produce them. Out of the blue an enquiry comes in for about 3,000 units, but a strong hint is given that nothing less than a 33 per cent discount will clinch the deal. What should you recommend? Using the costing information assembled so far, you can show the present breakdown of costs and arrive at your selling price.

$$\text{Unit cost breakdown} = 3.00$$
$$\text{Variable costs} = 1.43 \ (10{,}000 \text{ fixed costs} \div 7{,}000 \text{ units})$$
$$\text{Contribution to fixed costs}$$
$$\text{Contribution to meet profit objective}$$
$$= 1.43 \ (10{,}000 \text{ profit objective} \div 7{,}000 \text{ units})$$
$$\text{Selling price} = 5.86$$

As all fixed costs are met on the 7,000 units sold (or to be sold), the remaining units can be sold at a price that covers both variable costs and the profitability contribution, so you can negotiate at the same level of profitability, down to 4.43, just under 25 per cent off the current selling price. However, any selling

FIGURE 7.7   Break-even chart for special deals

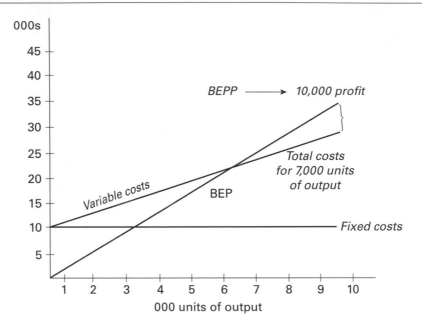

price above the 3.00 variable cost will generate extra profits, but these sales will be at the expense of your profit margin. A lower profit margin in itself is not necessarily a bad thing if it results in a higher return on capital employed, but first you must do the sums. There is a great danger with negotiating orders at marginal costs, as these costs are called, in that you do not achieve your break-even point and so perpetuate losses.

Dealing with multiple products and services

The examples used to illustrate the break-even point model were of necessity simple. Few if any businesses sell only one product or service, so a more general equation may be more useful to deal with real-world situations.

In such a business, to calculate your break-even point you must first establish your gross profit. This is calculated by deducting the money paid out to suppliers from the money received from customers.

For example, if you are aiming for a 40 per cent gross profit, expressed in decimals as 0.4, your fixed costs are 10,000 and your overall profit objective is 4,000, then the sum will be as follows:

$$\text{BEP} = \frac{10,000 + 4,000}{0.4} = \frac{14,000}{0.4} = 35,000$$

The examples used to illustrate the break-even point model were of necessity simple. So to reach the target you must achieve a 35,000 turnover. (You can check this out for yourself: look back to the previous example where the BEP was 7,000 units and the selling price was 5 each. Multiplying those figures gives a turnover of 35,000. The gross profit in that example was also 2 ÷ 5, or 40 per cent.)

Getting help with break-even

You have few options to get help with making break-even calculations. A friendly accountant can show you, and if your algebra is a bit rusty you can take a quick refresher at the BBC's Bite Size site (**www.bbc.co.uk/bitesize> ks3>Maths>Algebra>Equations**).

Alternatively there are a number of online spreadsheets and tutorials that will take you through the process. biz/ed (**www.bized.co.uk**>Virtual Worlds> Virtual Learning Arcade>Break-even Analysis) is a simulation that lets you see the effect of changing variables on a fairly complex break-even calculation.

Pricing strategies – the marketing options

Seemingly the simplest of the marketing choices it is often the most agonizing decision that MBAs are faced with. The subject transcends almost every area of a business. The economists get the ball rolling with ideas around the elasticity of demand. Set too high a price and no one comes to the dance; too low and your sales could go right off the scale, generating plenty of cost but very little profit. The accounts and production teams are concerned that sales will at least be sufficient to reach break-even in reasonable time. The strategists are worried about the signals in terms of corporate positioning that prices can send. However profitable a certain price may be for the business, it may just be so low that it devalues other products in your range. Apple, for example, has a position fairly and squarely at the innovator end of the product adoption cycle. Its customers expect to pay high prices for the privilege of being the first users of a new product. The iPod was positioned above the Walkman in price terms, though as the market for pocket sound devices was already mature there was scope to come into the market lower down the price spectrum.

Skim vs penetrate

Two generic pricing strategies need to be decided between before you can fine-tune your plans. Skimming involves setting a price at the high end of what you believe the market will bear. This would be a strategy to pursue if you have a very limited amount of product available for sale and would rather 'ration' than disappoint customers. It is also a way to target the innovators in your market who are happy to pay a premium to be amongst the first to have a new product. To be successful with this strategy you would need to be sure competitors can't just step in and soak up the demand that you have created.

Penetration pricing is the mirror image: prices are set at the low end, while being above your costs. Prices are competitive with the deliberate intention of eliminating your customers' need to shop around. Slogans such as 'everyday low prices' are used to emphasize this policy. The aim here is to grab as much of the market as you can before competitors arrive on the scene, and hopefully lock them out. The danger here is that you need a lot of volume either of product or hours sold before you can make a decent profit. This in turn means tying up more money for longer before you break even.

Dragon Lock, Cranfield enterprise programme participants (the executive puzzle makers), adopted a skim strategy when they launched their new product. Their product was easy to copy and impossible to patent, so they chose low price as a strategy to discourage competitors and to swallow up the market quickly.

Danger of low pricing

Aside from the obvious possible problems of the cash-flow implications of stretching out the break-even horizon and quality/image issues, it is an immutable law that raising prices is a whole lot more difficult than lowering them. It is less of a problem if the market as a whole is moving up, but raising a price because you set it too low in the first place is a challenge, to say the least.

Value pricing

Another consideration when setting your prices is the value of the product or service in the customers' mind. Their opinion of price may have little or no relation to the cost, and they may be ignorant of the price charged by the competition, especially if the product or service is a new one. In fact, many consumers perceive price as a reliable guide to the value they can expect to receive. The more you pay, the more you get. With this in mind, had Dyson launched his revolutionary vacuum cleaner, with its claims of superior performance, at a price below that of its peers, then some potential customers might have questioned those claims. In its literature Dyson cites as the inspiration for the new vacuum cleaner the inferior performance of existing products in the same price band. A product at six times the Dyson price is the one whose performance Dyson seeks to emulate. The image created is that, although the price is at the high end of general run-of-the-mill products, the performance is disproportionately greater. The runaway success of Dyson's vacuum cleaner would tend to endorse this argument.

Real-time pricing

The stock market works by gathering information on supply and demand. If more people want to buy a share than sell it, the price goes up until supply and demand are matched. If the information is perfect (that is, every buyer and seller knows what is going on), the price is optimized. For most businesses this is not a practical proposition. Their customers expect the same price every time for the same product or service – they have no accurate idea what the demand is at any given moment.

However, for businesses selling on the internet, computer networks have made it possible to see how much consumer demand exists for a given product at any time. Anyone with a point-of-sale till could do the same, but the reports might come in weeks later. This means online companies could change their prices hundreds of times each day, tailoring them to certain circumstances or certain markets, and so improve profits dramatically. easyJet, the budget airline, does just this. It prices to fill its planes, and you could pay anything from £30 to £200 (including airport taxes) for the same trip, depending on the demand for that flight. Ryanair and Eurotunnel have similar price ranges based on the basic rule – discounted low fares for early reservations and full fares for desperate late callers.

Internet auction pricing

Once the prerogative of the fine art and antiques markets, auctioning is a fast-growing pricing strategy for a whole host of very different types of business. The theory of auctioning is simple. Have as many interested potential buyers as possible see an item, set a time limit for the transaction to be completed and let them fight it out. The highest bidder wins and in general you can get higher prices than by selling through traditional pricing strategies. eBay was a pioneer in the new auction house sector and is still perhaps the best known. But there are dozens of others appearing and other auction houses you can plug into.

Pay-what-you-like pricing

This strategy is based on the auction concept but buyers set their own price. The twist is that there is no limit on supply, so everyone can buy at the price they want to pay. The band Radiohead released its seventh album, *In Rainbows*, in October 2007 as a download on its website where fans could pay what they wished, from nothing to £99.99. Estimates by the online survey group comScore indicate that of the 1.2 million visitors to Radiohead's website, three out of five downloaders paid nothing while those paying averaged £3 per album. So, allowing for the freeloaders, the band realized £1.11 per album. The band reckon that was more than they would have made in a traditional label deal. In fact, the version of the album released in this way was not the definitive one. That was released three months later in CD format, going straight to number one in the USA and the UK.

A number of restaurateurs have experimented with this pricing strategy with some success, but it is as yet in its infancy. Still, eBay is only a 'baby' in terms of business model, so watch this space.

Review your products and services

Selling the wrong products to the wrong people at the wrong price is a sure-fire way to rack up costs with little prospect of getting a worthwhile return. Just because you are making a product or service and your customers are happy and coming back for more doesn't mean you should continue doing so. Sometimes, as the Unilever case study below shows, doing less now is the best way to end up with a better business in the future.

CASE STUDY   Unilever

In 2015 when Unilever published their accounts for the preceding year the chairman stated: 'Our growth model is based on a leaner, more agile Unilever.' Reporting turnover at €48.4 billion with their operating profit margin up 0.4 percentage points to 14.5 per cent, the chairman continued: 'Our business is growing ahead of our markets... the consistency of our delivery is underlined by the fact that our average growth over the last five years is 4.9 per cent, making us one of the most reliable performers in our industry.'

The genesis of Unilever's lean strategy can be traced back to the spring of 2009 when nearly every bank in the world was selling off any product group that was not core and even a few that were. The Royal Bank of Scotland put a fifth of its assets into a separate business ready to be sold off, leaving the management free to concentrate on the part that might possibly have a future. A decade earlier, in September 1999, Unilever, a €34 billion (£30/$50 billion) business employing some 300,000 people in 90 countries and the name behind such brands as Magnum, Omo, Dove, Knorr, Ben & Jerry's, Lipton, SlimFast, Iglo, Unox and Becel, announced its intention to focus on fewer, stronger brands in order to 'promote faster growth and improved margins'. Over the following four years Unilever set out to whittle its brands down to just 400 from the 1,600 it started out with. At the same time it shook up its top management, splitting the company into two separate global units, food, and home and personal care.

You don't have to take quite as long as Unilever did to remove products from your portfolio. Budget airline Ryanair took just a few days to cut back its winter flight schedule when faced with the cost rise imposed by the UK government's departure tax. It stripped 16 aircraft from Stansted routes, reducing its capacity by 40 per cent, switching to other less costly European bases. Ryanair took this decision four months before the new tax was due to come into effect.

Costing to eliminate unprofitable products and services

Not all of a business's products will always be profitable. Settling down to allocate 'real' fixed costs to products can be something of an eye-opener for managers. Look at the example in Table 7.2. The business manufactures three products. Product C is bulky, complicated and a comparatively slow seller. It uses all the same sorts of equipment, storage space and sales effort as products A and B, only more so. When fixed costs are allocated across the range, it draws the greatest share.

TABLE 7.2   Product profitability 1

	A	B	C	Total
Sales	30,000	50,000	20,000	100,000
Variable costs	20,000	30,000	10,000	60,000
Allocated fixed costs	4,500	9,000	11,500	25,000
Total costs	24,500	39,000	21,500	85,000
Operating profit	5,500	11,000	(1,500)	15,000

This proves something of a shock. Product C is losing money, so it has to be eliminated, which will produce the situation shown in Table 7.3.

Fixed costs will not change, so the 25,000 has to be reallocated across the remaining two products. This will result in profits dropping from 15,000 to 5,000; therefore our conventional product costing system has given the wrong signals. We have lost all the 'contribution' that Product C made to fixed costs, and any product that makes a contribution will increase overall profits. Because fixed costs cannot be ignored, it makes more sense to monitor contribution levels and to allocate costs in proportion to them.

Looking back to Table 7.2, we can see that the products made the following contributions (Contribution = sales − variable costs), shown in Table 7.4.

TABLE 7.3   Product profitability 2

	A	B	Total
Sales	30,000	50,000	80,000
Variable costs	20,000	30,000	50,000
New allocated fixed costs	8,333	16,667	25,000
Total costs	28,333	46,667	75,000
Operating profit	1,667	3,333	5,000

TABLE 7.4   Allocating fixed costs by contribution level

		Contribution	%	Fixed cost allocated
Product	A	10,000	25	6,250
	B	20,000	50	12,500
	C	10,000	25	6,250
Total		40,000	100	25,000

Now we can recast the product profit-and-loss account using this marginal costing basis, as shown in Table 7.5. Not only should we not eliminate Product C, but because in contribution terms it is our most profitable product, we should probably try to sell more.

TABLE 7.5   Marginal costing product profit-and-loss account

	A	%	B	%	C	%	Total
Sales	30,000		50,000		20,000		100,000
Marginal costs	20,000		30,000		10,000		60,000
Contribution	10,000	33	20,000	40	10,000	50	40,000
Fixed costs	6,250		12,500		6,250		25,000
Product profit	3,750	13	7,500	15	3,750	19	15,000

Strip out unnecessary product cost

Even where products and services are profitable, there are opportunities to strip out cost. One of the most productive areas to start with is to establish exactly what customers really value and what they don't. IKEA, for example, decided early on that its core market segment was happy to assemble many products themselves. Where other furniture stores sold tables, chairs and beds already built, IKEA sold them flat-packed for self-assembly. That cut out several layers of cost: the product didn't have to be fully manufactured, it didn't occupy much store or warehouse space, and it didn't have to be delivered as customers would take the product home with them. This last feature, incidentally, is an extra benefit for IKEA's customers, who don't want to wait the weeks and sometimes months that other suppliers take to get product delivered – and they don't want to have to wait in for deliveries either. IKEA passes part of these cost savings on to their customers in lower prices and puts the rest on its bottom line.

Online video courses and lectures

14 ways to raise your prices (and keep your customers): Part of the Business Essentials series from Hixsons Chartered Certified Accountants and Business Advisors, produced in conjunction with Bournemouth & Poole College: **www.youtube.com/watch?v=adpn8AeObXU**

Introduction to Managing Price: London School of Business and Finance: **www.youtube.com/watch?v=k-MjWF2I428**

Pricing Objectives and Strategies: Alanis Business Academy: **www.youtube.com/watch?v=gPAGip9GOIU**

Pricing Tactics & Strategies: Professor Kim Donahue, Kelley School of Business: **www.youtube.com/watch?v=0U_6Huw2gFo**

Online video case studies

Amazon FBA Pricing Strategies: Pricing High and Still Making the Sale: **www.youtube.com/watch?v=_iUudUP7LcM**

Biomarker Pricing Case Study: sawtoothsoftware: **www.youtube.com/watch?v=3luVaxfF-3I**

Fedex Case Study: Rod McNealy, Johnson & Johnson Marketing Executive, Wharton Lecturer, presenting the Federal Express (Fedex) Case Study on Strategic Pricing to Princeton audience: **www.youtube.com/watch?v=B2rF3cTg0Mc**

Shangri-La Hotels: Managing Price. London School of Business and Finance Course: **http://freevideolectures.com/Course/2749/Marketing-Management#**

Sichuan Garden: Harvard Business School professor Ben Edelman was overcharged four dollars for his Chinese food takeout order and went to battle with the restaurant over the mix-up: **www.youtube.com/watch?v=RPf_Lf83rJo**

Sony Playstation price war with the Xbox 360: Cnet: **http://video.cars.aol.co.uk/the-xbox-360-vs-the-ps3-price-war-260107988**

People: managing the marketing organization

8

- Structural options
- Line and staff relationships
- Building and leading teams
- Making rewards relevant
- Understanding motivation
- Handling change

Marketing managers often believe that the most important aspects of marketing lie in areas such as creating sensational advertising campaigns, launching innovative and well-designed products or creating brand identity. Not to denigrate these factors in any way, but the single most prevalent reason for a marketing strategy failing lies in its implementation and by extension the people that carry out marketing tasks. Often known as the fifth 'P' of the marketing mix (see Chapter 3 for more on the marketing mix), it is the selection of people to implement strategy and the way in which they are organized that contribute most to success. Stated like that it sounds a fairly simple task. Just work your way through those headings and you should be able to get the desired results. Unfortunately, people both individually and collectively are rarely malleable and are infinitely variable in their likely responses to situations. McKinsey & Company, in a piece of research entitled 'The "moment of truth" in customer service', looked at the way employees manage the critical interactions that are important to customers. Their study included this quote from Jim Nordstrom, the former co-president of Nordstrom: 'People will work hard when they are given the freedom to do the job the way they think it should be done, when they treat customers the way they like to be treated' (**www.mckinsey.com/insights/ organization/the_moment_of_truth_in_customer_service**).

However, by understanding and applying the following principles and concepts, the MBA student can improve an organization's chances of achieving its objectives.

Marketing strategy vs structure, people and systems

This is the 'Which came first?' question, akin to that of the chicken and the egg. Unless you are starting up a new marketing organization on a greenfield site with no people other than yourself and only a pile of cash, every business situation involves some compromise between the ideal and the possible when it comes to people and structures.

The theory is clear. An organization's strategy, itself a product of its business environment, determines the shape of the organization structure, the sort of people it will employ and how they will be managed, controlled and rewarded. But in the real world the business environment is constantly changing as the economy fluctuates, competitors come and go and consumer needs, desires and aspirations alter. In any event, a business is limited in its freedom of action. However violent and essential a change in strategy, a business will rarely be free to hire and fire staff at will simply to change direction. The exception is in the case of a complete closure or withdrawal from an activity such as that of Marks & Spencer's controversial closure of its French outlets in 2001. This move was considered vital to the survival of the whole business and despite May Day protests in France the company's shares rose 7 per cent on the announcement.

Figure 8.1 is a useful aid to understanding how to approach organizational behaviour. The concentric circles are a metaphor to remind us of the circular nature of the subject. You can't just tackle one area without having an impact on others.

Structures – the options

Just as the skeleton is the structure that holds a body together, a business and its various departments including marketing also have their framework. The goal of any framework is to provide some boundaries while at the same time allowing the whole 'body' flexibility to respond to go about its business. While human bodies keep a very similar skeleton to the one they start out with, a business has a number of very different organizational structures to choose from. Also, it is unlikely that any one structure will be appropriate throughout an organization's life.

FIGURE 8.1   A framework for understanding organizational behaviour

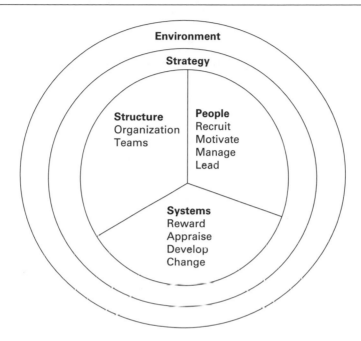

For an organization a structure has to perform the following functions:

- show who is responsible for what and to whom;
- define roles and responsibilities;
- establish communication and control mechanisms;
- lay out the ground rules for cooperation between all parts of the organization;
- set out the hierarchy of authority, power and decision making.

There are two major building blocks used in shaping an organization's structure beyond the level of the individual:

- the organizational chart;
- team composition.

There is nothing permanent about the organization of the marketing function, as the Cisco case study illustrates.

CASE STUDY   Cisco Systems – organizational evolution

On 11 February 2015, John Chambers, Cisco chairman and CEO, reported that Q2 Revenue for their current financial year was $11.9 billion, an increase of 7 per cent year over year, no mean achievement for what the company acknowledged as 'a volatile economic environment'. Chambers, who obtained his MBA from Kelley School of Business, Indiana University, joined Cisco in 1983 as senior vice president, Worldwide Sales and Operations, as part of the team responsible for the start-up. The CEO continued in his Q2 statement to emphasize that 'our strong momentum is the direct result of how well we have managed our company transformation over the last three plus years'. Cisco's organizational evolution had been going on for much longer than three years. Barely a decade after husband and wife Len Bosack and Sandy Lerner, both working for Stanford University, invented the technology to enable them to e-mail each other from different buildings on the campus, Cisco was already embarking on its first major structural change.

Today Cisco Systems is a world leader in networking for the internet, and is now a multinational corporation, with over 75,000 employees in more than 115 countries. Today Cisco solutions are the networking foundations for service providers, small and medium-sized business and enterprise customers who include corporations, government agencies, utilities and educational institutions. Since starting, Cisco has undergone several major changes in organizational structure, the latest being:

- In April 1997 Cisco structured its products and solutions into three customer segments: enterprise, small/medium business, and service provider. The organizational structure was altered to address two major new market opportunities: the service provider migration to internet protocol (IP) services and the adoption of IP products by small and medium-sized businesses through channel distribution. To that point Cisco had a product-focused structure.

- In August 2001 Cisco announced a transition from its three lines of businesses – enterprise, service provider and commercial – to allow the company to focus specifically on technology areas such as access, aggregation, internet switching and services, ethernet access, network management services, core routing, optical, storage, voice and wireless.

- In December 2007 Cisco announced a new organizational structure to position itself for growth in new markets and cater to the demands of new and emerging markets in China, Brazil and India. The new structure also set out to address the challenges imposed by the next phase of internet growth centred on the demands of growth in video and collaborative and networked web 2.0 technologies.

- In December 2012 Cisco announced a global strategy – Tomorrow Starts Here – designed to position Cisco for the next 10 years into a global leader in connecting the previously unconnected 'Internet of Everything'. A company spokesperson said 'transforming Cisco requires making tough, tough decisions', whilst announcing 12,000 people would go as part of 'reallocation of resources'.

Chambers, in a recent interview with McKinsey and Company, the US management consultancy company, explained that to move the company from one that 'sold plumbing and routers' to becoming 'the most trusted business advisor as well as the most trusted technology adviser' required a change in organization structures. Cisco's future Chambers claims, requires 'collaboration and teamwork, with a structured process behind it. And that's the key.'

Organizational charts

Pictorial methods of describing how organizations work have been around for centuries. Both the Roman and Prussian armies had descriptions of their hierarchical structures and the latter incorporated line and staff relationships. There is also some evidence that the ancient Egyptians documented their methods for organizing and dividing workers on major projects such as the pyramids. However, Daniel C McCallum is generally credited with developing the first systematic set of organizational charts in 1855, to organize railroad building on an efficient basis. The trigger for his innovation was the discovery that the building costs per mile of track did not drop with the length of line being built, contrary to logic. The inefficiencies were being caused by poor organization.

Basic hierarchical organization

This simple structure has everyone or part of the organization reporting to one person. It works well when the organization is small, decisions are simple or routine and communications are easy.

This basic structure can be based around one of several groupings, including:

- functions such as sales, new product development, market research, PR or advertising;

FIGURE 8.2   Basic hierarchical organization chart

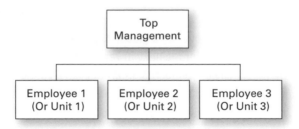

- geography such as country or region;
- product or service groups;
- customer or market segments such as trade, consumers, new accounts or key accounts.

Span of control

The number of people a manager can have reporting to him or her in a hierarchy is governed by the span of control. With few people reporting, the span of control is termed narrow; with more it is termed wide.

A narrow span of control means any one manager has fewer people reporting to him or her, so communications should be better and control easier. However, as the organization grows, that usually means creating more and more layers of management, so negating any earlier efficiency.

A wide span of control, also known as a flat management structure, involves having many people or units reporting to one person. This usually means having fewer layers of management, but it does call for a greater level of skill from those doing the managing. The nature of the tasks being carried out by subordinates will limit the capacity to run a flat organization. For example, a regional manager responsible for identical units such as branches of a supermarket chain, supported by good and well-developed control systems, may be able to have 10 or more direct reports. But if the organization comprises very different types of unit – for example, retail outlets, central bakeries, garages, factories, accounts departments and sales teams – the ability of any one manager to handle that diversity will be limited.

A further factor to take into account is the skill level of both managers and managed. A more highly skilled workforce can operate with a wider span of control as they will need less supervision and a higher-skilled manager can control a greater number of staff.

Line and staff organization

One way to keep an organization structure flat as the enterprise gets bigger and more complex is to introduce staff functions that take over some of the common duties of unit managers. For example marketing managers could probably handle their own recruitment, selection and training of staff while they have a dozen or so people in their domain. Once that expands to hundreds, and if growth is also impacting on other management areas such as sales and marketing, then it may be more efficient to create a specialist HR unit to support the line marketing managers.

Staff positions support line managers by providing knowledge and expertise but the buck ultimately stops with the line manager. Three type of authority are created in a line and staff organization, so alongside some efficiencies lies the possibility for conflict:

- Line authority goes down the chain of command, giving those further up the right and responsibility to instruct those below them to carry out specific tasks.
- Staff authority is the right and responsibility to advise line managers in certain areas. For example, an HR staffer will advise a line marketing manager on redundancy terms, conditions of employment and disciplinary issues.
- Functional authority or limited line authority gives a staff person the ultimate sanction over particular functions such as safety or financial reporting.

There are possibilities for conflict in the relationship between line and staff but these can be minimized in two ways. In the first instance, staff people report to their own superiors who have line authority over them. Second, line and staff personnel can be organized into teams with shared goals and objectives.

Functional organization

In a functional organization the staff and line managers all report to a common senior manager. This places more of a burden on senior management, who have a wider span of control and a greater variety of tasks to take responsibility

FIGURE 8.3 Line and staff organization chart

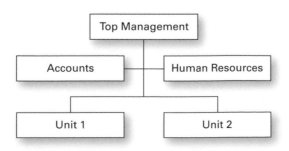

FIGURE 8.4   Functional organization chart

for. However, this structure concentrates all responsibility in one person and so minimizes the area for conflict. It may also deny an organization the high level of expertise that comes with having a professional staff function. For example, this would leave the onus for being fully conversant with current employment law on a production manager, rather than giving him or her access to staff advice. He or she can, of course, read up on the law themself, but that is not quite as good as having it as part of an everyday skill and experience base.

Matrix organization

A matrix organization gives two people line authority for interlocking areas of responsibility. In Figure 8.5 you can see that a manager is responsible for sales of product group 1 in both Europe and Asia. However, a manager is also responsible for the sales of all product groups within his or her continent.

FIGURE 8.5   Matrix organization chart

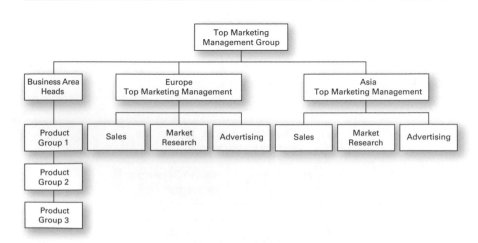

The aim of a matrix structure is to ensure all key areas in an organization have a line manager responsible for championing them. There is still the possibility for conflict of interest. For example, the person responsible for a product group may try to get more attention for his or her product in a particular market than it really warrants. In theory the managers in matrix organizations are senior enough to iron out their differences. That is not always the case in practice and in such cases their mutual boss has to resolve the issue.

Strategic business unit (SBU)

SBUs are in effect separate enterprises with full responsibility for their own profit or loss, either right down to net profit or as far back as the marketing margin (see Chapter 12 for more on margins). In a business where most of the costs are in service, advertising, branding or internet fulfilment, it would be quite possible for this type of SBU to be virtually a stand-alone venture, except for treasury, accounting and tax functions. They may themselves be organized in any one of the above structures. If they don't have their own specialist staff function, they may buy it in from the parent company when required. This maintains the concept of full profit accountability.

SBUs are further divided into those that simply have control over current revenue and expenditure and 'investment centres' that can make capital expenditure decisions such as investing in new product research and development or buying into joint ventures and other strategic relationships.

FIGURE 8.6   Strategic business unit (marketing) organization chart

Teams

Teams are the component parts of a business's structure and their effective creation and operation are a key way to get exceptional results from an organization. A group of people, even if they work together, are not necessarily a team. Look at Figure 8.7. This compares some of the characteristics of a sports team with those of a random collection of people that meet for a game. You can see immediately what needs to be done to weld people into a team.

FIGURE 8.7   Groups are not the same as teams

Sports team	Sports club
• Has the right number of players for the game	• Just the number of people who turn up
• Everyone has a clearly defined role	• Positions of players decided on the day
• Concrete and measurable objectives	• Often the aims have never been explained and where they have, different people have different aims
• An obvious competitor for the team to unite against	• Sometimes the internal competition is more important than winning a game
• A coach to train and improve players' game	• Training is ad hoc
• Right equipment for the game	• The right equipment is sometimes missing and not all players have the right equipment

Successful teams have certain features in common. They all have strong and effective leadership, clear objectives, appropriate resources, the ability to communicate freely throughout the organization, the authority to act quickly on decisions, a good balance of team members, the ability to work collectively, and a size appropriate to the task.

Team types

Teams can be made up of anything from five to 20 people. Anything above 20 is usually too unwieldy and will take up more resources than an organization can afford to devote to one aspect of the business.

Business teams

These are a group of people tasked with managing functions and achieving specific results over the longer term. In this example, there are three of these covering sales, administration and warehouse/dispatch. So, for example, the sales team is expected to meet sales targets and the dispatch team to get goods to customers on time. In practice every firm will have its own definition of business functions.

Project teams

These are often cross-functional, made up of people from different areas. These can be assembled for any period of time to look at a particular project. In this example we have assumed that each of these teams has been asked to look at how each function could be made more efficient. The value of having someone from other functions in these teams is to ensure that too parochial a view is not taken.

Taskforce teams

These are short-term bodies put together quickly to look at one narrow issue or specific problem. For example, if you proposed changing your business's working hours, a taskforce could look at the implications for everyone inside and outside the firm and report back. Then a decision based on the best information provided by people most affected by the change could be made.

Team roles

However talented the soloists are in an organization, in the end it's orchestras that make enough 'noise' to make things happen. But teams don't just occur naturally. The presumption that people are going to work together is usually a mistake. Chaos is more likely than teamwork.

Cultures in businesses have very different pedigrees and can pull the organization in very different directions. Take one successful new internet business, for example, where people came from financial services, retail and more recently technology. The company's roots were in financial services. Its competitors were banks and brokerage firms and its employees had moved around the sector in search of the ultimate accolade, to become vice-presidents. The focus was inward, towards hierarchy and title. The business's second cohort of employees came from retailing, the staff of their one-time expanding branch network. For retailers the focus is outwards, towards the customer. Their success was measured in the market and the best salespeople had the greatest respect and power. The third group, and the most recent, was the technologists. For these people success was measured by technical expertise. Titles were irrelevant and their main concern was for the completion of the project. Their loyalty was not to the hierarchy but to the principles of the project itself and to their team.

When putting people with disparate cultures into teams because of their particular professional or job skills, if the team is to function effectively the balance of behavioural styles has to mesh too. While there are various methods of categorizing team roles, the following are the key roles identified by Meredith Belbin while a research fellow at Cranfield (**www.belbin.com**), which need to be taken if a team is to work effectively:

Chairman/team leader. Stable, dominant, extravert. Concentrates on objectives. Does not originate ideas. Focuses people on what they do best.

Plant. Dominant, high IQ, introvert. A 'scatterer of seeds' who originates ideas. Misses out on detail. Trustful but easily offended.

Resource investigator. Stable, dominant, extravert and sociable. Lots of contacts with the outside word. Strong on networks. Salesperson, diplomat, liaison officer. Not an original thinker.

Shaper. Anxious, dominant, extravert. Emotional and impulsive. Quick to challenge and to respond to a challenge. Unites ideas, objectives and possibilities. Competitive. Intolerant of wooliness and vagueness.

Company worker. Stable, controlled. A practical organizer. Can be inflexible but likely to adapt to established systems. Not an innovator.

Monitor evaluator. High IQ, stable, introvert. Goes in for measured analysis, not innovation. Unambiguous and often lacking enthusiasm. But solid and dependable.

Team worker. Stable, extravert, but not really dominant. Much concerned with individuals' needs. Builds on others' ideas. Cools things down when tempers fray.

Finisher. Anxious introvert. Worries over what could go wrong. Permanent sense of urgency. Preoccupied with order. Concerned with following through.

Building and running a team

The following are the five essential elements to establishing and running effective teams:

Balanced team roles. You have to start building a team by recognizing that people are different. Every team member must not only have his or her 'technical' skills such as being an accountant or salesperson. He or she must also have a valuable team role. Experts in team behaviour have identified the key team profiles that are essential if a team is to function well. Any one person may perform more than one of these roles. But if too many people are competing to perform one of the roles, or one or more of these roles is neglected, the team will be unbalanced. They will perform in much the same way as a car does when a cylinder misfires.

Shared vision and goal. It is essential that the team has ownership of its own measurable and clearly defined goals. This means involving the team in marketing planning and strategy. It also means keeping the communications channels open as the business grows. The founding team knew clearly what they were trying to achieve and, as they probably shared an office, they shared information as they worked. But as the group gets larger and new people join, it will become necessary to help the informal communication systems to work better. Briefing meetings, social events and bulletin boards are all ways to get teams together and keep them facing the right way.

Shared language. To be a member of a business team, people have to have a reasonable grasp of the language of business. It's not much use exhorting people to increase market share or reduce debtor days if they have only the haziest notion of what those terms mean, why they matter or how they can influence the results. So you need to develop rounded business skills across all the core team members through continuous training, development and coaching.

Compatible personalities. While having different Belbin team profiles is important, it is equally vital to have a team who can get on with one another. They have to be able to listen to and respect others' ideas and views. They need to support and trust one another. They need to be able to accept conflict as a healthy reality and work through it to a successful outcome.

Good leadership. First-class leadership is perhaps the most important characteristic that distinguishes winning teams from the also-rans. However good the constituent parts, without leadership a team rapidly disintegrates into a rabble bound by little but a pay cheque.

The board of directors

One team stands apart from all the others within an organization – the board of directors, usually known simply as 'the board'. It is the team every MBA needs to know and understand and aspire to joining. Directors in major or public companies have a role outside that of simply heading up a function, even one as important as marketing, though they may perform one of the functions too. There is often confusion as to where the ultimate power rests in a company – with the directors or the shareholders. In private companies they are often one and the same body but in public companies, even where family ties remain, they are distinct and separate. In law a company is an entity separate from both its shareholders and directors. According to a company's articles of association some powers are exercised by directors, certain other powers may be reserved for the shareholders and exercised at a general meeting. If the powers of management are vested in the directors, then they and they alone can exercise these powers. The only way in which shareholders can control the exercise of powers by directors is by altering the articles, or by refusing to re-elect directors of whose actions they disapprove. Some of a director's duties, responsibilities and potential liabilities are:

- To act in good faith in the interests of the company; this includes carrying out duties diligently and honestly.

- Not to carry on the business of the company with intent to defraud creditors or for any fraudulent purpose.
- Not knowingly to allow the company to trade while insolvent; directors who do so may have to pay for the debts incurred by the company while insolvent.
- Not to deceive shareholders and to appoint auditors to oversee the accounting records.
- To have regard for the interests of employees in general.
- To comply with the requirements of the Companies Acts, such as providing what is needed in accounting records or filing accounts.

Composition of the board

The board is made up of two types of directors, internal and external, and typically the board would exercise major decisions through a number of committees:

Internal directors. Usually headed up by a chairman who runs board meetings, a chief executive officer (CEO) or managing director who runs the operating business, and a number of other directors.

External directors. Known as non-executive directors, these are usually people of stature and experience who can act as both a source of wise independent advice and a check on any wilder elements on a board.

Committees. The main board committees are those that oversee remuneration (particularly for directors), auditing, social responsibility (and 'green' matters), mergers and acquisitions and regulatory affairs.

People

If structures are the skeleton of an organization, people are its blood and guts. Douglas McGregor, a founding faculty member of MIT's Sloan School of Management, began his management classic, *The Human Side of Enterprise*, published in 1960, with the question: 'What are your assumptions (implicit as well as explicit) about the most effective way to manage people?' This seemingly simple question led to a fundamental revolution in management thinking. McGregor went on to claim: 'The effectiveness of organizations could be at least doubled if managers could discover how to tap into the unrealized potential present in their workforces.'

Finding the right people, keeping them on side, motivating, managing and rewarding them are the defining distinctions between the most successful organizations and the mediocre. Over the past 30 years or so, organizations have acquired centralized HR (human resources) departments whose purpose is to facilitate people issues, as they often quaintly term their work. McGregor anticipated their arrival with this pithy quote: 'It is one of the favorite pastimes of management to decide, from within their professional ivory tower, what help the field organization needs and then to design and develop programs for meeting these needs. Then it becomes necessary to get the field organization to accept the help provided. This is normally the role of the Change Manager; to implement the change that no one asked for or wants.'

None of this is to suggest that HR departments can't contribute to helping with 'people issues'. It's just that people issues are too important to exclude their immediate superiors from. At the very least, MBA skills include a sound grasp of the key tasks that the HR department is charged with performing.

Management by Walking Around (MBWA)

Management by Walking Around, sometimes with wandering transposed for walking, usually reduced to the acronym, MBWA, is one of the best-known and most enduring management techniques. The term describes an unstructured approach to hands-on, direct participation by the managers in the work-related affairs of their subordinates, in contrast to the rigid and distant command style of management popularized by earlier management theorists. In MBWA practice, managers spend a significant amount of their time making informal visits to work area and listening to employees, collect qualitative information, listen to suggestions and complaints, and keep a finger on the pulse of the organization.

As a management technique it was first brought to prominence by W Edwards Deming, an American statistician renowned for initiating the idea of TQM (Total Quality Management). Deming's view was that 'If you wait for people to come to you, you'll only get small problems. You must go and find them. The big problems are where people don't realize they have one in the first place'. In Japan, a country where Deming spent much of his life, managers are strong advocates of 'Genchi Genbutsu' – meaning 'Go and See'. NASA had a hand in the MBWA heritage, but the first documented use by a business corporation came in 1973 at Hewlett-Packard, where founders, Bill Hewlett and Dave Packard's philosophy encouraged their executives to know their people, understand their work, and make themselves more visible and accessible. Based on respect for people and the belief that most people just wanted to do a good job if they were handled with respect, this was the near opposite of Henry Ford's top-down command management style. HP being an engineering firm measured everything. They tracked the effect on morale, time spent to get a job done and performance against the number of times the boss went to the coal face. The message was clear. The more managers went to see what was being done the better were the results by almost every criterion.

MBWA got its big break when Tom Peters, in his successful and influential 1982 book *In Search of Excellence*, co-authored with Robert Waterman, included lessons learned from HP and other companies that used a similar decentralized, relaxed, collegial management style – and the term MBWA immediately became popular and included in the MBA lexicon.

What MBWA can achieve

Using MBWA, you can favourably influence the following:

1 Morale – Being heard and recognized goes a long way to making people often feel better about their jobs and their organization. MBWA makes those opportunities available.

2 Productivity – MBWA promotes informal, open and regular discussions, so people will more likely feel free to come to you with their ideas.

3 Approachability – When your team see you as a person and not just a boss, they'll be more likely to tell you what's going on. You'll get the chance to learn about issues before they become problems.

4 Trust – Organizations characterized by a high degree of trust are often the most successful. Test this concept yourself by contrasting how you react to a request from someone you trust to someone you don't. As your team gets to know you better, they'll trust you more and as a consequence share more information.

5 Business knowledge – The further away you are from customers and operation the less of a feel you will have for day-to-day operations and their problems. Getting out and learning what happening on a regular basis will give you a better understanding of the true current situation.

6 Accountability – Budgets and appraisals are relatively blunt tools used at their best to give a general sense of direction. When you meet regularly and informally with your team, agreements you make are much more likely to be committed to and achieved.

Despite the obvious benefits to being successful with MBWA, it takes more than just sauntering through your factory, office, warehouse, or retail outlet. MBWA isn't a 'walk in the park', it's a determined and genuine effort to understand your staff, what they do, and what you can do to make their work more effective.

To introduce MBWA successfully make it part of your managers' performance evaluation and incorporate their achievements in this area into their reward package. Remember what gets measured gets done and what gets rewarded gets done again.

MBWA in a virtual world

Multi-site, global businesses can present some difficulties when it comes to working MBWA. If your team are scattered around five continents and a dozen time zones you could spend more time at airports than with your team. These are a few ways to work around this difficulty and so bridge the gap between the times when face-to-face visits are possible.

Skype and videoconferencing

Skype with its internet chat and phone functions brings back the real-time aspect, and to a certain extent the spontaneity if people leave Skype running at their workstations. Videoconferencing using the inbuilt camera on a PC notebook is another way to recoup some of the impulsiveness inherent in MBWA. Neither Skype nor videoconferencing are quite as effective as a heart-to-heart around the coffee machine, but from time to time can be a reasonable approximation.

Project and function management software tools (eg Basecamp, Salesforce)

Structured project and function management is necessary, even when MBWA is being used. Web-based solutions like Basecamp and Salesforce have the advantage of being central repositories for information, event scheduling and progress reports whilst being visible to you as the manager. But while you can see what is happening with your team anywhere anytime, such software does not readily provide the insights or opportunities to develop the trusting relationships that MBWA can offer.

Google Docs – real-time work collaboration

Tools such as Google Docs let teams work together from different geographical locations, producing documents and commenting on them. Despite different time zones for example, executives can 'visit' projects to add their own remarks. With no real-time or face-to-face contact whilst exposing an employee's work to constant management scrutiny of the executive, this reduces spontaneity and can be demoralizing.

CASE STUDY   Pizza Hut

Jens Hofma, Pizza Hut's CEO, received his MBA from IMD, Switzerland. Before joining Pizza Hut he worked for Nestle and McKinsey in Switzerland and KFC Germany. Pizza Hut UK sees three million diners pass through its doors every month. According to their website 'An estimated 23 per cent of the British population has eaten a Pizza Hut pizza in the last 12 weeks!'

Jens Hofma spends half a day each fortnight serving tables at a Pizza Hut restaurant as a way of keeping informed about the real-time experience for his customers and shop-floor staff. Hofma claims that 'It's very easy when you are running a largish organization to lose a sense of reality. You are going from meeting to meeting and sometimes you pop into a restaurant and it's a bit like a celebrity visit and you don't get a true picture of what it's like'. So even after a long day at the company's head office in Borehamwood, Hertfordshire, Hofma heads for one of their 330 restaurants, dons a uniform and puts in a four-hour shift. What started off as an effort to get to know the company in the first few months back in 2009 when he was parachuted in to stem a cash haemorrhage, has turned into a habit.

Hofma arrived in 2009 to a business in trouble. Frank and Dan Carney opened the first Pizza Hut in Wichita, Kansas back in 1958 and by 1972 they had approximately 1,000 stores across the United States. In 1973 Pizza Hut went international with restaurants in Japan, Canada and England. The first UK Pizza Hut opened in Islington, London. Four years later PepsiCo bought the business and the next few decades saw multiple ownership changes. Whitbread joined forces with PepsiCo in 1982 taking the UK portfolio to 50 outlets. In 1997 PepsiCo decided to focus on their drinks business and under new ownership the business lost focus.

That 'true picture' that Hofma found out on his walkabouts was that of a company in the grips of what he openly describes as an 'identity crisis'. Pizza Hut posted pre-tax losses of £12.12m for the 52 weeks to 29 November 2009, a slight improvement on the £13.31m loss the previous year, according to accounts filed at Companies House this week. Its last UK profit of £6.88m was back in 2006.

The loss reinforced the view that Pizza Hut had failed to keep up with the dining-out aspirations of British people in the way it's more upmarket rival, Pizza Express, had. The problems at Pizza Hut also came at a time when the pizza delivery specialist Domino's was on a roll. The prevailing view back in 2009 was of a slightly tired brand that had missed out on the 'casual dining' market. Pizza Express, TGI Friday and a number of other pasta chains, such as Prezzo and Bella Italia, had been a bit more aspirational and innovative in terms of new products on the menu and their interiors. 'The UK went, in barely a decade, from being one of the least competitive restaurant markets to one of the most competitive in the world,' says Hofma.

With the backing of turnaround venture fund Hofma has refurbished nearly a quarter of the company's 330 strong estate. From 2012 the business moved into modest profits.

Systems

If the structure is the skeleton and people are the blood and guts, systems are the rules and procedures that enable an organization to function effectively and to prepare itself for the changes ahead.

Appraisals

An appraisal is almost certainly an MBA's first point of contact with an organization's systems and the most likely one to cause dissatisfaction and frustration. Although supposedly not about blame, reward or even praise, that's often how it ends up. Its output is direction and advice to help everyone perform better and be able to achieve career goals.

There are plenty of standard appraisal systems and procedures; many are little more than a tick-boxes-and-rating process; others are built around buzzwords such as '360 degree appraisals', meaning that staff below and above as well as peers have an input into the process.

There are really only four ground rules for successful appraisals:

- The appraisal needs to be seen as an open two-way discussion between people who work together rather than simply a boss– subordinate relationship; and it should be prepared for in advance. Discussion should be focused on achievements, areas for improvement, overall performance, training and development and career expectations and not salary (which is for a separate occasion).

- It should be results orientated rather than personality orientated. The appraisal interview starts with a review against objectives and finishes by setting objectives for the next period.

- Appraisals should be regular and timely – at least annually, perhaps more frequently in periods of rapid change. New employees should be appraised in their first three months.

- Sufficient time should be allowed and the appraisal needs to be carried out free from interruptions.

Managing change

The story told in business schools to illustrate the dangers of ignoring the need for change is that of the hypothetical frog dropped into a pot of boiling water. The immediate impact of a radically different environment spurs the frog into action, leaping out of the pot. The same frog placed in the same pot, where the initial temperature is much lower, will happily allow itself to be boiled to death, failing to recognize the danger if the process is slow enough.

The first task of a leader, therefore, is to define an organization's purpose and direction. This inevitably means changing those in response to changing circumstances.

Why change is necessary

The need for change comes from two main directions: either a new impetus from outside or inside the organization, or from the natural evolution of the organization itself.

Impetus-driven change

The following are the primary sources of the impetus for change that disturb the equilibrium of an organization:

- New management. This doesn't always trigger change but the temptation to tamper with even the best of organizations is usually too much for a 'new broom'. The person appointed almost invariably will want to put his or her stamp on strategy and structure; if all was really so hunky-dory why appoint him or her in the first place?

- Competitor behaviour. This can be either new entrants or existing players changing the dynamics in your markets by competing with better products, lower prices or smarter operations.

- Technology. Changes here can hit whole business sectors. For example, the advent initially of online DVD services and more recently of broadband delivery has profoundly changed the environment for the retail video rental business.

- Economic, political or legal environment. This includes such factors as business cycles altering demand levels radically, changes of government with consequent shifts in expenditure and taxation, and regulatory changes such as those affecting the tobacco industry and its ability to promote its wares.

Natural evolution

Organizations are in some ways like living organisms and have a natural progression from birth through childhood, adolescence, adulthood, senility and death. Some stages in the process for an organization are easily recognizable. All have a start and finish date and though their life span varies, for businesses at least the average is around 35 to 38 years. Some last much longer; there is a small club for businesses who have been around for over 250 years. (Japan's 1,400-year-old Kongo Gumi may be the oldest business enterprise, but guns (Beretta), banking (Rothschild) and alcoholic drinks (the Gekkeikan brewery, founded in 1627) also feature strongly.)

The phases of growth

Larry Greiner, a Harvard professor, identified the key phases an organization has to go through in its path to maturity. See Figure 8.8.

Churchill and Lewis (Churchill, N C and Lewis, V L, 1983, The five stages of small business growth, *Harvard Business Review*, May–June) refined this for small businesses. Each phase of growth calls for a different

FIGURE 8.8   The five phases of growth

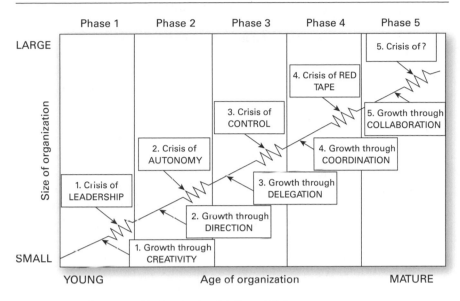

SOURCE: L E Greiner, *Harvard Business Review*, July/August 1972

approach to managing the organization. Sometimes strong leadership is required; at others a more consultative approach is appropriate. Some phases call for more systems and procedures, some for more cooperation between staff. Often leaders believe taking on another salesperson, a few hundred thousand square metres of space or another bank loan can solve the problems of growing up. This approach is rather like suggesting that the transition from infancy to adulthood could be accomplished by nothing more significant than providing larger clothes.

Managing the process

While change is inevitable and unpredictable in its consequences, this doesn't mean that it can't be managed as a process. The following are the stages in managing change:

- Tell them why. Change is better accepted when people are given a compelling business reason. Few bankers would question the need for change after the 2008–09 debacles at Bear Stearns, Société Générale, Northern Rock and RBS.
- Make it manageable. Even when people accept what needs to be done, the change may just be too big for anyone to handle. Breaking it down into manageable bits can help.

- Take a shared approach. Involve people early, asking them to join you in managing change. Give key participants some say in shaping the change right from the start. This will reduce the feeling that change is being imposed and more brains will be brought to bear on the problem.
- Reward success early. Flag up successes as quickly as possible. Don't wait for the year end or the appraisal cycle. This will inspire confidence and keep the change process on track.
- Expect resistance. Kurt Lewin, a German-born professor at the Massachusetts Institute of Technology, was one of the first researchers to study group dynamics and how change can be best effected in organizations. In a 1943 article entitled 'Defining the field at a given time', published in the *Psychological Review*, Lewin described what is now known as force field analysis. This is a tool that you can use to anticipate resistance to change and plan to overcome it. See Figure 8.9.
- Recognize that change takes longer than expected. Three researchers (Adams, J, Hayes, J, & Hopson, B) explained in *Transition: Understanding and managing personal change* (1976, Martin Robinson, London) the six stages that people go through when experiencing change and hence the reason the process takes so long. The stages are: immobilization or shock, disbelief, depression, acceptance of reality, testing out the new situation, rationalizing why

FIGURE 8.9 Force field analysis template

What is the problem/ change issue?			
Where are we now?			
Where do we want to get to?			
What/who are the main forces at work?	Driving forces	Neutral forces	Resisting forces
What action can we take to help driving forces, encourage neutral forces to help and to overcome resisting forces?			

it's happening and then final acceptance. Most major changes make things worse before they make them better. More often than not, the immediate impact of change is a decrease in productivity as people struggle to cope with new ways of working, while they move up their own learning curve. The doubters will gloat and even the change champions may waver. But the greatest danger now is pulling the plug on the plan and either adopting a new plan or reverting to the status quo. To prevent this 'disappointment', it is vital both to set realistic goals for the change period and to anticipate the time lag between change and results.

Monitoring staff morale

One way to both identify the need for change and to keep track of progress while implementing change is to carry out regular surveys of employee attitudes, opinions and feelings. HR-Survey (**www.hr-survey.com**>Employee Opinions) and Custom Insight (**www.custominsight.com**>View Samples> Sample employee satisfaction survey) provide fast, simple, and easy-to-use software to carry out and analyse HR surveys. They both have a range of examples of surveys that you can see and try before you buy, and which might help to stimulate your thinking.

Online video courses and lectures

Forget big change, start with a tiny habit: BJ Fogg, director of the Persuasive Tech Lab at Stanford University, talks to TEDx: **www.youtube.com/watch?v=AdKUJxjn-R8**

Leadership skills: Lauren Rodda and Amanda Mok, MIT Open Courseware: **http://ocw.mit.edu/high-school/humanities-and-social-sciences/leadership-training-institute/video-lectures/lecture-5/**

Make Meaning in Your Company: Guy Kawasaki, founder and Managing Director of Garage Technology Ventures talks at Stanford: **http://ecorner.stanford.edu/authorMaterialInfo.html?mid=1171**

The Power of Habit: Charles Duhigg, Pulitzer Prize-winning writer talks to TEDx: **www.youtube.com/watch?v=OMbsGBlpP30**

Prepare Your Brain for Change: Margaret Moore, CEO of Wellcoaches Corporation talks to Harvard Business Review: **https://hbr.org/2013/04/prepare-your-brain-for-change/**

Restructuring your organization for the digital age: Adobe Summit 2014: **http://tv.adobe.com/watch/adobe-summit-2014-emea/restructuring-your-organisation-for-the-digital-age/**

Six keys to leading positive change: Rosabeth Moss Kanter, Harvard Business School talks to TEDx, a program of local, self-organized events: **www.youtube.com/watch?v=owU5aTNPJbs**

Teamwork and communication: Lauren Rodda and Amanda Mok, MIT
Open Courseware: **http://ocw.mit.edu/high-school/humanities-and-social-sciences/leadership-training-institute/video-lectures/lecture-4/**

Three Myths of Behavior Change – What You Think You Know That You
Don't: Jeni Cross a sociology professor at Colorado State University
talks to TEDx: **www.youtube.com/watch?v=l5d8GW6GdR0**

Online video case studies

Cisco CEO John Chambers talks on Teamwork and
Collaboration to Harvard Business Review:
https://hbr.org/2008/10/cisco-ceo-john-chambers-on-tea

General Services Administration: Former GSA Chief Information
Officer Casey Coleman, talks about change management at GSA:
www.youtube.com/watch?v=gPyPKLkSm5c

Starbucks: Tom Peters returns to his favourite topic from In
Search of Excellence, Managing by Wandering Around, as
exemplified by Howard Schultz, Starbucks CEO:
www.youtube.com/watch?v=2UIY0Vykc_Y

Maths for marketing

- Decision-making tools
- Statistical methods
- Making forecasts
- Assessing cause and effect
- Making profitable marketing investments
- Ensuring survey reliability
- Managing marketing operations

Marketing executives collect an inordinate amount of data, usually supported by an IT (Information Technology) department that processes it. However, it falls to the application of analysis techniques carried out by marketers, usually those with MBAs, to interpret the data and explain its significance or otherwise. Bald information on its own is rarely of much use. If salespeople start leaving in large numbers, customers start complaining and debtor payment delinquencies are on the rise, these facts on their own may tell you very little. Are these figures close to average, or is it the mean or the weighted average that will reveal their true importance? Even if the figures are bad you need to know if they are outside the range you might reasonably expect to occur in any event.

Rotterdam School of Management, Erasmus University (**www.rsm.nl/mba/international-full-time-mba/curriculum-teaching**), for example, runs an elective 'Quantitative platform for business' where students investigate the whole range of quantitative methods available for problem solving. This business school considers the subject important enough to put it into term 1 in their Foundations of Management subjects. EMLYON (**www.em-lyon.com/english**) confines its teaching to 'Business statistics' covering 'the essential quantitative skills that will be required of you throughout the programme'. MIT Sloan School of Management (**http://mitsloan.mit.edu/mba/program/firstsem.php**)

has a teaching module, 'Data, models, and decision' in its first semester that 'introduces students to the basic tools in using data to make informed management decisions'.

But before you could even get into a top business school such as Wharton, Harvard or Chicago in the USA, INSEAD, London Business School or Cranfield in Europe, or Nanyang Business School (Singapore) or Ipade (Mexico), you need to take the Graduate Management Admissions Test (GMAT) or the very similar Graduate Record Examinations (GRE) which became a serious alternative in 2005 when Stanford decided to accept it for MBA admissions. Used by some 1,800 business schools worldwide, the GMAT has been recognized for over 50 years as a proven and reliable measurement to assess candidates' skills and predict their success on MBA programmes. The GMAT is administered in 94 centres around the world and given under standard conditions with the highest level of security to ensure that scores are comparable across applicants. It costs $250 to take, wherever the test is taken. The test itself takes two and a half hours and comprises tests in three areas: analytical writing (analysis of an issue and of an argument), quantitative section (problem solving and data sufficiency), and verbal (reading comprehension, critical reasoning and sentence correction). The average score is currently around 500. Less prestigious business schools look for a GMAT score of 550 and a score upwards of 660 will make you a competitive candidate at most business schools. You are up against everyone else taking the test, so as the average scores move up, so does the required score.

A lot of MBA candidates flunk the maths element of this test and even some who get through need remedial work in this area. Dartmouth's Tuck School of Business MBA programme runs a pre-orientation maths refresher, familiarly known as math camp, which is in effect a crash course in MBA maths skills. MIT's Sloan, Stanford and Penn's Wharton run similar refreshers, and Professor Peter Regan, who started the Tuck programme, runs MBAmath.com, a for-profit online maths course available to anyone on a subscriber basis.

To perform to the standard expected of an MBA, you will need a good grounding in the relevant maths and what follows should be seen as the minimum.

Quantitative research and analysis

The purpose of quantitative research and analysis is to provide managers with the analytical tools necessary for making better management decisions. The subject, while not rocket science, requires a reasonable grasp of mathematical concepts. It is certainly one area that many attending business school find challenging. But as figures on their own are often of little help in either understanding the underlying facts or choosing between alternatives, some appreciation of probability, forecasting and statistical concepts is essential. It is an area where with a modicum of application an MBA can demonstrate skills that will make him or her stand out from the crowd.

Decision theory

Blaise Pascal (1623–62), the French mathematician and philosopher who with others laid the foundations for the theory of probability, is credited with inaugurating decision theory or decision making under conditions of uncertainty. Until Pascal's time the outcomes of events were considered to be largely in the hands of the gods. He instigated a method for using mathematical analysis to evaluate the cost and residual value of various alternatives so as to be able to choose the best decision when all the relevant information is not available.

Decision trees

Decision trees are a visual as well as valuable way to organize data so as to help make a choice between several options with different chances of occurring and different results if they do occur. Trees (see Figure 9.1) were first used in business in the 1960s but became seriously popular from 1970 onwards when algorithms were devised to generate decision trees and automatically reduce them to a manageable size.

Making a decision tree requires these steps to be carried out initially, from which the diagram can be drawn:

- Establish all the alternatives.
- Estimate the financial consequences of each alternative.
- Assign the risk in terms of uncertainty allied with each alternative.

Figure 9.1 shows an example decision tree. The convention is that squares represent decisions and circles represent uncertain outcomes. In this example the problem being decided on is whether to launch a new product or revamp an existing one. The uncertain outcomes are whether the result of the decision will be successful (£10 million profit), just okay (£5 million profit) or poor (£1 million). In the case of launching a new product, the management's best estimate is that there is a 10 per cent (0.1 in decimals) chance of success, a 40 per cent chance it will be okay and a 50 per cent chance it will result in poor sales. Multiplying the expected profit arising from each possible outcome by the probability of its occurring gives what is termed as an 'expected value'. Adding up the expected values of all the possible outcomes for each decision suggests in this case that revamping an old product will produce the more profit.

The example is a very simple one and in practice decisions are much more complex. We may have intermediate decisions to make, such as whether to invest heavily and bring the new product to market quickly, or whether to spend money on test marketing. This will introduce more decisions and more uncertain outcomes represented by a growing number of 'nodes', the points at which new branches in the tree are formed.

FIGURE 9.1   Example decision tree

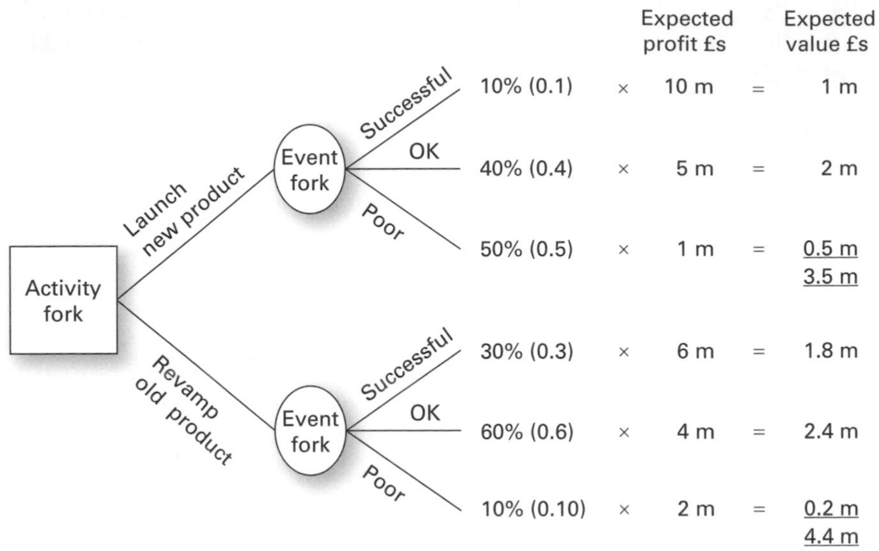

			Expected profit £s		Expected value £s
	Successful	10% (0.1)	×	10 m	=	1 m
Event fork	OK	40% (0.4)	×	5 m	=	2 m
	Poor	50% (0.5)	×	1 m	=	0.5 m / 3.5 m
	Successful	30% (0.3)	×	6 m	=	1.8 m
Event fork	OK	60% (0.6)	×	4 m	=	2.4 m
	Poor	10% (0.10)	×	2 m	=	0.2 m / 4.4 m

Activity fork — Launch new product — Event fork; Revamp old product — Event fork

Statistics

Statistics are the set of tools that we use to help us assess the truth or otherwise of something we observe. For example, if the last 10 phone calls a company received were all cancelling orders, does that signal that a business has a problem, or is that event within the bounds of possibility? If it is within the bounds of possibility, what are the odds that we could still be wrong and really have a problem? A further issue is that usually we can't easily examine the entire population so we have to make inferences from samples and unless those samples are representative of the population we are interested in and of sufficient size, we could still be very wrong in our interpretation of the evidence. At the time of writing there is much debate as to how much of a surveillance society Britain has become. The figure of 4.2 million cameras, one for every 14 people, is the accepted statistic. However, a diligent journalist tracked down the evidence to find that extrapolation of a survey of a single street in a single town was how that figure had been arrived at.

Central tendency

The most common way statistics are considered is around a single figure that purports in some way to be representative of a population at large. There are three principal ways of measuring tendency; these are the most often confused and frequently misrepresented set of numbers in the whole field of statistics.

To analyse anything in statistics you first need a 'data set' such as the following for the selling prices of a company's products:

Product 1: selling price 30;

Product 2: selling price 40;

Product 3: selling price 10;

Product 4: selling price 15;

Product 5: selling price 10.

The mean (or average)

This is the most common tendency measure and is used as a rough-and-ready check for many types of data. In the example above, adding up the prices – 105 – and dividing by the number of products – five – you arrive at a mean, or average, selling price of 21.

The median

The median is the value occurring at the centre of a data set. Recasting the figures above puts Product 4's selling price of 15 in that position, with two higher and two lower prices. The median comes into its own in situations where the outlying values in a data set are extreme, as they are in our example, where in fact most of the products sell for well below 21. In this case the median would be a better measure of the central tendency. You should always use the median when the distribution is skewed. You can use either the mean or the median when the population is symmetrical as they will give very similar results.

The mode

The mode is the observation in a data set that appears the most; in this example it is 10. So if we were surveying a sample of the customers of the company in this example we would expect more of them to say they were paying 10 for their products, though as we know the average price is 21.

Variability

As well as measuring how values cluster around a central value, to make full use of the data set we need to establish how much those values could vary. The two most common methods employed are range and standard deviation from the mean.

Range

The range is calculated as the maximum figure minus the minimum figure. In the example being used here that is 40 – 10 = 30. This figure gives us an idea of how dispersed the data is and so how meaningful the average figure alone might be.

Standard deviation from the mean

This is a rather more complicated concept as you need first to grasp the central limit theorem, which states that the mean of a sample of a large population will approach 'normal' as the sample gets bigger. The most valuable feature here is that even quite small samples are normal. The bell curve, also called the Gaussian distribution – named after Johann Carl Friedrich Gauss (1777–1855), a German mathematician and scientist – shows how far values are distributed around a mean. The distribution, referred to as the standard deviation, is what makes it possible to state how accurate a sample is likely to be. When you hear the results of opinion polls predicting elections based on samples as small as 1,000, these are usually reliable within four percentage points, equivalent to 19 times out of 20, you have a measure of how important this concept is.

Figure 9.2 is a normal distribution that shows that 68.2 per cent of the observations of a normal population will be found within 1 standard deviation of the mean, 95.5 per cent within 2 standard deviations, and 99.7 per cent within 3 standard deviations. So almost 100 per cent of the observations will be observed in a span of 6 standard deviations, 3 below the mean and 3 above the mean. The standard deviation is an amount calculated from the values in the sample. (You can get free tutorials on this and other aspects of statistics at Web Interface for Statistics Education (**http://wise.cgu.edu**). This is a service provided by Claremont Graduate University.)

FIGURE 9.2   Normal distribution curve (bell) showing standard deviation

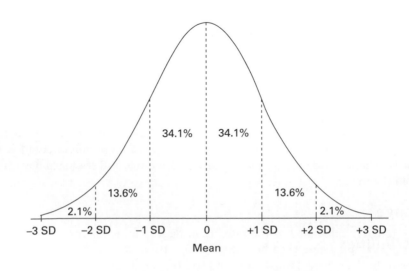

Forecasting

Sales drive much of a business's activities; they determine cash flow, stock levels, production capacity and ultimately how profitable or otherwise a business will be, so unsurprisingly much effort goes into attempting to predict future sales. A sales forecast is not the same as a sales objective. An objective is what you want to achieve and will shape a strategy to do so. A forecast is the most likely future outcome given what has happened in the past and the momentum that provides for the business.

Any forecast is made up of three components and to get an accurate forecast you need to decompose the historical data to better understand the impact of each on the end result.

- Underlying trend. This is the general direction, up, flat or down, over the longer term, showing the rate of change.
- Cyclical factors. These are the short-term influences that regularly superimpose themselves on the trend. For example, in the summer months you would expect sales of certain products, swimwear, ice cream and suntan lotion to be higher than in the winter. Ski equipment would probably follow a reverse pattern.
- Random movements. These are irregular, random spikes up or down, caused by unusual and unexplained factors.

Using averages

The simplest forecasting method is to assume that the future will be more or less the same as the recent past. The two most common techniques that use this approach are:

- Moving average. This takes a series of data from the past, say the last six months' sales, adds them up, divides by the number of months and uses that figure as being the most likely forecast of what will happen in month seven. This method works well in a static, mature marketplace where change happens slowly, if at all.
- Weighted moving average. This method gives the most recent data more significance than the earlier data since it gives a better representation of current business conditions. So before adding up the series of data each figure is weighted by multiplying it by an increasingly higher factor as you get closer to the most recent data.

Exponential smoothing and advanced forecasting techniques

Exponential smoothing is a sophisticated averaging technique that gives exponentially decreasing weights as the data gets older, and conversely more recent data are given relatively more weight in making the forecasting. Double and triple exponential smoothing can be used to help with different types of trend. More sophisticated still are Holt's and Brown's linear exponential smoothing approaches and the Box–Jenkins model, named after two statisticians; these apply autoregressive moving average models to find the best fit of a time series.

Fortunately all an MBA needs to know is that these and other statistical forecasting methods exist. The choice of which is the best forecasting technique to use is usually down to trial and error. Various software programs will calculate the best-fitting forecast by applying each technique to the historical data you enter. Then wait and see what actually happens and use the technique whose forecast is closest to the actual outcome. Professor Hossein Arsham of the University of Baltimore provides a useful range of tools showing how different forecasting techniques perform (**http://home.ubalt.edu/ntsbarsh/ business-stat/stat-data/forecast.htm**). Duke University's Fuqua School of Business, consistently ranked amongst the top 10 US business schools in every single functional area, provides this helpful link to all their lecture material on forecasting: **www.duke.edu/~rnau/411home.htm**.

Causal relationships

Often when looking at data sets it will be apparent that there is a relationship between certain factors. Look at Figure 9.3, which is a chart showing the monthly sales of barbeques and the average temperature in the preceding month for the past eight months.

It's not hard to see that there appears to be, as we might expect, a relationship between temperature and sales in this case. By drawing the line that most accurately represents the slope, called the line of best fit, we can have a useful

FIGURE 9.3   Scatter diagram example

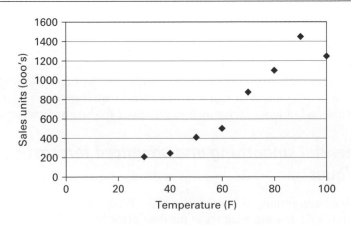

tool for estimating what sales might be next month, given the temperature that occurred this month (see Figure 9.4).

FIGURE 9.4   Scatter diagram – line of best fit

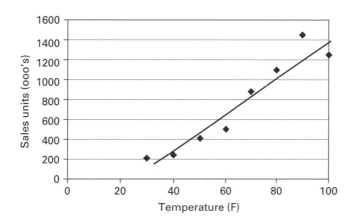

The example used is a simple one and the relationship obvious and strong. In real life there is likely to be much more data and it will be harder to see if there is a relationship between the 'independent variable', in this case temperature, and the 'dependent variable', sales volume. Fortunately there is an algebraic formula known as 'linear regression' that will calculate the line of best fit for you.

There are then a couple of calculations needed to test if the relationship is strong (it can be strongly positive or even if strongly negative it will still be useful for predictive purposes) and significant. The tests are known as R-Squared and the Student's t-test, and all an MBA needs to know is that they exist and you can probably find the software to calculate them on your computer already. Otherwise you can use Web-Enabled Scientific Services & Applications (**www.wessa.net/slr.wasp**) software, which covers almost every type of statistical calculation. The software is free online and provided through a joint research project with K U Leuven Association, a network of 13 institutions of higher education in Flanders.

For help in understanding these statistical techniques, read *The Little Handbook of Statistical Practice*, by Gerard E Dallal of Tufts; this is available free online (**www.jerrydallal.com/LHSP/LHSP.htm**). At Princeton's website (**http://dss.princeton.edu/online_help/analysis/interpreting_regression.htm**), you can find a tutorial and lecture notes on the subject as taught to its Master of International Business students.

Surveys and sample size

Surveys are the most common research method used in organizations to get a handle on almost every aspect of performance, from measuring sales force morale or assessing customer satisfaction, to getting the views of almost any stakeholder group on almost any issue. MBAs will certainly have to know how to get surveys done and if working in a small organization they may well have to do it themselves. Chapter 2 covers the practical aspects of preparing and executing surveys, but to be sure of the degree to which they likely to be meaningful you need a modest grasp of maths.

The size of the survey undertaken is vital to its accuracy. You frequently hear of political opinion polls taken on samples of 1,500–2,000 voters. This is because the accuracy of your survey clearly increases with the size of sample, as the following example shows:

With a random sample of ...	95 per cent of surveys are right within ... percentage points
250	6.2
500	4.4
750	3.6
1,000	3.1
2,000	2.2
6,000	1.2

So, if on a sample size of 600, your survey showed that 40 per cent of women in the town drove cars, the true proportion would probably lie between 36 and 44 per cent. A sample of 250 completed replies is about the minimum to provide meaningful information on which reliance can be placed.

Creative Research Systems survey software provide this Sample Size Calculator as a public service together with some information on the terms that you need to know (**www.surveysystem.com/sscalc.htm**).

Marketing operations

Marketing operations are the processes used to get the optimum amount of output at the lowest cost. Success is measured by being able to meet delivery promises while hitting profit margin objectives. Marketing operations achieve this by identifying possible resource conflicts, directing sufficient resources to achieve tasks on time, and by minimizing stock and work in progress levels.

The techniques used to facilitate marketing operations that an MBA should understand include the following.

Gantt charts

Henry Gantt, a mechanical engineer, management consultant and associate of Frederick Taylor's, showed how an entire process could be described in terms of both tasks and the time required to carry them out. He developed what became known as the Gantt chart to help with major infrastructure projects, including the Hoover Dam and the US Interstate highway system around 1910. By laying out the information on a grid with tasks on one axis and their time sequence along the other, it was possible to see at a glance an entire production plan as well as highlight potential bottlenecks. Gantt charts can be used for any task, not just production scheduling, as Figure 9.5, giving an example of how a website design project could be planned, demonstrates.

FIGURE 9.5 Gantt chart showing weekly tasks for a website design project

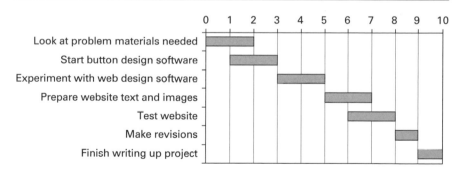

Critical path method (CPM)

A more sophisticated way to schedule operations was developed in the late 1950s. DuPont, the US chemical company, first used CPM to help with shutting down plants for maintenance. Later the US Navy adapted and improved it for use on the Polaris project. CPM uses a chart (see Figure 9.6 below) showing all the tasks to be carried out to complete a scheduled activity, the sequence in which they have to be carried out and how long each event, as tasks are known, will take to be completed. The critical path is the route through the network that will take the longest amount of time. The significance of the critical path is that any delays in carrying out events on this path will delay the whole project. Tasks not on the critical path have more

FIGURE 9.6 Critical path method applied

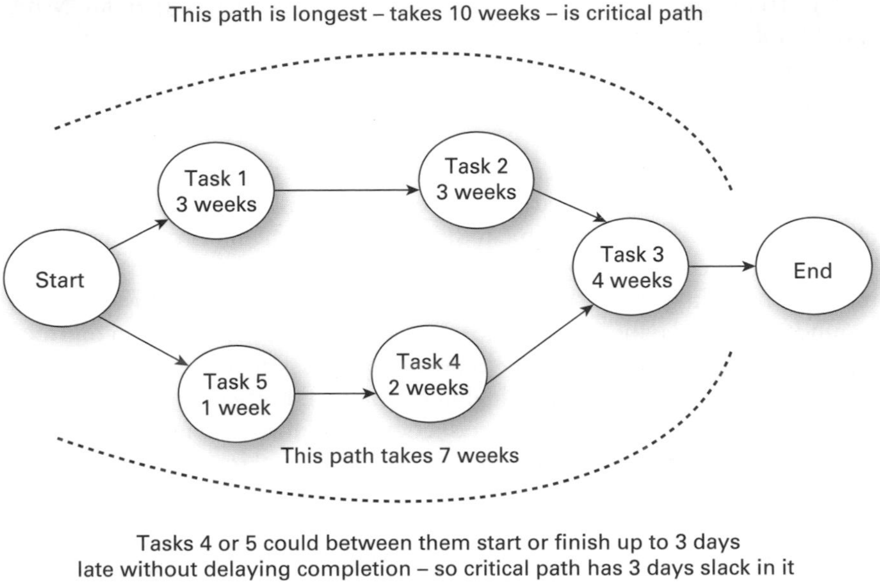
This path is longest – takes 10 weeks – is critical path
Start
Task 1
3 weeks
Task 2
3 weeks
Task 3
4 weeks
End
Task 5
1 week
Task 4
2 weeks
This path takes 7 weeks
Tasks 4 or 5 could between them start or finish up to 3 days
late without delaying completion – so critical path has 3 days slack in it

leeway and may be slipped without affecting the end date of the project. This is called slack or float.

Marketing managers use this technique and the others described below for major projects such as new product launches, opening new outlets and planning advertising and promotion campaigns.

The steps in the critical planning method process are:

- Identify the events.
- Decide on the sequence in which they must be carried out.
- Draw the network.
- Calculate the completion time for each event.
- Identify the longest and hence critical path.
- Keep the chart updated as events unfold.

Programme evaluation and review technique (PERT) and Activity Network, also known as an 'Activity-on-node diagram', are more sophisticated forms of CPM that allow for a degree of randomness in activity start and completion times.

Linear programming

In 1947, George Dantzig, an American mathematician, developed an algorithm (a mathematical technique) that could help resolve problems involving operational constraints. His algorithm could, for example, help with situations where several products could be produced but material, labour or machine capacity is insufficient to make all that's demanded. The challenge is to decide what mix of products can be produced that will make the maximum profit and then plan accordingly. Unfortunately, the iterative nature of producing solutions using Dantzig's algorithm proved so tedious that until cheap computers arrived it remained an academic idea of interest only to mathematics students.

The Dantzig algorithm comprises an objective, the quantity to be optimized, for example profit, nutrient content, water flow or production of one particular product out of several, along with any variables and constraints, for example a certain minimum amount of water must flow.

Queuing theory

Agner Krarup Erlang, a Danish engineer who worked for the Copenhagen Telephone Exchange, had the problem of estimating how many circuits were needed to provide an acceptable telephone service. He found out by empirical observation that the relationship between the number of circuits and the number of telephone customers who could be provided with an acceptable level of service was not as obvious as it at first seemed. For example, in his experiments, where one circuit was provided on a network, adding just one more could reduce waiting time by over 90 per cent, rather than just halving it as simple logic might suggest. He published the first paper on queuing theory in 1909 and this new operations-scheduling technique was born.

Queuing theory can help answer operational questions such as these for a service business such as a restaurant, bank or call centre. Given the present resources:

- How long will a customer have to wait before they are served?
- How long will it take for the service to be completed?
- How big a waiting area will be needed for the queue?
- What is the probability of a customer having to wait longer than a given time interval before he or she is served? This is the classic service standard problem, calling for, say, 'All telephone calls to be answered within 10 rings'.
- What is the average number of people in the queue?
- What is the probability that the queue will exceed a certain length? This can cause congestion in a bank or supermarket.
- What time period will the server be fully occupied and how much idle time is it likely to have, bearing in mind this is a cost to be minimized?

The technique can be used for any operational problem where efficiency is determined by calculating the optimal number of channels required to meet a level of demand. J E Beasley, formerly of the Tanaka Business School

(Imperial College) and currently Professor of Operational Research at Brunel University, provides helpful notes on the subject at this web link: **http:// people.brunel.ac.uk/~mastjjb/jeb/or/queue.html**.

Marketing investment decisions

If the cost of capital in a business, that is, the interest costs on debt and the dividends and other costs of equity (see Chapter 12 for a fuller description of these terms), is 15 per cent, taking on any new activity that makes less than that figure will be lowering the performance, hardly an MBA type of activity.

Investment decisions, where cost and revenue implications last over several years, perhaps even decades, fall into a number of categories:

- Bolt-on investments. These are where an investment will be supporting and enhancing an existing operation – for example, if additional spending is required for a website to provide the clicks where the bricks aspect of sales already exists.

- Stand-alone single project. An example here would be where a new product or market is put under the spotlight. This involves a simple accept or reject decision.

- Competing projects. These require a choice that produces the best results, either because only one can be pursued or because of limited finance. Examples here would be whether to open a branch in Spain or Italy first, whether to launch new product A or B.

What follows is an examination of the financial aspects of investment decisions. There may well be other strategic reasons for taking investment decisions, including those that might be more important than finance alone. For example, it could be imperative to deny a competitor a particular opportunity; or it could be that achieving a national or global strategy calls for disproportionate expenses in one or more areas. However, there are *no* circumstances when any marketing investment decision should not be subjected to proper financial appraisal and so at least show the cost of accepting a lower return than required by the cost of capital being used.

Also, it's important to note that any methodology for appraising investments requires that cash is used rather than profits, for reasons that will become apparent as the techniques are explained. Profit is not ignored; it is simply allowed to work its way through in the timing of events.

Payback period

The most popular method for evaluating investment decisions is the payback method. To arrive at the payback period you have to work out how many years it takes to recover your cash investment. Table 9.1 shows two investment

TABLE 9.1 The payback method

	Investment A	Investment B
Initial cash cost NOW (Year 0)	20,000	40,000
Net cash flows		
Year 1	1,000	10,000
Year 2	4,000	10,000
Year 3	8,000	16,000
Year 4	7,000	4,000
Year 5	5,000	28,000
Total cash in over period	25,000	68,000
Cash surplus	5,000	28,000

projects that require respectively 20,000 and 40,000 cash now in order to get a series of cash returns spread over the next five years.

Although both propositions call for different amounts of cash to be invested, we can see that both recover all their cash outlays by year 4. So we can say these investments have a four-year payback. But as a matter of fact, investment B produces a much bigger surplus than the other project and it returns half our initial cash outlay in two years. Investment A has only returned a quarter of our cash over that time period.

Payback may be simple, but it is not much use when it comes to either dealing with timing or comparing different investment amounts.

Discounted cash flow

We know intuitively that getting cash in sooner is better than getting it in later. In other words, a pound received now is worth more than a pound that will arrive in one, two or more years in the future because of what we could do with that money ourselves, or because of what we ourselves have to pay out to have use of that money (see discussion on cost of capital, above). To make sound investment decisions we need to ascribe a value to a future stream of earnings to arrive at what is known as the present value. If we know we could earn 20 per cent on any money we have, then the maximum we would be prepared to pay for a pound coming in one year hence would be around 80p. If we were to pay one pound now to get a pound back in a year's time we would in effect be losing money.

The technique used to handle this is known as discounting and the process is termed discounted cash flow (DCF); the residual discounted cash is called the net present value.

TABLE 9.2   Using discounted cash flow (DCF)

	Cash flow A	Discount factor at 15% B	Discounted cash flow A × B
Initial cash cost NOW (Year 0)	20,000	1.00	20,000
Net cash flows			
Year 1	1,000	0.8695	870
Year 2	4,000	0.7561	3,024
Year 3	8,000	0.6575	5,260
Year 4	7,000	0.5717	4,002
Year 5	5,000	0.4972	2,486
Total	25,000		15,642
Cash surplus	5,000	Net present value	(4,358)

The first column in Table 9.2 shows the simple cash flow implications of an investment proposition; a surplus of £5,000 comes after five years from putting £20,000 into a project. But if we accept the proposition that future cash is worth less than current cash, the only question we need to answer is: How much less? If we take our cost of capital as a sensible starting point, we would select 15 per cent as an appropriate rate at which to discount future cash flows. To keep the numbers simple and to add a small margin of safety, let's assume 15 per cent is the rate we have selected (this doesn't matter too much, as you will see in the section on internal rate of return).

The formula for calculating what a pound received at some future date is:

$$\text{Present value (PV)} = £P \times 1 \div (1 + r)^n$$

where £P is the initial cash cost, r is the interest rate expressed in decimals and n is the year in which the cash will arrive. So if we decide on a discount rate of 15 per cent, the present value of a pound received in one year's time is:

$$\text{PV} = £1 \times 1 \div (1 + 0.15)^1 = 0.87 \text{ (rounded to two decimal places)}$$

So we can see that our £1,000 arriving at the end of year 1 has a present value of £870; the £4,000 in year 2 has a present value of £3,024 and by year 5 present value reduces cash flows to barely half their original figure. In fact, far from having a real payback in year 4 and generating a cash surplus of £5,000, this project will make us £4,358 worse off than we had hoped to be if we required to make a return of 15 per cent. The project, in other words, fails to meet our criteria using DCF but may well have been pursued using payback.

Internal rate of return (IRR)

DCF is a useful starting point but does not give us any definitive information. For example, all we know about the above project is that it doesn't make a return of 15 per cent. In order to know the actual rate of return we need to choose a discount rate that produces a net present value of the entire cash flow of zero, known as the internal rate of return. The maths is time-consuming but Kaplan Financial (**http://kfknowledgebank.kaplan.co.uk**), an accountancy training provider, have tools for working out payback, discounted cash flow, internal rate of return and many more calculations relating to capital budgeting. You have to register on the site before downloading its free capital budgeting spreadsheet suite and tutorial. From the home page you should click on 'Download Center' and 'Download Financial Metrics Lite for Microsoft Excel'. Using this spreadsheet, you will see that the IRR for the project in question is slightly under 7 per cent, not much better than bank interest and certainly insufficient to warrant taking any risks for.

Online video courses and lectures

A Brief Comparison of Qualitative and Quantitative Research Methods: Professor Shawn Clankie, Otaru University of Commerce: **www.youtube.com/watch?v=LYqDKEsy9gE**

Capital Budgeting: Oral Roberts University. Dr Ray Gregg, Accounting Professor at ORU: **www.youtube.com/watch?v=6YAJ1yN5r98**

Decision Making in a Complex and Uncertain World: University of Groningen, Netherlands: **www.futurelearn.com/courses/ complexity-and-uncertainty**

Descriptive and Inferential Statistics: Alanis Business Academy: **www.youtube.com/watch?v=bvUZ1NH_quA**

Forecasting – Time series models – Simple Exponential smoothing, Prof G Srinivasan, Department of Management Studies, IIT Madras: **www.youtube.com/watch?v=k9dhcflyOFc**

Identifying Qualitative and Quantitative Variables: Alanis Business Academy: **www.youtube.com/watch?v=4K9PVYqiA4c**

Introduction to probability and statistics: MIT Open Courseware: **http://ocw.mit.edu/courses/mathematics/18-05-introduction-to-probability-and-statistics-spring-2014/this-course-at-mit/#Video**

Linear Programming and Duality: MIT Open Courseware as it was taught by Dr Jeremy Orloff and Dr Jonathan Bloom in Spring 2014: **http://ocw.mit.edu/courses/mathematics/18-086-mathematical-methods-for-engineers-ii-spring-2006/video-lectures/lecture-28-linear-programming-and-duality/**

Measures of Central Tendency and Dispersion: Alanis Business Academy: **www.youtube.com/watch?v=DgC3DdnBtE4**

Population and Sample Means: Alanis Business Academy: **www.youtube.com/watch?v=E25i4FHFe2U**

Online case studies

Adobe: Marketing by the numbers: How Adobe puts the data back into its marketing: **http://tv.adobe.com/watch/adobe-summit-2014-emea/marketing-by-the-numbers-how-adobe-puts-the-data-back-into-its-marketing/**

Carson Dellosa: Steve Griffin, Carson Dellosa's CTO describes how Mariner and Carson Dellosa, a publisher of educational books and tools, improved the ability to analyse point-of-sale data beginning with a pilot project and then moving into building a complete business intelligence framework: **www.youtube.com/watch?v=LmdmHfPaVbg**

What Sherlock Holmes Can Teach Us About Decision Making – Maria Konnikova at the RSA: **www.youtube.com/watch?v=JfZd2oLllMw**

Marketing and the law

10

- Dealing with trading regulations
- Advertising standards
- Innovation issues
- Employment rules
- Behaving ethically in the market

Some business schools take law very seriously. For example, at Northwestern University's Kellogg School and George Washington University, MBA students can take a joint MBA and JD (juris doctor), the basic professional degree for lawyers. Babson in Wellesley, Massachusetts has law as one of its core subjects. Penn State, on the other hand, offers only an optional module in the second year on 'Business law for innovation and competition'.

Other than very large businesses it is not usual to have either a qualified lawyer or a legal department in businesses in the UK. Such services are usually bought in on either a contractual or ad hoc basis. Law is an imprecise field. As Henry L Mencken, the American journalist and critic, so succinctly expressed it, 'a judge is a law student who marks his own examination papers'.

The complexity of commercial life means that, sooner or later, your marketing activities will involve taking, or defending yourself against, legal action. It may be a contract dispute with a customer, or a former employee might claim to have been fired without reason.

Ignorance does not form the basis of a satisfactory defence, so every MBA needs to know enough law to know when he or she might need legal advice, however high his or her standard of ethics and social responsibility may be.

While the standards and application of the legal issues that have a bearing on marketing vary greatly from country to country, what follow are areas of near-universal importance. International sources of information on how these issues are covered are listed.

The Doing Business law library operated by World Bank is the world's largest free online collection of business laws and regulations. It links to official government sources wherever possible and is updated regularly. Covering 189 countries you can find out everything from the rules on opening and closing a business to trading across borders, employment laws, enforcing contracts and much more (**www.doingbusiness.org/law-library**).

Trading regulations

Organizations are heavily regulated in almost every sphere of their trading operations. Some types of business require a permit before they can even start trading and all businesses have to comply with certain standards when it comes to advertising, holding information or offering credit. Following are the regulations that govern the trading activities of most business ventures.

Getting a licence or permit

Some businesses, such as those working with food or alcohol, employment agencies, minicabs and hairdressers, need a licence or permit before they can set up in business at all. Even playing music in public, recorded or live, or putting tables and chairs on a pavement require permission from someone. Your local authority planning department can advise you what rules will apply to your business.

You can get information on business licences and permits on these websites.

Australia (**www.business.gov.au/registration-and-licences/Pages/ default.aspx**)

Canada (**www.canadabusiness.ca/eng/page/2843/**)

New Zealand (**www.business.govt.nz/starting-and-stopping/ entering-a-business/starting-a-business#licenses-consents-permits**)

South Africa (**http://joburg.org.za/index.php?option=com_content&task =view&id=416&Itemid=58**)

UK (**www.gov.uk/licence-finder**)

United States (**www.sba.gov/category/navigation-structure/starting- managing-business/starting-business/obtain-business-licenses-**)

Advertising and descriptive standards

Any advertising or promotion you undertake concerning your business and its products and services, including descriptions on packaging, leaflets and instructions and those given verbally, have to comply with the relevant regulations. You can't just make any claims you believe to be appropriate for your business. Such claims must be decent, honest and truthful, and take into account your wider responsibilities to consumers and anyone else likely to be affected; if you say anything that is misleading or fails to meet any of these tests, then you could leave yourself open to being sued.

Complaints, returns and refunds

Customers buying products are entitled to expect that the goods are 'fit for purpose' in that they can do what they claim and, if the customer has informed you of a particular need, that they are suitable for that purpose. The goods also have to be of 'satisfactory quality', that is, durable and without defects that would affect performance or prevent their enjoyment. For services you must carry the work out with reasonable skill and care and provide it within a reasonable amount of time. The word 'reasonable' is not defined and is applied in relation to each type of service. So, for example, repairing a shoe might reasonably be expected to take a week, while three months would be unreasonable.

If goods or services don't meet these conditions, customers can claim a refund. If they have altered the product or waited an excessive amount of time before complaining or have indicated in any other way that they have 'accepted', they may not be entitled to a refund but may still be able to claim some money back for a period of up to six years.

Distance selling and online trading

Selling by mail order via the internet, television, radio, telephone, fax or catalogue requires that you comply with some additional rules over and above those concerning the sale of goods and services described above. In summary, you have to provide written information, an order confirmation and the chance to cancel the contract. During the cooling-off period, customers have the unconditional right to cancel within seven working days, provided they have informed you in writing by letter, fax or e-mail.

Protecting customer data

If you hold personal information on a computer on any living person, customer or employee, for example, then there is a good chance you need to comply with some legal regulation. Consumers International (CI), the global federation of consumer organizations established in 1985, argues convincingly that consumer protection plays a crucial role in building a fairer, safer world. They regularly assess the state of consumer protection around the world through a global survey of its 58 country member organizations. The main instrument of consumer protection is the Consumer Protection Act (CPA) with 78 per cent of all countries using such a measure. The CPA adoption rate is almost directly correlated with a country's level of economic development. Eighty-five per cent of countries in Western Europe and North America have CPA legislation whilst the figure for Sub-Saharan Africa is just 63 per cent (**www.consumersinternational.org/news-and-media/resource-zone/**).

Employment legislation

Employing people is something of a legal minefield from potential discrimination when hiring to unfair employment terms when firing unsatisfactory employees. Work records have to be kept, health and safety conditions monitored, pay and conditions considered and taxes collected for onward transfer to relevant government departments. As if that were not enough every country, even in relatively harmonized areas such as Europe and the United States, have their own idiosyncratic conditions. These organizations will provide a good starting point to keep on top of employment law:

- World Bank Group. Doing Business – Labour Market Regulation – covers such aspects as Difficulty of hiring, Rigidity of hours, Difficulty of redundancy, Redundancy costs (in salary weeks), Social protection and labour disputes (**www.doingbusiness.org/data/exploretopics/labor-market-regulation**)
- WorldEmploymentLaw.com (**www.worldemploymentlaw.com**) provides up-to-date labour law for the United States, the UK, Russia and a handful of other countries.

CASE STUDY

'In 2015, and given its very solid balance sheet, our Group intends to pursue its 2016 strategic plan in a determined and disciplined manner,' was the reasoned statement on the website of one of France's foremost institutions. The 'About us' section on the website went on to expand on the company's history offering to take readers on a 'digital journey, via 50 surprising and unusual objects, to help you discover Société Générale's history from 1864 to the present day'.

What was absent from these headline statements was that Société Générale reported a trading loss of €4.9 billion on 24 January 2008 after liquidating €50 billion in what the bank says were unauthorized futures positions taken by a relatively junior trader, Jerome Kerviel. The bank claims that Kerviel forged documents and e-mails to suggest he had hedged his positions. But Kerviel insists that his bosses at SocGen, as the bank is generally known, must have been aware of his massive risk taking, and turned a blind eye as long as he was making money for the bank.

Kerviel plans to file a complaint for unfair dismissal and extract compensation from his employer based around three points of defence. Société Générale appears to have terminated his contract without a face-to-face meeting, as is required by French labour laws. Second, the bank's losses may only have occurred while unwinding Kerviel's positions in January 2008, during what was an unprecedented period of global stock market turbulence. This situation makes it unclear exactly how much responsibility Kerviel bears for the total losses.

Third, he had no obvious motive and seems not to have made personal profit from his trades. In fact, his behaviour has made him a folk hero in France, with over 150 Facebook groups showing an interest in his fate.

His chances of success in an unfair dismissal case look at least fair. In April 2007, Laura Zubulake, 44, won £15.5 million from UBS in New York after a male executive said she was fired because she was 'old and ugly and she can't do the job'. Three years earlier Elizabeth Weston received a £1 million settlement from Merrill Lynch over a colleague's 'lewd' comments over a Christmas lunch.

Although Kerviel's actions put him at the top of the 'rogue trader' list, he is unlikely to head the unfair dismissal stakes. That title is likely to go to six women, five of them employees in New York and one at the London office of German-owned bank Dresdner Kleinwort Wasserstein. They are suing for £800 million over allegations that the company refused to promote them and discriminated against them by allowing after-hours trips to strip clubs for male colleagues and humiliating sexual banter in the office.

Intellectual property

The holy grail for competitive marketing strategy is to have a product or service with sufficient unique advantage to make it stand out from others in the market. It is equally important that such an advantage cannot be easily copied. In other words, there is a barrier to entry preventing others from following the same path to riches. The advantage can be anything from the business name (The Body Shop), a catchy slogan ('Never knowingly undersold' – John Lewis), some technological wizardry (Dolby Noise Reduction), an instantly recognizable logo (Google) or even a jingle such as that used by Microsoft's Windows during start-up.

The generic title covering this area is 'intellectual property', usually shortened to IP, and it splits down into a number of distinct areas. Businesses spend a lot of time and money creating and protecting IP, so you need at least an appreciation of the legal issues involved. The case below is an example of how things can go wrong from the outset.

CASE STUDY

When Mark Zuckerberg, then aged 20, started Facebook from his college dorm back in 2004 with two fellow students, he could hardly have been aware of how the business would pan out. Facebook is a social networking website on which users have to put their real names and e-mail addresses in order to register, then they can contact current and past friends and colleagues to swap photos, news and gossip. Within three years the company was on track to make $100 million sales, partly on the back of a big order from Microsoft that appeared to have its sights on Facebook as either a partner or an acquisition target.

Zuckerberg in his jeans, Adidas sandals and a fleece, looks a bit like a latter-day Steve Jobs, Apple's founder. He also shares something else in common with Jobs. He has a gigantic intellectual property legal dispute on his hands. For three years he had to deal with a law suit brought by three fellow Harvard students who claim, in effect, that he stole the Facebook concept from them.

Patents

A patent can be regarded as a contract between an inventor and the state. The state agrees with the inventor that if he or she is prepared to publish details of the invention in a set form and if it appears that he or she has made a real advance, the state will then grant the inventor a 'monopoly' on the invention for 20 years. The inventor uses the monopoly period to manufacture and sell his or her innovation; competitors can read the published specifications and glean ideas for their research, or they can approach the inventor and offer to help to develop the idea under licence.

However, the granting of a patent doesn't mean the proprietor is automatically free to make, use or sell the invention themselves, since to do so might involve infringing an earlier patent that has not yet expired.

A patent really only allows the inventor to stop another person using the particular device that forms the subject of the patent. The state does not guarantee validity of a patent either, so it is not uncommon for patents to be challenged through the courts.

What you can patent

What inventions can you patent? The basic rules are that an invention must be new, must involve an inventive step and must be capable of industrial exploitation.

You can't patent scientific/mathematical theories or mental processes, computer programs or ideas that might encourage offensive, immoral or antisocial behaviour. New medicines are patentable but not medical methods of treatment. Neither can you have just rediscovered a long-forgotten idea (knowingly or unknowingly).

If you want to apply for a patent, it is essential not to disclose your idea in non-confidential circumstances. If you do, your invention is already 'published' in the eyes of the law, and this could well invalidate your application.

Copyright

Copyright gives protection against the unlicensed copying of original artistic and creative works – articles, books, paintings, films, plays, songs, music, engineering drawings. To claim copyright, the item in question should carry this symbol: © (author's name) (date). You can take the further step of recording the date on which the work was completed. This, though, is an unusual precaution to take and probably only necessary if you anticipate an infringement.

Copyright protection usually lasts for 70 years after the death of the person who holds the copyright, or 50 years after publication if this is later.

Copyright is infringed only if more than a 'substantial' part of your work is reproduced (ie issued for sale to the public) without your permission, but since there is no formal registration of copyright, the question of whether or not your work is protected usually has to be decided in a court of law.

Designs

You can register the shape, design or decorative features of a commercial product if it is new, original, never published before or – if already known – never before applied to the product you have in mind. Protection is intended to apply to industrial articles to be produced in quantities of more than 50. Design registration applies only to features that appeal to the eye – not to the way the article functions.

Protection lasts for around 25 years. You can handle the design registration yourself, but, again, it might be preferable to let a specialist do it for you. There is no register of design agents but most patent agents are well versed in design law.

Trademarks and logos

A trademark is the symbol by which the goods or services of a particular manufacturer or trader can be identified. It can be a word, a signature, a monogram, a picture, a logo or a combination of these.

To qualify for registration, the trademark must be distinctive, must not be deceptive and must not be capable of confusion with marks already registered. Excluded are misleading marks, national flags, royal crests and insignia of the armed forces. A trademark can only apply to tangible goods, not services (although pressure is mounting for this to be changed).

To register a trademark, you or your agent should first conduct preliminary searches at the trademarks branch of the Patent Office to check there are no conflicting marks already in existence. You then apply for registration on the official trademark form and pay a fee (currently £200). Registration is initially for 10 years. After this, it can be renewed for periods of 10 years at a time, indefinitely.

It isn't mandatory to register a trademark. If an unregistered trademark has been used for some time and could be construed as closely associated with a product by customers, it will have acquired a 'reputation', which will give it some protection legally, but registration makes it much simpler for the owners to have recourse against any person who infringes the mark. Registration is usually for around 10 years, and is renewable.

CASE STUDY

Wagamama, a small London-based restaurant chain, which has prospered by selling Japanese noodles to city trendies, saw the need to protect its idea as the main plank of its business strategy.

Alan Yau, who founded the business, came to the UK as an 11-year-old economic immigrant from Hong Kong. He joined his father running a Chinese takeaway in King's Lynn, Norfolk. Within 10 years he was running two Chinese restaurants of his own, one of which is close to the British Museum. From the outset he had plans to run a large international chain of restaurants.

Yau's food style is healthy, distinctive and contemporary. Wagamama conjures up someone who is a bit of a spoilt brat in Japanese, and the word lodged in Yau's mind. His informal communal dining room, opened under the Wagamama banner, received favourable reviews, and the queues, which have become an essential part of the Wagamama experience, started forming. Realizing he had an idea with global potential, Yau took the unusual step of registering his trademark worldwide. It cost £60,000. But within two years that investment began to pay off. A large listed company opened an Indian version of Wagamama. The concepts looked similar enough to lead ordinary people to think the two businesses were related. As Yau felt he could lose out, he decided to sue. The case was heard quickly and within three months Yau had won and his business idea was safe – at least for the five years his trademark protection runs for.

Founded in April 1992 in Bloomsbury, London, the company now operates in Australia, Belgium, Cyprus, Denmark, Dubai, Egypt, Greece, Ireland, the Netherlands, New Zealand, Switzerland, Turkey, the UK and the USA. It was voted London's most popular restaurant by *Zagat* readers every year since 2006 and as an official 'Super Brand' in 2008.

Names

Business and domain names involve a cross-section of IP issues. A good name, in effect, can become a one- or two-word summary of your marketing strategy: Body Shop, Toys R Us, Kwik-Fit are good examples. Many companies add a slogan to explain to customers and employees alike 'how they do it'. Cobra Beer's slogan, 'Unusual thing, excellence' focuses attention on quality and distinctiveness. The name, slogan and logo combine to be the most visible tip of the iceberg in a corporate communications effort and as such need a special effort to protect.

Business name

When you choose a business name, you are also choosing an identity, so it should reflect:

- who you are;
- what you do;
- how you do it.

Given all the marketing investment you will make in your company name, you should check with a trademark agent whether you can protect your chosen name (descriptive words, surnames and place names are not normally allowed except after long use). It will be accepted unless there is another company with that name on the register or the Registrar considers the name to be obscene, offensive or illegal.

By putting the term 'business names' into the World Intellectual Property Organization search pane you will bring up the relevant country's legislation (**www.wipo.int/portal/en/**).

Registering domains

Internet presence requires a domain name, ideally one that captures the essence of your business neatly so that you will come up readily on search engines and is as close as possible to your business name. Once a business name is registered as a trademark (see earlier in this chapter) you may (as current case law develops) be able to prevent another business from using it as a domain name on the internet.

Registering a domain name is simple but as hundreds of domain names are registered every day and you must choose a name that has not already been registered, you need to have a selection of domain names to hand in case your first choice is unavailable. These need only be slight variations – for example, Cobra Beer could have been listed as Cobra-Beer, CobraBeer or even Cobra Indian Beer, if the original name was not available. These would all have been more or less equally effective in terms of search engine visibility.

WIPO (World Intellectual Property Organization) formed in 1967 is the global forum for intellectual property services, policy, information and cooperation operating as a self-funding agency of the United Nations. Their directory link (**www.wipo.int/directory/en/**) gives details of the organization responsible for IP matters in their 188 member states as well as information on national laws and statistics on disputes.

Ethics in marketing

This subject is perhaps the most controversial and disputed in terms of the teaching methodology and content used in business schools. A recent survey on corporate social responsibility education in Europe found that while most business schools had some content in this area, only a quarter had a specific topic, module or elective covering the ground. Since 2015, courses in corporate social responsibility (CSR), ethics, sustainability or business and society have been a requirement for 68 per cent of MBAs, up from 45 per cent in 2003 and 34 per cent in 2001. Most had the subject embedded in various other subject areas, for example under titles such as a combination of 'accounting, corporate governance, law and public governance' or 'stake-holder management'. Others had ethics and social responsibility covered in the context of specific disciplines – ethical accounting systems or marketing and ethics. Georgia Tech College of Management's MBA set as a business ethics paper the task 'Analyze Sarbanes–Oxley from both conceptual and implementation perspectives', which is largely a single issue of directors' responsibilities to investors.

There is widespread use of practitioner speakers from business or non-governmental organizations as well as case studies from industry, and these methods dwarf the more academic methods (lectures, tutorials) used in other subject areas. Tuck School of Business at Dartmouth, for example, teaches a 'brief mini course' based on discussions of ethical issues encountered by its faculty in cases involving its experience 'particularly on the functional areas of business as exercised in both the USA and the global marketplace, where different local practices and cultural norms seem to muddy the ethical water'. The academics, however, are on the march! Nottingham University Business School has an International Centre for Corporate Social Responsibility and a Professor of CSR. INSEAD has a chaired professor of Business Ethics and Corporate Responsibility, though the focus there appears to be very much around ethical consumerism, deception in marketing and marketing ethics.

However Jonathan P Doh and Peter Tashman in their research findings on how the top 50 business schools taught social responsibility concluded: 'Our results suggest that the institutionalization of CSR, sustainability and sustainable development is far from extensive. These subjects do appear to be diffusing through the business school curricula, but with uneven records of adoption and diverse methods of implementation by faculty' (Doh, J P and Tashman, P (2014) Half a world away: The integration and assimilation of corporate social responsibility, sustainability, and sustainable development in business school curricula, *Corporate Social Responsibility and Environmental Management*, **21** (3), pp 131–42).

Defining areas of responsibility

Actions for which a person or group of people can be held accountable and so commended or blamed, disciplined or rewarded, are said to lie within their sphere of responsibility. Anything that lies outside our control also lies beyond the scope of our responsibilities. Ethics, known in academic circles as moral philosophy, is concerned with classifying, defending, and proposing concepts of right and wrong behaviour in the way in which we discharge our responsibilities. While many responsibilities lie within the scope of the law – shareholders' protection, discrimination at work, misleading advertising and so forth – both in those areas and the grey area that surrounds them lies the province of ethics and social responsibility. Right and wrong in themselves are often not too difficult to separate. The problem usually stems from competing 'rights' – giving shareholders a better return vs saving the planet, for example, and the inherent selfishness of humans. Many, if not all, of our actions are triggered by self-interest. In fact, much of the justification for capitalism's attraction lies in the 'invisible hand' theory advanced by Adam Smith in his defining book, *The Wealth of Nations*.

Business ethics defines the categories of duty for which we are morally responsible. Lists of moral duties and rights can be lengthy and overlapping. The duty-based theory advanced by British philosopher W D Ross (1877–1971), provides a short list of duties that he believed reflects our actual moral convictions:

- fidelity: the duty to keep promises;
- reparation: the duty to compensate others when we harm them;
- gratitude: the duty to thank those who help us;
- justice: the duty to recognize merit;
- beneficence: the duty to improve the conditions of others;
- self-improvement: the duty to improve our virtue and intelligence;
- non-maleficence: the duty to not injure others.

Ross recognized that there will be occasions when we must choose between two conflicting duties. For example, should your business be involved in any way with products that facilitate abortions? On one side of that moral argument lies beneficence in improving the conditions of women and on the other non-maleficence in not doing injury to the unborn child. You can find out more about the theoretical aspects of ethics on the Internet Encyclopedia of Philosophy (**www.iep.utm.edu/e/ethics.htm**) and on related business issues on the free Management Library website (**www.managementhelp.org/ethics/ethxgde.htm**).

CASE STUDY   Unilever – embedding ethics

The spring of 2015 was a busy period for Unilever, the British–Dutch multinational consumer goods company co-headquartered in Rotterdam, Netherlands, and London, UK. In March 2015 it acquired the iconic British skincare brand REN Skincare and the month before it topped the list of companies which file the most patents a year, according to the European Patent Office (EPO).

Its beginnings were more humble. In 1887 William Hesketh Lever, already a highly successful soap manufacturer, was looking for a new site for his factory to allow him to expand. The site needed to be near to a river for importing raw materials, and a railway line for transporting the finished products. The 56 acres of unused marshy land at the site that became Port Sunlight, named after his soap, was far more than he needed simply for manufacturing purposes. Lever had something more all-embracing in mind. His stated aims were to create an environment that allowed his workers 'to socialise and Christianise business relations and get back to that close family brotherhood that existed in the good old days of hand labour'. His intention was to extend his responsibilities beyond making money for himself and to share that, albeit on his own terms, with everyone who worked for him. Between 1899 and 1914 Lever built some 800 houses, taking an active part in the design himself. The community's population of 3,500 shared allotments, public buildings including the Lady Lever Art Gallery, schools, a concert hall, open-air swimming pool, church, and a temperance hotel. His cottage hospital, built in 1907, continued until the introduction of the National Health Service in 1948. He also introduced schemes for welfare, education and the entertainment of his workers, and encouraged recreation and organizations that promoted art, literature, science or music.

Unilever, as the company is now known, has carried the Lever values and vision on into corporate life. The company's behaviour in all affairs is governed by a set of clear, stated and communicated guidelines. Starting with its core value –

'As a multi-local multinational we aim to play our part in addressing global environmental and social concerns through our own actions, and working in partnership with stakeholders at local, national and international levels' – the company has developed a comprehensive set of principles to guide its behaviour in all aspects of its work. The guidelines that Unilever expects employees to work to include always working with integrity with 'the highest standards of corporate behaviour towards everyone we work with, the communities we touch, and the environment on which we have an impact'. The full value statement can be seen on the company website at: (**www.unilever.com/sustainable-living-2014/our-approach-to-sustainability/values-and-standards**).

Resolving conflict

Unfortunately, however ethical and socially responsible an organization is, it will at some stage, perhaps even frequently, find itself pursuing a strategy that upsets other stakeholder groups. A recent example of one such conflict was Shell's decision, announced in April 2008, to pull out of the London Array wind farm. This £2 billion project for 341 turbines capable of producing 1,000 megawatts of power was a key part of the UK government's strategy to produce 15 per cent of UK energy needs from renewable sources by 2015, with an aspiration to raise that to 20 per cent by 2020. Given that in 2008 renewable energy accounted for only 2 per cent of output in the UK, the London Array was seen as important, perhaps vital, to achieving those goals. But Shell had to weigh up the consequences of upsetting the UK government, Friends of the Earth, and its other German and Dutch partners in the project, with other concerns. Shell's view was that the costs of wind farms were simply spiralling out of control, with steel prices rising with increased world demand from such countries as China and India. In any event, world turbine production was booked up years in advance. Shell already had stakes in 11 wind farms producing over 1,100 megawatts and reckoned as a company it could make the same contribution to the environment at a much lower cost to its shareholders, but probably on another continent and in another technology.

Resolving stakeholder conflicts calls for tact and communications and the recognition that while you can't please everyone, you can still be ethical. About 1 per cent of Shell's investments are in green projects. For example, a company subsidiary, Shell Solar, has played a major role in the development of first-generation CIS (copper indium diselenide) thin-film technology. This Shell believes to be the most commercially viable form of photovoltaic solar technology to generate electricity from the sun's energy. Together with its joint venture partner in this project, Saint Gobain, Shell has a pilot plant under construction in Saxony, Germany that will produce sufficient solar panels to save 14,000 tonnes of CO_2 per year. So stakeholders such as the UK government and Denmark's DONG Energy in the London Array project had to be weighed up against Saint Gobain, with the German government being party to both strategies through the participation of that country's energy giant, E.ON. All the while, Shell was under pressure to match its historical profit growth.

Authenticity Consulting (**www.authenticityconsulting.com/misc/long.pdf**) has a useful checklist to help with decisions about resolving stakeholder conflict.

Whistleblowers – an ethical longstop

Not surprisingly, the people most likely to know about unethical or socially irresponsible behaviour are those working in the organization itself. Governments around the world have adopted measures to encourage a flow of information on ethical problems and fraud from whistleblowers – that is, anyone employed or recently employed by a public body, business organization or charity who reveals evidence of wrongdoing. Whistleblowers have also been given a measure of legal protection. In the USA the Lloyd–La Follette Act of 1912 started the ball rolling, giving federal employees the right to provide Congress with information, and was followed by a patchwork of laws covering such fields as water pollution, the environment, the Sarbanes–Oxley Act (2002) to deal with corporate fraud and the Whistleblower Protection Enhancement Act (2007). In the UK the Public Interest Disclosure Act (1998) and various laws enacted by the European Union and other governments provide a framework of legal protection for individuals who disclose information.

Many firms too have established ways to attract information on frauds being committed against them including 24-hour hotlines and corporate ethics offices. For example, Vodafone's 'Speak up' programme, launched in 2006–07, provides suppliers and employees working in its supply chain with a means of reporting any ethical concerns (**www.vodafone.com/start/responsibility/supply_chain/whistle-blowing.html**).

The National Whistleblowers Centre (**www.whistleblowers.org**) focuses on exposing government and corporate misconduct, promoting ethical standards and protecting the jobs and careers of whistleblowers. They can provide further background on the subject.

Is ethical marketing a profitable strategy?

There is plenty of anecdotal evidence that ethical and socially responsible organizations are better places to work. At the very least, being ethical provides an organization with an insurance policy limiting its exposure to a range of legal liabilities for faulty products, misleading advertising, price fixing and discrimination at work, for example. But evidence on whether being ethical helps a business organization to become and stay more profitable is less clear.

But that still begs the question of what constitutes 'good'. The FTSE4Good Index (**www.ftse.com/products/indices/FTSE4Good**) sets out to measure the performance of companies that meet globally recognized corporate responsibility standards. For inclusion, a company can't be involved in the extraction or processing of uranium. That only serves to highlight the problem of deciding what is ethical and what is not. For example, is mining uranium for nuclear power really more harmful than, say, switching to biofuels, which, aside from probably releasing between two and nine times more carbon gases over the next 30 years than fossil fuels, will almost certainly cause food prices to stay high, particularly in the developing world? Or is the motor industry, whose products kill more people every year than the armaments industry, a more ethical and socially responsible sector?

However, a small but growing band of business schools believes there is enough mileage in social responsibility and ethics to launch 'green' MBA programmes that emphasize a triple bottom line, also known as TBL or 3BL: profit, people, planet. Corporate Knights, The Magazine for Clean Capitalism, that produces a ranking for green and sustainable MBA programmes now produces a ranking for the most Green business schools. Two Canadian business schools come out top and the UK's Exeter Business School (which hosts the sustainability-focused One Planet MBA Program) is third. The full list is published at **www.corporateknights.com/reports/2013-sustainable-mba/**.

'Social Responsibility' took something of a knock in September 2015 when Volkswagen fell from grace. Recently ranked as the 11th best in the world for its CSR (Corporate Social Responsibility) work by The Reputation Institute, in 2014, it collected the "Gold Medal Award for Sustainable Development" from the non-profit World Environment Center and its own sustainability report runs to 156 pages. There is a view gaining ground that CSR departments are simply providing an insurance policy allowing companies to take risk with their own internal standards.

Online video courses and lectures

Fault in Contract Law: 'Let Us Never Blame a Contract Breaker.' Richard Posner, Senior Lecturer in Law at the University of Chicago Law School and Judge on the US Court of Appeals for the Seventh Circuit: **www.youtube.com/watch?v=GvlDdJpF5oM**

IBM Study: Corporate Social Responsibility a survey based on responses from top executives at more than 250 companies worldwide: **www.youtube.com/watch?v=PdkYieDuVvY**

Introduction to Business Law: Richard Ertel, Adjunct Professor at Nassau Community College. This is the first in a series of short videos, each under an hour. The other topics covered include: Intellectual property,

Employment law, Sole proprietorships, Partnerships, Limited partnerships, Limited liability companies, Contracts, Negligence and Bankruptcy: **www.youtube.com/channel/UCpi5XVTME57RDLB-VN-SDaA**

Introduction to European Business Law: Run periodically by the faculty of Lund University, Sweden. Founded in 1666 and ranked among the world's top 100 universities: **www.coursera.org/course/europeanbusinesslaw**

Law and the Entrepreneur: This course highlights the critical legal and business issues entrepreneurs face as they build and launch a new venture. Run periodically by the faculty of Northwestern University: **www.coursera.org/course/law**

The Law of Agency: George Geis, University of Virginia School of Law Vice Dean: **www.youtube.com/watch?v=L_tsPzj27-0**

Laws that choke creativity: Lawrence Lessig, TED speaker: **www.ted.com/talks/larry_lessig_says_the_law_is_strangling_creativity?language=en#**

Making Mischief in the Blogosphere – Legally Speaking: University of California Television (UCTV): **www.youtube.com/watch?v=CHhl27cuJuY**

Market Segmentation: Professor Michal Barzuza of the University of Virginia School of Law discusses the Rise of Nevada as a Liability-Free Jurisdiction: **www.youtube.com/watch?v=QxepEieffUc**

The Political and Judicial Elements of American Capitalism: Professor Rae of Yale University uses the Merck-Vioxx business case to highlight political elements of US capitalism, including government regulatory agencies, federalism, lobbying, regulatory capture, tort law and liability, and patent law: **http://oyc.yale.edu/political-science/plsc-270/lecture-14**

Practical Ethics run occasionally by Peter Singer, a professor at Princetown University: **www.coursera.org/course/practicalethics**

Social Media and the Law: How Our Ideas of 'Privacy' Changing and Why it Matters: Duke Law School review recent legal developments that take social media into account: **www.youtube.com/watch?v=Huboy9EWMiM**

What is Corporate Social Responsibility (CSR)? Professor Thomas Beschorner, University of St Gallen, Switzerland: **www.youtube.com/watch?v=E0NkGtNU_9w**

Online video case studies

Apple vs Samsung – Jobs on iPhone Patent: **www.youtube.com/watch?v=Fz_nZ2n4UkM**

Apple vs Samsung: 10 juicy secrets from the courtroom, TechRadar: **www.youtube.com/watch?v=ilsKCJOxFSY**

Bhopal gas tragedy: Union Carbide not liable for claims, says US court – NewsX: **www.youtube.com/watch?v=FyHaaAXn0QU**

Billion dollar art battle steeped in WW2 history, 60 Minutes: **www.cbsnews.com/news/billion-dollar-world-war-ii-art-battle-60-minutes/**

Coca Cola. Corporate Social Responsibility: **www.youtube.com/watch?v=B7dDSHwFgKk**

Facebook: Ownership Contract Does Not Exist; Zuckerberg Comments on Lawsuit, SmarTrend News: **www.youtube.com/watch?v=rJLjD98QcZ4**

Gulf of Mexico Oil Spill, Legal Liability, Part 1. Witnesses testified on legal liability issues surrounding the Gulf of Mexico oil spill to the House Judiciary Committee. C-SPAN: **www.c-span.org/video/?293754-1/gulf-mexico-oil-spill-legal-liability-part-1**

Legal Battles: A Tale of Two GMs? DrivingSales News, 18 December 2014: **http://drivingsalesnews.com/legal-battles-a-tale-of-two-gms/**

Nike and Corporate Responsibility. Claire Anderson, Global Justice Final Project: **www.youtube.com/watch?v=xTB4thqyo5Q**

Primark on the racks. BBC Trust: **www.youtube.com/watch?v=OWio7NVOnaI**

Primark responds to the BBC Trust's Panorama verdict: **www.youtube.com/watch?v=hUSsG_tDDY0**

Starbucks. Being a Responsible Company: **www.starbucks.co.uk/responsibility**

Who owns Facebook and its 500 million users? Legal troubles over the ownership of the site. CNBC's Scott Cohn reports: **www.today.com/video/today/38358645#38358645**

Winklevoss Twins – Facebook was our idea – Tyler & Cameron. ViralFuture: **www.youtube.com/watch?v=KzN6XWDEmXI**

11

Marketing plans and budgets

- Marketing planning tools
- Marketing planning – the detail
- Preparing budgets
- Analysing performance against budget
- Information systems

In Chapter 3 we covered marketing strategy and the tools for determining the core direction of the marketing thrust. In Chapter 8 we looked at the tools and processes used to help shape the direction of the enterprise as a whole – vision, mission and objectives.

Strategy has three dimensions: the intellectual, analytical and thinking aspect used to devise broad strategic direction, the development and shaping of specific actions in pursuit of those strategies, and the implementation of strategy through the execution of business plans. If an organization gets it wrong in any of these areas the results it is aiming for may not be achieved, it may fall behind others in the market or in the worst case fail altogether. As we said in Chapter 3, getting all three areas right can be more of an art than a science.

Shaping marketing plans – tools and techniques

While Porter's Five Forces approach to marketing strategy formulation (see Chapter 3) is, as far as business schools are concerned at least, the standard starting point, there are also a number of other tools that an MBA needs to be familiar with to help to turn strategy into detailed marketing plans.

The following are the main tools and techniques an MBA will be expected to know and understand.

Ansoff growth matrix

Igor Ansoff, while Professor of Industrial Administration in the Graduate School at Carnegie Mellon University, published his landmark book, *Corporate Strategy*, in 1965, in which he explained a way of categorizing strategies as an aid to understanding the nature of the risks involved. He invited his students to consider growth options as a square matrix divided into four segments. The x-axis is divided into existing and new products, and the y-axis into existing and new markets. Ansoff assigned titles and level of risk to the resulting types of strategy. You can find out more about the matrix at **www.strategyvectormodel.com**>Ansoff Matrix.

- Market penetration involves selling more of your existing products and services to existing customers – the lowest-risk strategy.
- Product/service development involves creating extensions to your existing products or new products to sell to your existing customer base. This is more risky than market penetration, but less risky than market development.
- Market development involves entering new market segments or completely new markets, either in your home country or abroad. You will face new competitors and may not understand the customers as well as you do your current ones.
- Diversification is selling new products into new markets – the most risky strategy as both are relative unknowns. Avoid this strategy unless all others have been exhausted. Diversification can be further subdivided into four categories of increasing risk profile:
  - Horizontal diversification: entirely new product into current market;
  - Vertical diversification: move backwards into firm's suppliers or forwards into customer's business;
  - Concentric diversification: new product closely related to current products either in terms of technology or marketing presence but in a new market;
  - Conglomerate diversification: completely new product into a new market.

Boston matrix

Developed in 1969 by the Boston Consulting Group, this tool can be used in conjunction with the life-cycle concept (see Chapter 4) to plan a portfolio of product/service offers. The thinking behind the matrix is that a company's products and services should be classified according to their ability to either

FIGURE 11.1   Ansoff growth matrix

	Existing Products	New Products or Services
Existing Markets	**Market Penetration** Sell more of your existing products and services to existing customers – the lowest-risk strategy.	**Product/Service Development** Creating extensions to your existing products or new products to sell to your existing customer base.
New Markets	**Market Development** Entering new market segments or completely new markets either in your home country or abroad.	**Diversification** Selling new products into new markets; the most risky strategy as both are relative unknowns. Avoid unless all other strategies have been exhausted.

generate or consume cash against two dimensions: the market growth rate and the company's market share. Cash is used as the measure rather than profit, as that is the real resource used to invest in new offers. The objective then is to use the positive cash flow generated from 'cash cows', usually mature products that no longer need heavy marketing support budgets, to invest in 'stars', the fast-growing, usually newer products, positioned in markets in which the company already has a high market share – usually newer markets. 'Dogs' should be disinvested and 'question marks' limited in number and watched carefully to see if they are more likely to become stars or dogs.

FIGURE 11.2   Boston matrix

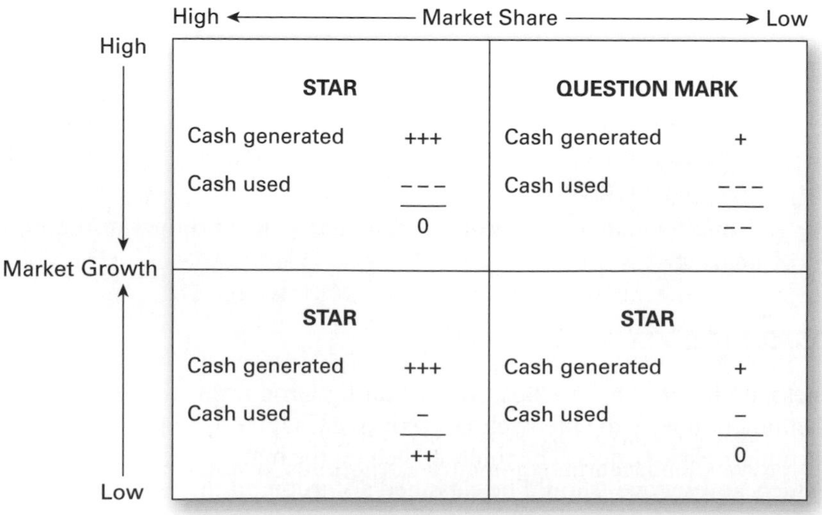

High ←————— Market Share —————→ Low

	High Market Share	Low Market Share
High Market Growth	**STAR** Cash generated +++ Cash used – – – ——— 0	**QUESTION MARK** Cash generated + Cash used – – – ——— – –
Low Market Growth	**STAR** Cash generated +++ Cash used – ——— ++	**STAR** Cash generated + Cash used – ——— 0

GE–McKinsey directional policy matrix

General Electric was much taken by the visual aspect of the Boston matrix and was using it to enhance its own performance while working with another consulting firm, McKinsey and Company. Between them in 1971 they came up with a variant and in some ways an improvement by substituting business strength and industry attractiveness for market share and market growth rate – the logic being that although these are subjective measures they are more accessible than market growth and share, as these are hard to establish and in any event the figures are themselves largely subjective suppositions based largely on opinions.

FIGURE 11.3   GE–McKinsey directional policy matrix

Other matrix variations

A dozen or so other similar matrices are in use, each with their own strengths and weaknesses. Arthur D Little, Inc, a management consultancy founded in 1886 and based in Cambridge, Massachusetts, came up with its own matrix in the late 1970s using competitive position and industry maturity as the directions. Two business school professors, Gary Hamel (London Business School) and C K Prahalad (University of Michigan), developed a matrix in 1994 as an aid in setting specific acquisition and deployment goals. Other academics (in the USA Charles W Hofer and Dan Schendel, and in the UK Cranfield colleagues Malcolm McDonald and Cliff Bowman) as well as companies such as Shell have all added twists to the basic matrix strategy tool.

The Boston Growth Matrix is explained at
www.valuebasedmanagement.net/methods_bcgmatrix.html

This is a tutorial showing how to create BCG Matrix in Excel:
http://best-excel-tutorial.com/56-charts/176-bcg-matrix

The GE McKinsey Growth Matrix is explained at
www.mbaknol.com/strategic-management/gemckinsey-matrix/

Long-run return pyramid

Another helpful marketing planning tool is the long-run return pyramid, which is in effect a checklist of growth options. None of the options are mutually exclusive and the tool does not provide for any form of evaluation. Nevertheless, it can be a valuable aide-memoire to ensure that no stone has been left unturned during the strategic review process. The pyramid's pedigree is unknown, but it is loosely based on DuPont's return-on-investment pyramid, used to trace all the performance ratios that influence return on investment. The pyramid in the form shown in Figure 11.4 is attributed to Robert Brown, a senior academic at Cranfield School of Management.

FIGURE 11.4   Long-run return pyramid

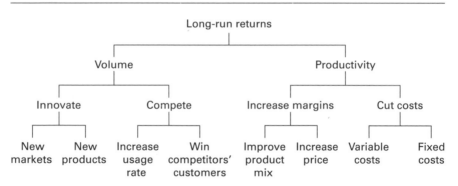

Marketing and business plans

All the thinking that goes into devising and shaping marketing planning has to be set out in a form that will ensure that it can be successfully implemented. That form is a marketing plan, which itself is part of a wider plan for the business as a whole, setting out in detail the role each part of the organization has to play for the next three to five years. That period is needed because recognizing an opportunity, developing a product or service to exploit it and bringing that product to market all take time and the plan has to encompass all these stages to be of any value. The dichotomy here is that while strategy takes time for the results to show, the world in which the business is implementing its plans is changing. Three- and five-year business plans need to be reviewed fundamentally each year and progress monitored at least quarterly.

Preparing marketing and business plans is a task that MBAs are invariably expected to be able to carry out, so this section describes the total structure of the plan within which the marketing function plays a key role. Exactly how large that role is will depend on organization structure adopted (see Chapter 8). If the marketing organization is a strategic business unit with full profit accountability, then there will in effect be no difference between the business and marketing plans.

Preparing these plans calls for a broad level of understanding of all aspects of the business – cash flow, profit margins, funding issues, marketing and selling, staffing and structures, production, operations, research and development, supply chain, etc – that few others in the organization are likely to have. It is an opportunity for an MBA to broaden and deepen his or her relationships with all key executives as well as the board of directors. So often tedious and always time-consuming, the task of preparing business plans should be welcomed as a career progression opportunity par excellence.

Structure of the marketing and business plan

The plan is in essence the route map from where the business is to where it wants to get and how it will go about getting to its destination: roles and responsibilities of key players, the resources required in terms of money, people and materials and so forth. While there is much debate about exactly what should go into the business plan and how it should be laid out, there is no doubt that it is the essential tool for ensuring that a well-thought-out marketing strategy is executed successfully too.

What follows is the suggested general layout for a business plan as used on the MBA programme at Cranfield; from observation at international business plan competitions, it seems to be fairly universal.

Executive summary

This is the most important part of the plan and will form the heart of any presentation to the board, shareholders or prospective investors. Written last, it should be punchy, short – ideally one page but never more than two – and should enthuse any reader. Its primary purpose is to excite and inspire an audience to want to read the rest of the business plan.

The executive summary should start with a succinct table showing past performance in key areas and future objectives. This will give readers a clear view of the business's capacity to perform as well as the scale of the task ahead.

The executive summary should continue with sections covering the following areas:

- What the primary products/services are and why they are better than or different from what is around now.

TABLE 11.1   Executive summary – history and projections

	Last year	This year	Business area	Year 1	Year 2	Year 3, etc
Sales turnover by:						
Product/ service						
Market segment 1						
Market segment 2, etc						
Total sales						
Gross profit %						
Operating profit %						
Total staff numbers						
Sales staff numbers						
Capital employed						
Return on capital employed						

- Which markets/customer groups will most need what you plan to offer and why.
- How close you are to being ready to sell your product/service and what, if anything, remains to be done.
- Why your organization has the skills and expertise to execute this strategy; if new or additional people are required, who they are or how you will recruit them.
- Financial projections showing in summary the sales, profit, margins and cash position over the next three to five years.

- How the business will operate, sketching out the key steps from buying in any raw materials through to selling, delivering and getting paid.
- What physical resources – equipment, premises – the plan calls for.

The contents – putting flesh on the bones

Unlike the executive summary that is structured to reveal the essence of your business proposition, the plan itself should follow a logical sequence such as this:

- Vision. A vision's purpose is to stretch the organization's reach beyond its grasp. Generally, few people concerned with the company can see how the vision is to be achieved, but all concerned agree that it would be great if it could be. Once your vision becomes reality, it may be time for a new challenge, or perhaps even a new business.
- Mission. A mission statement explains concisely what you do, who you do it for and why you are better than or different from others operating in your market. It should be narrow enough to give focus yet leave enough room for growth. Above all, it should be believable to all concerned.
- Objectives. These are the big-picture numbers such as market share, profit, return on investment, that are to be achieved by successfully executing the chosen strategy.
- Operations. This area covers any processes such as manufacture, assembly, purchasing, stock holding, delivery/fulfilment and website.
- Financial projections. Detailed information on sales and cash flow for the period of the plan, showing how much money is needed, for what, by when and what would be the most appropriate source of those funds – long- or short-term borrowings, equity, factoring or leasing finance for example.
- Premises. What space and equipment will be needed and how your home will accommodate the business while staying within the law.
- People. What skills and experience do you have that will help run this business and implement the chosen strategy; what other people will you need and where will you find them?
- Administrative matters. Do you have any intellectual property on your product or service; what insurance will you need; what changes, if any, will be needed to the accounting and control and record systems?
- Milestone timetable. This should show the key actions you have still to take to be ready to achieve major objectives and the date by which these will be completed.

- Appendices. Use these for any bulky information such as market studies, competitors' leaflets, customer endorsements, technical data, patents, CVs and the like that you refer to in your business plan.

The marketing plan – in detail

The above is a basic summary of the contents of the business plan, each section of which will be in rather more detail. For the marketing department that detail will include:

- market projections and forecasts by product, market and market segment (see Chapter 9 for more on forecasting techniques);
- competitor analysis – SWOT (see Chapter 3 for more on strengths, weaknesses, opportunities and threats as well as other tools for analysing competitors);
- specific growth objectives by product/service category, using Ansoff and Boston matrices (see earlier in this chapter);
- major new product/service launches and new market entry goals;
- advertising and promotion actions and schedules (see Chapter 5);
- distribution and channel-to-market routes (see Chapter 6)
- detailed pricing by product/service and market segment, including discounts and offers (see Chapter 7);
- customer retention methods and goals;
- sales force size, structure and incentives;
- market research tasks and programmes (see Chapter 2).

All these topics are covered in this book and by using the index and table of contents you can find your way to them quickly.

Using marketing planning software

There are a number of free software packages that will help you through the process of writing a marketing plan. The ones listed below include some useful resources, spreadsheets and tips that may speed up the process, but are not substitutes for finding out the basic facts about your market, customers and competitors:

Marketing MO, an offshoot of Moderandi Inc, have an App 'for building sustainable, profitable growth delivering the marketing strategy, processes and operational tactics for creating sustainable success'. Costs from £200/$299, but you can try it for free (**www.marketingmo.com/**).

MarketingPlan Now is a full-featured site that lets you create a complete marketing plan for free. Not only does the site let you make your marketing plan, it provides free training resources to help you develop an intelligent, insightful, and accurate marketing plan. You can get a full professional audit of your marketing plan for £120/$180 (**www.marketingplannow.com/**).

Mplans is part of a network of Palo Alto Software sites dedicated to helping entrepreneurs and marketers create plans. They have a number of free aids and examples of marketing plans as well as their software, Sales and Marketing Pro which costs £110 ($163) helps you design your marketing plan and sales strategy using a marketing system they claim has been 'praised by experts like Entrepreneur Magazine and Harvard Business School' (**www.paloalto.com/ sales_and_marketing_plan_software/features/marketing_plans/**).

Budgets and variances

Budgeting is the principal interface between the marketing department and the finance department. As a staff function (see Chapter 8 for more on line and staff functions), the finance department will assist managers in preparing a detailed budget for the year ahead for every area of the organization – this is in effect the first year of the marketing plan. MBAs are invariably expected to play a role in facilitating the process within their department. Budgets are usually reviewed at least halfway through the year and often quarterly. At that review a further quarter or half year can be added to the budget to maintain a one-year budget horizon. This is known as a rolling quarterly (half yearly) budget.

Budget guidelines

Budgets should adhere to the following general principles:

- The budget must be based on realistic but challenging goals. These are arrived at by both a top-down 'aspiration' of senior management and a bottom-up forecast of what the department concerned sees as possible.
- The budget should be prepared by those responsible for delivering the results – the salespeople should prepare the sales budget and the advertising and promotion people the A&P budget. Senior managers must maintain the communication process so that everyone knows what other parties are planning for.
- Agreement to the budget should be explicit. During the budgeting process, several versions of a particular budget should be discussed. For example, the boss may want a sales figure of 2 million, but the sales team's initial forecast is for 1.75 million. After some debate, 1.9 million may be the figure agreed upon. Once a figure is agreed, a virtual contract exists that declares a commitment from employees to achieve the target and commitment from the employer to be

satisfied with the target and to supply resources in order to achieve it. It makes sense for this contract to be in writing.

- The budget needs to be finalized at least a month before the start of the year and not weeks or months into the year.
- The budget should undergo fundamental reviews periodically throughout the year to make sure all the basic assumptions that underpin it still hold good.
- Accurate information reviewing performance against budgets should be available seven to 10 working days before the month's end.

Variance analysis

Explaining variances is also an MBA-type task, so performance needs to be carefully monitored and compared against the budget as the year proceeds, and corrective action must be taken where necessary. This has to be done on a monthly basis (or using shorter time intervals if required), showing both the company's performance during the month in question and throughout the year so far.

Looking at Table 11.2, we can see at a glance that the business is behind on sales for this month, but ahead on the yearly target. The convention is to put all unfavourable variations in brackets. Hence, a higher-than-budgeted sales figure does not have brackets, while a higher materials cost does. We can also see that, while profit is running ahead of budget, the profit margin is slightly behind (−0.30 per cent). This is partly because other direct costs, such as labour and distribution in this example, are running well ahead of budget.

TABLE 11.2   The fixed budget

Heading	Month			Year to date		
	Budget	Actual	Variance	Budget	Actual	Variance
Sales	805*	753	(52)	6,358	7,314	956
Materials	627	567	60	4,942	5,704	(762)
Materials margin	178	186	8	1,416	1,610	194
Direct costs	74	79	(5)	595	689	(94)
Gross profit	104	107	3	820	921	101
Percentage	**12.92**	**14.21**	**1.29**	**12.90**	**12.60**	**(0.30)**

* Figures indicate thousands of pounds

Flexing the budget

A budget is based on a particular set of sales goals, few of which are likely to be exactly met in practice. Table 11.3 shows a company that has used £762,000 more materials than budgeted. As more has been sold, this is hardly surprising. The way to manage this situation is to flex the budget to show what, given the sales that actually occurred, would be expected to happen to expenses. Applying the budget ratios to the actual data does this. For example, materials were planned to be 22.11 per cent of sales in the budget. By applying that to the actual month's sales, a materials cost of £587,000 is arrived at.

Looking at the flexed budget in Table 11.3, we can see that the company has spent £19,000 more than expected on the material given the level of sales actually achieved, rather than the £762,000 overspend shown in the fixed budget.

TABLE 11.3   The flexed budget

Heading	Month			Year to date		
	Budget	Actual	Variance	Budget	Actual	Variance
Sales	753*	753	–	7,314	7,314	–
Materials	587	567	20	5,685	5,704	(19)
Materials margin	166	186	20	1,629	1,610	(19)
Direct costs	69	79	(10)	685	689	(4)
Gross profit	97	107	10	944	921	(23)
Percentage	12.92	14.21	1.29	12.90	12.60	(0.30)

*Figures indicate thousands of pounds

The same principle holds for other direct costs, which appear to be running £94,000 over budget for the year. When we take into account the extra sales shown in the flexed budget, we can see that the company has actually spent £4,000 over budget on direct costs. While this is serious, it is not as serious as the fixed budget suggests.

The flexed budget allows you to concentrate your efforts on dealing with true variances in performance.

The following website has a downloadable Excel spreadsheet, Annual Marketing Budget Template (**www.score.org/resources/annual-marketing-budget-template**) which you can use to estimate your annual marketing expenses. This spreadsheet provides space for market research, communications, sales and event support, marketing travel, advertising, and online marketing. The template can be modified as needed to fit your business needs. Once you are satisfied with your projection, use the profit and loss projection (**www.score.org**>Business Tools>Template Gallery>Profit and Loss Projection (3 Years)) to complete your budget.

Seasonality and trends

The figures shown for each period of the budget are not the same. For example, a sales budget of £1.2 million for the year does not translate to £100,000 a month. The exact figure depends on two factors:

- The projected trend may forecast that, while sales at the start of the year are £80,000 a month, they will change to £120,000 a month by the end of the year. The average would be £100,000.

- By virtue of seasonal factors, each month may also be adjusted up or down from the underlying trend. You could expect the sales of heating oil, for example, to peak in the autumn and tail off in the late spring.

See also Chapter 9 for more on forecasting.

Online video courses and lectures

Best marketing strategy ever! Steve Jobs Think different: **www.youtube.com/watch?v=keCwRdbwNQY**

Diversification Strategy: Prof Vikas Kumar, Università Bocconi: **www.youtube.com/watch?v=L7-M7S0mDq0**

Good Strategy/Bad Strategy: the difference and why it matters: Delivered by Professor Richard Rumelt, the Harry and Elsa Kunin Professor of Business and Society at UCLA Anderson at the London School of Economics and Political Science (LSE): **www.youtube.com/ watch?v=UZrTl16hZdk**

How to Create a Marketing Plan – A Step by Step Guide: Business Training Made Simple part of the Made Simple Group is a London-based training company: **www.youtube.com/watch?v=YlFpM1UAEaE**

Methods of Entry into Foreign Markets: HSI – Holt and Sons International: **www.youtube.com/watch?v=GtPZZ-CzfkE**

A MIT Nuts & Bolts: Business Plans – Refining and Presenting your Venture Idea, Joe Hadzima, Senior Lecturer at MIT Sloan School of Management: **www.youtube.com/watch?v=AdI-E-_InCl**

Philip Kotler: Marketing Strategy, delivered to The London Business Forum: **www.youtube.com/watch?v=biIOOPuAvTY**

Online video case studies

Beyond the Golden Arches: Inside McDonald's with Bloomberg TV: **www. bloomberg.com/news/videos/b/3259b1fa-b60c-4dd1-8efd-4c29ce44fc9e**

Customer acquisition strategies in a competitive banking market: Anthony Thomson Metro Bank's Co-founder, speaking at Marketforce's The Future of Retail Banking conference in November 2012: **www.youtube.com/watch?v=T_X224BH3EA**

UC Berkeley Business Plan Competition Finalist Presentations and Awards Ceremony. The Haas School of Business presents the eight finalist teams from a record-breaking 110 entries. The finalists were competing for $45,000 in prizes: **www.youtube.com/watch?v=k4NlDNmAaGM**

UW Business Plan Competition 2012 Final Round Presentation – from Foster School of Business: **https://vimeo.com/43505531**

12 Additional core general MBA subjects

- Understanding accounting reports
- Sourcing finance
- Interpreting financial data
- Setting the strategic direction
- Motivating and managing

Every MBA student, whether he or she takes a general programme or one that specializes in a particular discipline, as this book does, will be required to study the four core disciplines. These contain the basic tools that an MBA will use or need to refer to more or less every working day and comprise:

Marketing. The subject of this book.

Finance and accounting. The construction of the key accounting reports – profit and loss, cash flow and balance sheet. The tools required to access a business's financial health and performance. Finance covers the vital areas of where a business gets its money from and the risks and responsibilities associated with each of those sources.

Organizational behaviour. Organizing, inspiring, motivating, rewarding and managing both individuals and teams are the enduring challenge in organizations as they grow and develop. Often people are the defining advantage that one organization has and can sustain over its competitors.

Strategy. This is the unifying discipline, often called business strategy. It deals with the core purpose of an enterprise and how it should respond to the challenges of a fast-changing environment. It centres not just on how strategy is shaped with the recognition that no organization can be truly great in the absence of shared goals, values and a sense of purpose – a shared picture of the future of the enterprise.

This chapter contains the essential tools within each of those disciples to enable an MBA Marketing student to bring their skills to bear and play a more rounded role in shaping and implementing the direction of the organization they work in but are inhibited by their lack of fundamental business knowledge.

Accounting and finance

The dividing line between accounting and finance is blurred. In basic terms accounting is considered to be everything concerned with the process of recording financial events, producing the key financial reports – cash flow, profit and loss, income statement and balance sheet – and ensuring such recordings are in compliance with the prevailing rules. Finance is the area concerned with where the money to run a business actually comes from in order to be accounted for. In order to be able to understand and interpret the accounts, using such tools as ratios, you need a reasonable grasp of both these areas, though the ratios themselves are generally considered to be in the accounting domain.

In many business schools you will find an array of options in addition to the core elements of this discipline. At the London Business School, for example, you will find on the menu: asset pricing, corporate finance, hedge funds, corporate governance, investments, mergers and acquisitions, capital markets and international finance. Members of the finance group also run the BNP Paribas Hedge Fund Centre, the Centre for Corporate Governance, the Private Equity Institute and the London Share Price Database. At Cass Business School, City of London, you will find options on behavioural finance and on dealing with financial crime and derivatives. In this chapter there is all that you would find in the core teaching that you need to understand and sufficient to move on to more esoteric aspects of finance, should the need ever arise.

Accounting

Although accounting has become more complex, involving ever more regulations, and has moved from visible records written in books to key stokes in a software program, the purposes are the same:

- to establish what a business owns by way of assets;
- to establish what a business owes by way of liabilities;
- to establish the profitability, or otherwise, at certain time intervals, and how that profit was achieved.

Accounting is certainly not an exact science. Even the most enthusiastic member of the profession would not make that claim. There is considerable scope for interpretation and educated guesswork, as all the facts are rarely available when the accounts are drawn up. For example, we may not know for certain that a particular customer will actually pay up, yet unless we have firm evidence that it won't – for example, if the business is failing – then the value of the money owed will appear in the accounts.

Obviously, if accountants and managers had complete freedom to interpret events as they will, no one inside or outside the business would place any reliance on the figures, so certain ground rules have been laid down by the profession as to reporting structures and methods, to help get a level of consistency into accounting information.

Cash flow

There is a saying in business that profit is vanity and cash flow is sanity. Both are necessary, but in the short term – and often that is all that matters in business as it struggles to get a foothold in the shifting sands of trading – cash flow is life or death. The rules on what constitutes cash are very simple: it has to be just that, or negotiable securities designated as being as good as cash. Cash flow is looked at in two distinct and important ways:

- as a projection of future expected cash flows;
- as an analysis of where cash came from and went to in an accounting period and the resultant increase or decrease in cash available.

The future is impossible to predict with great accuracy but it is possible to anticipate likely outcomes and be prepared to deal with events by building in a margin of safety. The starting point for making a projection is to make some assumptions about what you want to achieve and testing those for reasonableness.

Take the situation of High Note, a business being established to sell sheet music, small instruments and CDs to schools and colleges, which will expect trade credit and members of the public who will pay cash. The owner plans to invest 10,000 and to borrow 10,000 from a bank on a long-term basis. The business will require 11,500 for fixtures and fittings. A further 1,000 will be needed for a computer, software and a printer. That should leave around 7,500 to meet immediate trading expenses such as buying in stock and spending 1,500 on initial advertising. Hopefully customers' payments will start to come in quickly to cover other expenses such as wages for book-keeping, administration and fulfilling orders. Sales in the first six months are expected to be 60,000 based on negotiations already in hand, plus some cash sales that always seem to turn up. The rule of thumb in the industry seems to be that stock is marked up by 100 per cent; so 30,000 of bought-in goods sell on for 60,000.

On the basis of the above assumptions it is possible to make the cash flow forecast set out in Table 12.1. It has been simplified and some elements such as VAT and tax have been omitted for ease of understanding.

The maths in the table is straightforward: the cash receipts from various sources are totalled, as are the payments. Taking one from the other leaves a cash surplus or deficit for the month in question. The bottom row shows the cumulative position. So, for example, while the business had 2,450 cash left at the end of April, taking the cash deficit of 1,500 in May into account, by the end of May only 950 (2,450 – 1,500) cash remains.

TABLE 12.1 High Note six-month cash flow forecast

Month	April	May	June	July	Aug	Sept	Total
Receipts							
Sales	4,000	5,000	5,000	7,000	12,000	15,000	48,000
Owners' cash	10,000						
Bank loan	10,000						
Total cash in	*24,000*	*5,000*	*5,000*	*7,000*	*12,000*	*15,000*	
Payments							
Purchases	5,500	2,950	4,220	7,416	9,332	9,690	39,108
Rates, electricity, heat, telephone, internet, etc	1,000	1,000	1,000	1,000	1,000	1,000	
Wages	1,000	1,000	1,000	1,000	1,000	1,000	
Advertising	1,550	1,550	1,550	1,550	1,550	1,550	
Fixtures/fittings	11,500						
Computer, etc	1,000						
Total cash out	*21,550*	*6,500*	*7,770*	*10,966*	*12,882*	*13,240*	
Monthly cash							
Surplus/deficit(–)	2,450	(1,5C0)	(2,770)	(3,966)	(832)	1,760	
Cumulative cash balance	2,450	950	(1,820)	(5,786)	(6,668)	(4,908)	

Cash flow spreadsheet

You can do a number of 'What if?' projections to fine-tune cash flow projections, using spreadsheets. *Entrepreneur* has a calculator to help you in an analysis of factors that impact your net cash flow and produce projections of future cash flows based on various alternative marketing planning decisions as to profit margins, stock levels and the amount of credit given to customers (**www.entrepreneur.com/calculators/cashflowcalculator.html**).

Statement of cash flows for the year

A cash flow statement summarizes exactly where cash came from and how it was spent during the year. At first glance it seems to draw on a mixture of transactions included in the profit and loss account and balance sheet for the same period end, but this is not the whole story. Because there is a time lag on many cash transactions, for example, tax and dividend payments, the statement is a mixture of some previous year and some current year transactions; the remaining current year transactions go into the following year's cash flow statement during which the cash actually changes hands. Similarly, the realization and accrual conventions relating to sales and purchases respectively result in cash transactions having a different timing from when they were entered in the profit and loss account.

To take an example: a company had sales of £5 million this year and £4 million last year and these figures appeared in the profit and loss accounts of those years. Debtors at the end of this year were £1 million and at the end of the previous year were £0.8 million. The cash inflow arising from sales this year is £4.8 million (£0.8 million + £5 million – £1 million) whereas the sales figure in the profit and loss account is £5 million.

For these reasons it is not possible to look at just this year's profit and loss account and balance sheet to find all the cash flows. You need the previous year's accounts too. The balance sheet will show the cash balance at the period end but will not easily disclose all the ways in which it was achieved. Compiling a cash flow statement is quite a technical job and some training plus inside information are needed to complete the task. Nevertheless, the bulk of the items can be identified from an examination of the other two accounting statements for both the current and previous years.

From an MBA perspective, it is understanding the requirement for a cash flow statement as well as the other two accounts that is important, as well as being able to interpret the significance of the cash movements themselves.

CASE STUDY   Global Waste Inc

Unaudited condensed cash flow statement for Global Waste Inc, established in 2013 as a supplier of container solutions for source-separated waste, is shown below. Initially one man and a desk, the company has grown rapidly to become a leading supplier of recycling solutions. Turnover by 2016 is running at over £30 million ($45 million) a year with operating profit in excess of £1 million ($1.5 million).

TABLE 12.2   Unaudited condensed cash flow statement for Global Waste Inc (for the six months ended 30 June 2016)

	Half year to 30 June 2016 £'000	Half year to 30 June 2015 £'000	Year 31 Dec 2015 £'000
Net cash flows from operating activities	2,242	3,879	1,171
Cash flows from investing activities			
Purchases of property, plant and equipment	(603)	(464)	(701)
Proceeds from sale of property, plant and equip	345	–	–
Purchase of intangible assets	(55)	(87)	(193)
Purchase of investments	(35)	–	–
Interest received	28	58	107
Net cash used in investing activities	(320)	(493)	(787)
Cash flows from financing activities			
Dividends paid	(310)	(283)	(422)
Proceeds from issue of shares	13	–	128
Net cash used in financing activities	(297)	(283)	(294)
Net increase in cash and cash equivalents	1,625	3,103	90
Cash and cash equivalents at beginning of period	2,126	2,036	2,036
Cash and cash equivalents at the end of period	3,751	5,139	2,126

The three columns represent the cash activities for two equivalent six-month periods and for the whole of the preceding year. The cash of £2.126 million generated to 31 December 2015 (bottom of the right-hand column) is carried over to the start of the June 2016 six-month period (second figure from bottom of left-hand column). By adding the net increase (or decrease) in cash generated in this period we arrive at the closing cash position.

The cash flow statement, then, gives us a complete picture of how cash movements came about: from normal sales activities, the purchase or disposal of assets, or from financing activities. This is an expansion of the sparse single figure in the company's closing balance sheet stating that cash in current assets is £3.751 million.

The profit and loss account (income statement)

If you look back to the financial situation in the High Note example, you will see a good example of the difference between cash and profit. After all, the business has sold 60,000 worth of goods that it only paid 30,000 for, so it has a substantial profit margin to play with. While 39,108 has been paid to suppliers, only 30,000 of goods at cost have been sold – meaning that 9,108 worth of instruments, sheet music and CDs are still in our stock. A similar situation exists with sales. We have billed for 60,000 but only been paid for 48,000; the balance is owed by debtors. The bald figure at the end of the cash flow projection showing High Note to be in the red to the tune of 4,908 seems to be missing some important facts.

The difference between profit and cash

Cash is immediate and takes account of nothing else. Profit, however, is a measurement of economic activity that considers other factors that can be assigned a value or cost. The accounting principle that governs profit is known as the 'matching principle', which means that income and expenditure are matched to the time period in which they occur.

So for High Note, the profit and loss account for the first six months would be as shown in Table 12.3.

The structure of the profit and loss statement

This account is set out in more detail for a business in order to make it more useful when it comes to understanding how a business is performing. For example, though the profit shown in our worked example is 8,700, in fact it would be rather lower. As money has been borrowed to finance cash flow, there would be interest due, as there would be on the longer-term loan of 10,000.

TABLE 12.3   Profit and loss account for High Note for the six months April–September

Sales		60,000
Less cost of goods to be sold		30,000
Gross profit		30,000
Less expenses:		
Heat, electric, telephone, internet, etc	6,000	
Wages	6,000	
Advertising	9,300	
Total expenses		21,300
Profit before tax, interest and depreciation charges		8,700

In practice we have four levels of profit:

- Gross profit is the profit left after all costs related to making what you sell are deducted from income.
- Operating profit is what's left after you take the operating expenses away from the gross profit.
- Profit before tax is what is left after deducting any financing costs.
- Profit after tax is what is left for the owners to spend or reinvest in the business.

For High Note this could look much as set out in Table 12.4.

TABLE 12.4   High Note's extended profit and loss account

Sales	60,000
Less the cost of goods to be sold	30,000
Gross profit	30,000
Less operating expenses	21,300
Operating profit	8,700
Less interest on bank loan and overdraft	600
Profit before tax	8,100
Less tax	1,827
Profit after tax	6,723

A more substantial business than High Note will have taken on a wide range of commitments. For example, as well as the owners' money, there may be a long-term loan to be serviced (interest and capital repayments); parts of the workshop or offices may be sublet, generating 'non-operating income'; and there will certainly be some depreciation expense to deduct. Like any accounting report it should be prepared in the best form for the user, bearing in mind the requirements of the regulatory authorities. The elements to be included are:

1 sales (and any other revenues from operations);
2 cost of sales (or cost of goods sold);
3 gross profit – the difference between sales and cost of sales;
4 operating expenses – selling, administration, depreciation and other general costs;
5 operating profit – the difference between gross profit and operating expenses;
6 non-operating revenues – other revenues, including interest, rent, etc;
7 non-operating expenses – financial costs and other expenses not directly related to the running of the business;
8 profit before income tax;
9 provision for income tax;
10 net income (or profit or loss).

Profit and loss spreadsheet

There is an online free Excel profit and loss spreadsheet on *Entrepreneur*'s website at **www.entrepreneur.com/formnet/form/939** with 25 expense columns and four income streams built in, which you can add, subtract or edit to suit your needs.

The balance sheet

A balance sheet is a snapshot picture at a moment in time. On the one hand, it shows the value of assets (possessions) owned by the business; on the other, it shows who provided the funds with which to finance those assets and to whom the business is ultimately liable.

Assets are of two main types and are classified under the headings of either fixed assets or current assets. Fixed assets come in three forms. First, there are the hardware and physical things used by the business itself and which are not for sale to customers. Examples of fixed assets include buildings, plant, machinery, vehicles, furniture and fittings. Next come intangible fixed assets, such as goodwill, intellectual property, etc, and these are also shown under the general heading 'fixed assets'. Finally, there are investments in other businesses. Other assets in the process of eventually being turned into cash from customers are called current assets, and include stocks, work in progress, money owed by customers and cash itself.

$$\text{Total assets = fixed assets + current assets}$$

Assets can only be bought with funds provided by the owners or borrowed from someone else – for example, bankers or creditors. Owners provide funds by directly investing in the business (say, when they buy shares issued by the company) or indirectly by allowing the company to retain some of the profits in reserves. These sources of money are known collectively as liabilities.

$$\text{Total liabilities}$$
$$\text{= share capital and reserves + borrowings and other creditors}$$

Borrowed capital can take the form of a long-term loan at a fixed rate of interest or a short-term loan, such as a bank overdraft, usually at a variable rate of interest. All short-term liabilities owed by a business and due for payment within 12 months are referred to as creditors falling due within one year, and long-term indebtedness is called creditors falling due after one year.

So far in our High Note example the money spent on 'capital' items such as the 12,500 spent on a computer and fixtures and fittings have been ignored, as has the 9,108 worth of sheet music, etc remaining in stock waiting to be sold and the 12,000 of money owed by customers who have yet to pay up. An assumption has to be made about where the cash deficit will be made up and the most logical short-term source is a bank overdraft.

For High Note at the end of September the balance sheet is set out in Table 12.5.

Balance sheet and other online tools

SCORE (**www.score.org/resources/balance-sheet-template**) is an Excel-based spreadsheet you can use for constructing your own balance sheet. You can find guidance on depreciation, handling stock and on the layout of the balance sheet profit and loss account and cash flow forecasts at Accounting Coach. This was set up by Harold Averkamp, CPA, MBA, to 'utilize the Internet for communicating a more clear explanation of accounting concepts to people in all parts of the world and at a low cost' (**www.accountingcoach.com/accounting-topics**). The basic information is free, which may be sufficient to get a good feel for the subject. The Pro version costs £33 ($49) and includes a series of short videos, lecture notes and exams in the main financial topics. The glossary has definitions of all the accounting terms you are ever likely to come across in the accounting world (see 'Dictionary of terms' tab).

Package of accounts

The cash flow statement, the profit and loss account and the balance sheet between them constitute a set of accounts, but conventionally two balance sheets, the opening and closing ones, are provided to make a 'package'. By including these balance sheets we can see the full picture of what has happened to the owner's investment in the business.

TABLE 12.5   High Note balance sheet at 30 September

Assets		
Fixed assets		
Fixtures, fitting, equipment	11,500	
Computer	1,000	
Total fixed assets		12,500
Working capital		
Current assets		
Stock	9,108	
Debtors	12,000	
Cash	0	
	21,108	
Less current liabilities (creditors falling due within one year)		
Overdraft	4,908	
Due to suppliers	0	
	4,908	
Net current assets		
[Working capital (CA-CL)]		16,200
Total assets less current liabilities		28,700
Less creditors falling due after one year		
Long-term bank loan		10,000
Net total assets		18,700
Capital and reserves		
Owner's capital introduced	10,000	
Profit retained (from P&L account)	8,700	
Total capital and reserves		18,700

TABLE 12.6   Package of accounts

Balance sheet at 31 Dec 2010 (£)		P & L for year to 31 Dec 2011 (£)		Balance sheet at 2011 (£)	
Fixed assets	1,000	Sales	10,000	Fixed assets	1,200
Working capital	1,000	less cost of sales	6,000	Working capital	1,400
	2,000	Gross profit	4,000		2,600
		less expenses	3,000		
Financed by		Profit before tax	1,000	Financed by	
Owners' equity	2,000	Tax	400	Owners' equity	2,000
		Profit after tax	600	Reserves	600
					2,600

Table 12.6 shows a simplified package of accounts. We can see from these that over the year the business has made £600 of profit after tax, invested that in £200 of additional fixed assets, £400 of working capital such as stock and debtors, balancing that off with the £600 put into reserves from the year's profits.

Analysing accounts

The main analytical approach is to examine the relationship of pairs of figures extracted from the accounts. A pair may be taken from the same statement, or one figure from each of the profit and loss account and balance sheet statements. When brought together, the two figures are called ratios. Miles per gallon or kilometres per litre, for example, are useful ratios for drivers checking one aspect of a vehicle's performance. Some financial ratios are meaningful in themselves, but their value mainly lies in their comparison with the equivalent ratio last year, a target ratio or a competitor's ratio.

Accounting ratios

Ratios used in analysing company accounts are clustered under five headings and are usually referred to as 'tests':

- tests of profitability;
- tests of liquidity;
- tests of solvency;
- tests of growth;
- market tests.

The profit and loss account and balance sheet in the tables earlier in this section will be used, where possible, to illustrate these ratios.

You can quickly see the consequences of marketing decisions on business performance. For example, extending credit terms and so taking longer to get paid, or developing products that fail to sell as forecasted will lead to reduced profitability and declining liquidity. Neither of these is desirable and as such the MBA Marketing needs to have a grasp of the tools required to analyse performance and anticipate the consequences.

Tests of profitability

There are six ratios used to measure profit performance. The first four are arrived at using only the profit and loss account and the other two use information from both that account and the balance sheet.

Gross profit This is calculated by dividing the gross profit by sales and multiplying by 100. In this example the sum is $30,000 \div 60,000 \times 100 = 50$ per cent. This is a measure of the value we are adding to the bought-in materials and services we need to 'make' our product or service; the higher the figure, the better.

Operating profit This is calculated by dividing the operating profit by sales and multiplying by 100. In this example the sum is $8,700 \div 60,000 \times 100 = 14.5$ per cent. This is a measure of how efficiently we are running the business, before taking account of financing costs and tax. These are excluded, as interest and tax rates change periodically and are outside our direct control. Excluding them makes it easier to compare one period with another or with another business. Once again the rule here is, the higher the figure, the better.

Net profit before and after tax Dividing the net profit before and after tax by the sales and multiplying by 100 calculates these next two ratios. In this example the sums are $8,100 \div 60,000 \times 100 = 13.5$ per cent and $6,723 \div 60,000 \times 100 = 11.21$ per cent. This is a measure of how efficiently we are running the business, after taking account of financing costs and tax. The last figure shows how successful we are at creating additional money to either invest back in the business or distribute to the owner(s) as either drawings or dividends. Once again the rule here is, the higher the figure, the better.

Return on equity This ratio is usually expressed as a percentage in the way we might think of the return on any personal financial investment. Taking the owners' viewpoint, their concern is with the profit earned for them relative to the amount of funds they have invested in the business. The relevant profit here is after interest, tax (and any preference dividends) have been deducted. This is expressed as a percentage of the equity that comprises ordinary share capital and reserves. So in this example the sum is: Return on equity = 6,723 ÷ 18,700 × 100 = 36 per cent.

Return on capital employed   This takes a wider view of company performance than return on equity by expressing profit before interest, tax, and dividend deductions as a percentage of the total capital employed, irrespective of whether this capital is borrowed or provided by the owners.

Capital employed is defined as share capital plus reserves plus long-term borrowings. Where, say, a bank overdraft is included in current liabilities every year and in effect becomes a source of capital, this may be regarded as part of capital employed. If the bank overdraft varies considerably from year to year, a more reliable ratio could be calculated by averaging the start- and end-year figures. There is no one precise definition used by companies for capital employed. In this example the sum is: Return on capital employed = 8,700 ÷ (18,700 + 10,000) × 100 = 30 per cent.

Tests of liquidity

In order to survive, companies must also watch their liquidity position, by which is meant keeping enough short-term assets to pay short-term debts. Companies go out of business compulsorily when they fail to pay money due to employees, bankers or suppliers.

The liquid money tied up in day-to-day activities is known as working capital, the sum of which is arrived at by subtracting the current liabilities from the current assets. In the case of High Note we have £21,108 in current assets and £4,908 in current liabilities, so the working capital is £16,200.

Current ratio   As a figure, the working capital doesn't tell us much. It is rather as if you knew your car had used 20 gallons of petrol but had no idea how far you had travelled. It would be more helpful to know how much larger the current assets are than the current liabilities. That would give us some idea if the funds would be available to pay bills for stock, the tax liability and any other short-term liabilities that may arise. The current ratio, which is arrived at by dividing the current assets by the current liabilities is the measure used. For High Note this is 21,108 ÷ 4,908 = 4.30. The convention is to express this as 4.30:1 and the aim here is to have a ratio of between 1.5:1 and 2:1. Any lower and bills can't be met easily; much higher and money is being tied up unnecessarily.

Quick ratio (acid test)   This is a belt-and-braces ratio used to ensure a business has sufficient ready cash or near cash to meet all its current liabilities. Items such as stock are stripped out because although these are assets, the money involved is not immediately available to pay bills. In effect, the only liquid assets a business has are cash, debtors and any short-term investment such as bank deposits or government securities. For High Note this ratio is: 12,000 ÷ 4,908 = 2.44:1. The ratio should be greater than 1:1 for a business to be sufficiently liquid.

Average collection period We can see that High Note's current ratio is high, which is an indication that some elements of working capital are being used inefficiently. The business has £12,000 owed by customers on sales of £60,000 over a six-month period. The average period it takes High Note to collect money owed is calculated by dividing the sales made on credit by the money owed (debtors) and multiplying it by the time period, in days; in this case the sum is as follows: $12,000 \div 60,000 \times 182.5 = 36.5$ days.

If the credit terms are cash with order or seven days, then something is going seriously wrong. If it is net 30 days, then it is probably about right. In this example it has been assumed that all the sales were made on credit.

Average payment period This ratio shows how long a company is taking on average to pay its suppliers. The calculation is as for average collection period, but substituting creditors for debtors and purchase for sales.

Days' stock held High Note is carrying £9,108 stock of sheet music, CDs, etc, and over the period it sold £30,000 of stock at cost. (The cost of sales is £30,000 to support £60,000 of invoiced sales as the mark-up in this case is 100 per cent.) Using a similar sum as with average collection period, we can calculate that the stock being held is sufficient to support 55.41 days' sales ($9,108 \div 10,000 \times 182.5$). If High Note's suppliers can make weekly deliveries, then this is almost certainly too high a stock figure to hold. Cutting stock back from nearly eight weeks (55.41 days) to one week (7 days) would trim 48.41 days or £7,957.38 worth of stock out of working capital. This in turn would bring the current ratio down to 2.68:1.

Circulation of working capital This is a measure used to evaluate the overall efficiency with which working capital is being used. That is the sales divided by the working capital (current assets − current liabilities). In this example that sum is $60,000 \div 16,420 = 3.65$ times. In other words, we are turning over the working capital over three and a half times each year. There are no hard-and-fast rules as to what is an acceptable ratio. Clearly, the more times working capital is turned over, stock sold for example, the more chance a business has to make a profit on that activity.

Tests of solvency

These measures see how a company is managing its long-term liabilities. There are two principal ratios used here, gearing and interest cover.

Gearing (or leverage) This measures as a percentage the proportion of all borrowing, including long-term loans and bank overdrafts, to the total of shareholders' funds, ie share capital and all reserves. The gearing ratio is sometimes also known as the debt/equity ratio. For High Note this is:

$(4,908 + 10,000) \div 18,800 = 14,908 \div 18,800 = 0.79{:}1$. In other words, for every £1 the shareholders have invested in High Note they have borrowed a further 79p. This ratio is usually not expected to exceed 1:1 for long periods.

Interest cover   This is a measure of the proportion of profit taken up by interest payments and can be found by dividing the annual interest payment into the annual profit before interest, tax and dividend payments. The greater the number, the less vulnerable the company will be to any setback in profits, or rise in interest rates on variable loans. The smaller the number, then the more risk that level of borrowing represents to the company. A figure of between 2 and 5 times would be considered acceptable.

Tests of growth

Growth is inevitably regarded as a measure of marketing virility. These ratios are arrived at by comparing one year with another, usually for elements of the profit and loss account such as sales and profit. So, for example, if next year High Note achieved sales of 100,000 and operating profits of 16,000, the growth ratios would be 67 per cent, that is, 40,000 of extra sales as a proportion of the first year's sales of 60,000; and 84 per cent, that is, 7,300 of extra operating profit as a percentage of the first year's operating profit of 8,700.

Some additional information can be gleaned from these two ratios. In this example we can see that profits are growing faster than sales, which indicates a healthier trend than if the situation were reversed.

Market tests

This is the name given to stock market measures of performance. Four key ratios here are:

Earnings per share = net profit ÷ shares outstanding. This measures the after-tax profit made by a company divided by the number of ordinary shares it has issued.

Price/earnings (PE) ratio = market price per share ÷ earnings per share. This measures the market price of an ordinary share divided by the earnings per share. The PE ratio expresses the market value placed on the expectation of future earnings, ie the number of years required to earn the price paid for the shares out of profits at the current rate.

Yield = dividends per share ÷ price per share. This measures the percentage return a shareholder gets on the 'opportunity' or current value of their investment.

Dividend cover = net income ÷ dividend. This measures the number of times the profit exceeds the dividend. The higher the ratio, the more retained profit to finance future growth.

Other ratios

There are a very large number of other ratios that businesses use for measuring aspects of their marketing performance in particular, such as:

- sales per unit of currency invested in fixed assets – a measure of the use of those fixed assets;
- sales per employee – showing if your headcount is exceeding your sales growth;
- profit per employee;
- sales per manager, per support staff, etc – showing the effectiveness of overhead spending.

Accounting Coach (see earlier in this chapter) provides a clear explanation of financial ratios and financial statement analysis. Business forms for computing 24 popular financial ratios are included in AccountingCoach PRO which costs £33 ($49) (**www.accountingcoach.com/financial-ratios/explanation**).

Combined ratios

No one would use a single ratio to decide whether one motor vehicle was a better or worse buy than another. Miles per gallon, kilometres per litre, miles or kilometres per hour, annual depreciation percentage and residual value proportion are just a handful of the ratios that would need to be reviewed. So it is with a business. A combination of ratios can be used to form an opinion on the financial state of affairs at any one time.

The best known of these combination ratios is the Altman Z-Score (**www.creditguru.com/CalcAltZ.shtml**), which uses a combined set of five financial ratios derived from eight variables from a company's financial statements linked to some statistical techniques to predict a company's probability of failure. Entering the figures into the on-screen template at the website above produces a score and an explanatory narrative giving a view on the business's financial strengths and weaknesses.

Finance

There are many sources of funds available to businesses. However, not all of them are equally appropriate to all businesses at all times. These different sources of finance carry very different obligations, responsibilities and opportunities for profitable business. Having some appreciation of these differences will enable managers and directors to make an informed choice.

Most businesses initially and often until they go public, floating their shares on a stock market, confine their financial strategy to bank loans, either long term or short term, viewing the other financing methods as either too complex or too risky. In many respects the reverse is true. Almost every finance source other than banks will to a greater or lesser extent share some of the risks of doing business with the recipient of the funds.

Figure 12.1 shows the funding appetite of various sources of funds. Venture capitalists, business angels and indeed any source of share capital will only be attracted to propositions that combine high growth potential with a high risk/reward potential. Banks and other lenders will be attracted to almost the opposite profile, looking instead to a stable, less risky proposition that at least offers some security to the capital sum they are putting up.

FIGURE 12.1   Funding appetite

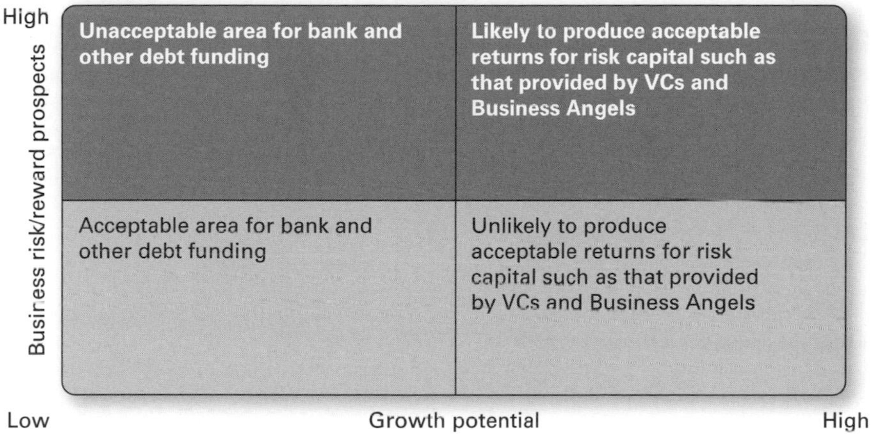

High	Unacceptable area for bank and other debt funding	Likely to produce acceptable returns for risk capital such as that provided by VCs and Business Angels
	Acceptable area for bank and other debt funding	Unlikely to produce acceptable returns for risk capital such as that provided by VCs and Business Angels

Business risk/reward prospects

Low   Growth potential   High

Debt vs equity

Despite the esoteric names – debentures, convertible loan stock, preference shares – businesses have access to only two fundamentally different sorts of money. Equity, or owner's capital, including retained earnings, is money that is not a risk to the business. If no profits are made, then the owner and other shareholders simply do not get dividends. They may not be pleased, but they cannot usually sue – and even where they can sue, it is the advisors who recommended the share purchase that will be first in line.

Debt capital is money borrowed by the business from outside sources; it puts the business at financial risk and is also risky for the lenders. In return for taking that risk they expect an interest payment every year, irrespective of the performance of the business. High gearing is the name given when a business has a high proportion of outside money to inside money. High gearing has considerable attractions to a business that wants to make high returns on shareholders' capital.

How gearing works   Table 12.7 shows an example of a business that is assumed to need 60,000 capital to generate 10,000 operating profits. Four different capital structures are considered. They range from all share capital (no gearing) at one end to nearly all loan capital at the other. The loan capital has to be 'serviced', that is, interest of 12 per cent has to be paid. The loan itself can be relatively indefinite, simply being replaced by another one at market interest rates when the first loan expires.

TABLE 12.7   The effect of gearing on shareholders' returns

Capital structure	No gearing N/A	Average gearing 1:1	High gearing 2:1	Very high gearing 3:1
Share capital	60,000	30,000	20,000	15,000
Loan capital (at 12%)	–	30,000	40,000	45,000
Total capital	60,000	60,000	60,000	60,000
Profits				
Operating profit	10,000	10,000	10,000	10,000
Less interest on loan	None	3,600	4,800	5,400
Net profit	10,000	6,400	5,200	4,600
Return on share capital =	10,000	6,400	5,200	4,600
	60,000	30,000	20,000	15,000
=	16.6%	21.3%	26%	30.7%
Times interest earned =	N/A	10,000	10,000	10,000
		3,600	4,800	5,400
=	N/A	2.8 times	2.1 times	1.8 times

Following the table through, you can see that return on the shareholders' money (arrived at by dividing the profit by the shareholders' investment and multiplying by 100 to get a percentage) grows from 16.6 to 30.7 per cent by virtue of the changed gearing. If the interest on the loan were lower, the return on shareholders' capital (ROSC) would be even more improved by high gearing, and the higher the interest, the lower the relative improvement in ROSC. So in times of low interest, businesses tend to go for increased borrowings rather than raising more equity, that is, money from shareholders.

At first sight this looks like a perpetual profit-growth machine. Naturally shareholders and those managing a business whose bonus depends on shareholders' returns would rather have someone else 'lend' them the money for the business than ask shareholders for more money, especially if by doing so they increase the return investment. The problem comes if the business does not produce 10,000 operating profits. Very often a drop in sales of 20 per cent means profits are halved. If profits were halved in this example, the business could not meet the interest payments on its loan. That would make the business insolvent, and so not in a 'sound financial position'.

Any decisions about gearing levels have to be taken with the level of business risk involved. Certain categories of venture are intrinsically more risky than others. Businesses selling staple food products where little innovation is required are generally less prone to face financial difficulties than, say, internet start-ups, where the technology may be unproven with a short shelf life and the markets themselves uncertain. See Figure 12.2.

FIGURE 12.2   Risk and gearing

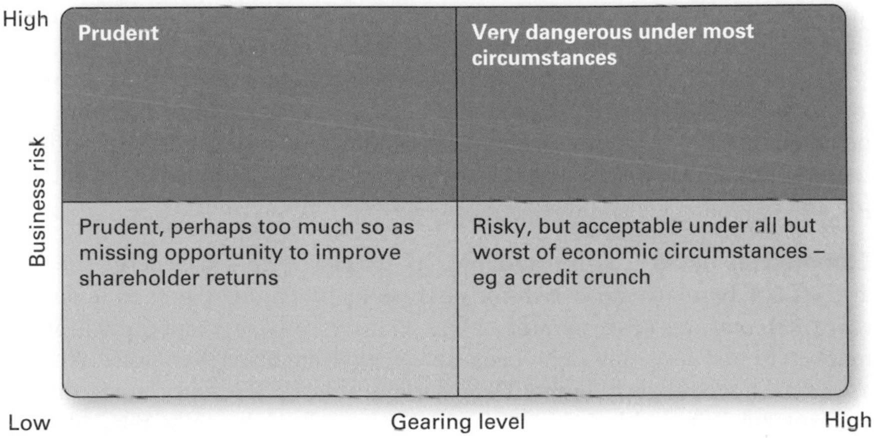

Business risk (vertical axis, Low to High); Gearing level (horizontal axis, Low to High).

Prudent	**Very dangerous under most circumstances**
Prudent, perhaps too much so as missing opportunity to improve shareholder returns	Risky, but acceptable under all but worst of economic circumstances – eg a credit crunch

Principal sources of debt

Debt finance and the regulation of such transactions are hardly new and their practice stretches back far before the arrival of such firms as Banca Monte dei Paschi di Siena SpA (MPS) in 1472, though that is now the oldest operating bank.

All debt providers try hard to take little or no risk but expect some reward irrespective of performance. They want interest payments on money lent, usually from day one, though sometimes they are content to roll interest payments up until some future date. While they hope the management is competent, they are more interested in securing a charge against any assets the business or its managers may own. At the end of the day they want all their money back. It would be more prudent to think of these organizations as people who will help you turn a proportion of an illiquid asset such as property, stock in trade or customers who have not yet paid up, into a more liquid asset such as cash, but of course at some discount.

Banks   Banks are the principal, and frequently the only, source of finance for nine out of every 10 unquoted businesses. Firms around the world rely on banks for their funding. They provide a wide variety of financial products from short-term day-to-day overdrafts to term loans running for a decade or more.

Bonds *et al*   Bonds, debentures and mortgages are all kinds of borrowing with different rights and obligations for the parties concerned. For a business a mortgage is much the same as for an individual. The loan is for a specific event, buying a particular property asset such as a factory, office or warehouse. Interest is payable and the loan itself is secured against the property, so should the business fail the mortgage can substantially be redeemed.

Companies wanting to raise funds for general business purposes, rather than as with a mortgage where a particular property is being bought, issue debentures or bonds. These run for a number of years, typically three years and upwards, with the bond or debenture holder receiving interest over the life of the loan, with the capital returned at the end of the period.

The key difference between debentures and bonds lies in their security and ranking. Debentures are unsecured and so in the event of the company being unable to pay interest or repay loans they may well get little or nothing back. Bonds are secured against specific assets and so rank ahead of debentures for any payout.

Commercial paper   Banks and big companies such as General Electric and AT&T regularly raise cash for operations by issuing paper to investors that often matures in six months or less. Private investors, especially money-market funds, buy this debt because as well as being very safe it pays an interest rate slightly higher than comparable US Treasury notes or UK government gilts. Although commercial paper is technically repayable in under six months, in practice the corporate borrower repays investors by issuing more paper, effectively paying back investors with more borrowed cash. The attraction to the borrower over other forms of lending is that as long as it matures before nine months (270 days) it doesn't have to be registered with any regulatory body, making it in effect 'off balance sheet', which in turn reduces gearing (see earlier in this chapter for more on gearing).

Asset finance   While most sources of debt finance allow their funds to be used for a wide spectrum of purposes, two important sources are predicated on a precise relationship between what a business has or will shortly have by way of assets, and what they are prepared to advance:

Leasing and hire purchase. Physical assets such as cars, vans, computers, office equipment and the like can usually be financed by leasing them, rather as a house or flat may be rented. Alternatively, they can be bought on hire purchase. This leaves other funds free to cover the less tangible elements in your cash flow.

Operating leases are taken out where you will use the equipment (for example, a car, photocopier, vending machine or kitchen equipment) for less than its full economic life. The lessor takes the risk of the equipment becoming obsolete, and assumes responsibility for repairs, maintenance and insurance. As you, the lessee, are paying for this service, it is more expensive than a finance lease, where you lease the equipment for most of its economic life and maintain and insure it yourself.

Hire purchase differs from leasing in that you have the option to eventually become the owner of the asset, after a series of payments. You can find a leasing company via the International Finance and Leasing Association (**www.ifla.com**), a network of leading finance companies all over the world. The website also has general information on terms of trade and code of conduct.

Discounting and factoring. Customers often take time to pay up. In the meantime you have to pay those who work for you and your less patient suppliers. So, the more you grow, the more funds you need. It is often possible to 'factor' your creditworthy customers' bills to a financial institution, receiving up to 80 per cent of the cash due from your customers more quickly than they would normally pay. The factoring company in effect buys your trade debts, and can also provide a debtor accounting and administration service. You will, of course, have to pay for factoring services. Having the cash before your customers pay will cost you a little more than normal overdraft rates. The factoring service will cost between 0.5 and 3.5 per cent of the turnover, depending on volume of work, the number of debtors, average invoice amount and other related factors.

Invoice discounting is a variation on the same theme, where you are responsible for collecting the money from debtors yourself. You can find an invoice discounter or factor through the International Factoring Association (**www.factoring.org**), which has a directory of factoring companies around the world, with the strongest coverage in North America.

Principal sources of equity

Businesses operating as a limited company or limited partnership have a potentially valuable opportunity to raise relatively risk-free money. It is risk free to the business but risky, sometimes extremely so, to anyone investing. Essentially this type of capital, known collectively as equity, consists of the issued share capital and reserves of various kinds. It represents the amount of money that shareholders have invested directly into the company by buying shares, together with retained profits that belong to shareholders but which the company uses as additional capital. As with debt, equity comes in a number of different forms with differing rights and privileges.

Private equity

There are three main sources of private equity: business angels, venture capital firms and corporate venture funding.

Business angels   One likely first source of equity or risk capital will be a private individual with his or her own funds and perhaps some knowledge of your type of business. In return for a share in the business, such investors will put in money at their own risk. They have been christened 'business angels', a term first coined to describe private wealthy individuals who back a play on Broadway or in London's West End.

Most angels are determined upon some involvement beyond merely signing a cheque and may hope to play a part in your business in some way. They are hoping for big rewards – one angel who backed Sage with £10,000 ($15,600) in its first round of £250,000 ($390,000) financing saw his stake rise to £40 million ($62 million).

These three organizations provide information on the angel process and have directories of local providers:

- EBAN (European Business Angel Network) with over 150 member organizations from 50 countries throughout Europe (**www.eban.org**)
- UK Business Angels Association (**www.ukbusinessangelsassociation.org.uk/member/directory**)
- The World Business Angels Association (**http://wbaa.biz/**)

Venture capital   Venture capitalists (VCs), sometimes unflatteringly referred to as vulture capitalists, are investing other people's money, often from pension funds. They have a different agenda from that of business angels, and are more likely to be interested in investing more money for a larger stake. In general, VCs expect their investment to have paid off within seven years, but they are hardened realists. Two in every 10 investments they make are total write-offs, and six perform averagely well at best. So, the one star in every 10 investments they make has to cover a lot of duds. VCs have a target rate of return of 30 per cent plus, to cover this poor hit rate.

Raising venture capital is not a cheap option and deals are not quick to arrange either. Six months is not unusual, and over a year has been known. Every VC has a deal done in six weeks in its portfolio, but that truly is the exception. Fees will run to hundreds of thousands of pounds, the sweetener being that these can be taken from the money raised.

US venture capital investment is around six times that of the UK. European venture capital as a whole is roughly the same size as for the UK, and the rest of the world about the same again.

The British Private Equity and Venture Capital Association (**www.bvca.co.uk**) and the European Private Equity and Venture Capital Association (**www.evca.com**) both have online directories giving details of hundreds of venture capital providers. The National Venture Capital Association in the USA has directories of international venture capital associations both inside and outside the United States (**www.nvca.org**>Resources).

You can see how those negotiating with or receiving venture capital rate the firm in question at The Funded website (**www.thefunded.com**) in terms of the deal offered, the firm's apparent competence and how good they are managing the relationship. There is also a link to the VC's website. The Funded has 20,572 members.

Corporate venturing   This is another type of business that is also in the risk capital business, without it necessarily being their main line of business. These firms, known as corporate venturers, usually want an inside track to new developments in and around the edges of their own fields of interest.

Sinclair Beecham and Julian Metcalfe, who started with a £17,000 ($26,500) loan and a name borrowed from a boarded-up shop, founding Pret A Manger, were not entrepreneurs content with doing their own thing. They had global ambitions and it was only by cutting in McDonald's, the burger giant, that they could see any realistic way to dominate the world. They sold a 33 per cent stake for £25 million ($39 million) in 2001 to McDonald's Ventures, LLC, a wholly owned subsidiary of McDonald's Corporation, the arm of McDonald's that looks after its corporate venturing activities. They joined forces with the corporate venturing arm of a big firm. They could also have considered Cisco, Apple Computers, IBM and Microsoft, who also all have corporate venturing arms.

According to Global Corporate Venturing (**www.globalcorporateventuring. com**), some 47 of the 100 biggest US companies are involved in venture investing. In the United States Google leads the field with 121 investments worth $5 billion. Elsewhere, the main action is in China and India where the value of corporate venturing investments made were $10 billion and $3 billion respectively.

Public equity

Stock markets are the place where serious businesses raise serious money. It's possible to raise anything from a few million to tens of billions; expect the costs and efforts in getting listed to match those stellar figures. The basic idea is that owners sell shares in their businesses, which in effect brings in a whole raft of new 'owners' who in turn have a stake in the businesses' future profits. When they want out they sell their shares on to other investors. The share price moves up and down to ensure that there are as many buyers as sellers at any one time.

Going public also puts a stamp of respectability on you and your company. It will enhance the status and credibility of your business, and it will enable you to borrow more against the 'security' provided by your new shareholders, should you so wish. Your shares will also provide an attractive way to retain and motivate key staff.

The world's stock markets   How many stock exchanges are there? All you may have heard of are the LSE (London Stock Exchange) and NYSE (New York Stock Exchange), with the more informed adding Frankfurt, Tokyo and perhaps Paris. Those guessing five, or even 10 or 20, are way off. The answer is around 200. There are currently at least 13 in the USA alone.

The big markets compete with alternative platforms and brokerage networks for market share and about a third of equities trading occurs off-exchange. You can find out more about most of the world stock markets on the University of Chicago website (**http://guides.lib.uchicago.edu/stock_ exchanges**) where exchanges are listed by continent and country. The World Federation of Exchanges (**www.world-exchanges.org**) is a useful source for facts and figures on these markets.

CASE STUDY   Cobra Beer

By 2015 Cobra dominated the UK's Indian restaurant market, being sold at more than 98 per cent of licensed curry houses. It is now also available at all the main supermarkets. The company had grown by an average 40 per cent every year since it was set up.

In 1990 Cambridge-educated and recently qualified accountant Karan Bilimoria started importing and distributing Cobra Beer, a name he chose because it appeared to work well in lots of different languages. He initially supplied his beer to complement Indian restaurant food in the UK. Lord Bilimoria, as he now is, started out with debts of £20,000, ($31,000), but from a small flat in Fulham and with just a Citroen 2CV by way of assets he has grown his business to sales of over £100 million ($156 million) a year. Three factors have been key to his success. Cobra was originally sold in large 660 ml bottles and so was more likely to be shared by diners. Also, as Cobra is less fizzy than European lagers, drinkers are less likely to feel bloated, and can eat and drink more. The third factor was Bilimoria's extensive knowledge through his training as an accountant of sources of finance for a growing business. He was fortunate in having an old-style bank manager who had such belief in Cobra that he agreed a loan of £30,000 ($47,000); since then Bilimoria has tapped into every possible type of funding (see Figure 12.3), including selling a 28 per cent stake in his firm in 1995.

Molson Coors, who have been in the beer business for 350 years, took a majority stake in the business in 2009, ensuring Cobra has access to sufficient funds for future growth. Sales of Cobra have continued to grow strongly, albeit at an average of 'either high single digit or 10 per cent'. They sell alongside Molson Coors portfolio of more than 100 beer brands including Coors Light, Molson Canadian, Miller Lite, Carling and Staropramen, as well as craft and specialty beers like Blue Moon and Creemore Springs.

FIGURE 12.3 Cobra Beer's financing strategy

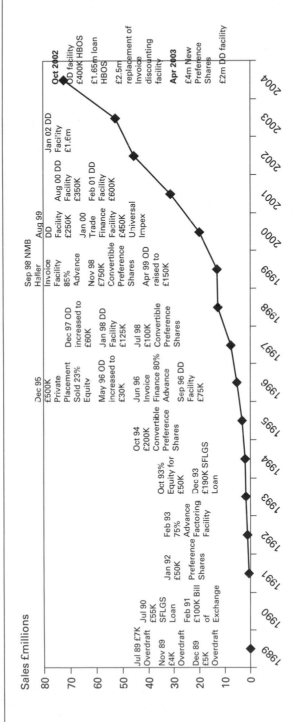

Crowdfunding

Crowdfunding business finance is a new game-changing concept that puts the power firmly into the hands of entrepreneurs looking to raise finance. Instead of one large investor putting money into a business, larger numbers of smaller investors contribute as little as £10 each to raise the required capital. Crowdcube, the first UK-based crowdfunding website, has now teamed up with Startups.co.uk so entrepreneurs will be able to both access information on raising finance and have direct access to an innovative way to solve the problem from one site (**www.crowdcube.com/partner/startups**).

Crowdcube was the first crowdfunding website in the world to enable the public to invest in and receive shares in UK companies, and has more than 10,000 registered members currently seeking investment opportunities. The platform has already raised more than £3 million for small businesses through its principal site, and hosted the world's first £1 million crowdfunding deal in November 2011. The range of businesses that have used this financing method is wide and getting wider. Darlington Football Club raised £291,450 from 722 investors over 14 days through Crowdcube to help fend off closure after going into liquidation. Oil supplier Universal Fuels has raised £100,000 through Crowdcube, making founder Oliver Morgan the youngest entrepreneur to successfully raise investment through the process.

CASE STUDY   Chilango – how the Burrito Bond was born

When former Skype employees Eric Partaker and Dan Houghton started Chilango they had in mind supplying mouth-watering Mexican food, something of a rarity when they launched seven years ago. Eric developed an appetite for tacos, burritos and the like in his native Chicago, but when he came to work in London was faced with a veritable Mexican cuisine desert. When Eric met Dan by coincidence also a Mexican food fanatic the pair made it their mission to plug what they saw as a gap in the market.

Eric Partaker, an American and Norwegian national, graduated from the University of Illinois at Urbana-Champaign with a Bachelor of Science degree in Finance, and is also an alumnus of Katholieke Universiteit Leuven, Belgium, where he studied History, Philosophy, and Literature. Dan is a Cambridge mathematics graduate, leaving with a 1st. They met up in 2005 when they were both on the new business ventures team reporting to the CEO of Skype Technologies.

By 2014 with seven London Mexican food outlets open, one opposite the Goldman Sachs headquarters, they had proved there was an appetite for their business model. But with each new restaurant costing around £500,000 to launch opening they discovered another gap – an urgent need for cash to achieve their goal to launch six new Chilango restaurants around London quickly.

In 2014 they hit the headlines for financial rather than culinary innovation. Using the crowdfunding website they set out to raise £1 million in two months offering 8 per cent interest with the capital to be repaid in four years. With the minimum investment set at £500, those putting up £10,000 get free lunch once a week at one of their restaurants. Hence the name 'Burrito Bond' was born.

One day after books on the bond opened, investments had already been received from executives in the food and drinks business, including the chief executive officer and chief financial officer of café-chain Carluccio's, the former CEO of Domino's Pizza UK and the former CEO of Krispy Kreme UK, according to the prospectus website. By 3 July 2014, according to information on the crowdfunding website the company had received £1,140,500 from 344 investors.

Organizational behaviour

Organizational behaviour (OB) is the whole rather amorphous area that deals with people, why they behave the way they do and how to create and manage an organization that can achieve the goals set for the business. As one CEO summarized it, the task is 'to get people to do what I want them to do because they want to do it'.

The single most prevalent reason for a strategy failing lies in its implementation; the analysis and planning behind a proposed course of action are rarely the root of the problem. That is more likely to lie in the selection of the people to implement strategy, their management, motivation, rewards and the way in which they are organized and led.

The structure of the organization is covered in Chapter 8, as it applies particularly to the marketing organization. What follows here are the other elements in the core of OB that the MBA Marketing will be expected to have an appreciation of.

Motivation

As a subject for serious study, motivation is a relatively new 'science'. Thomas Hobbes, the 17th-century English philosopher, suggested that human nature could best be understood as self-interested cooperation. He claimed motivation could be summarized as choices revolving around pain or pleasure. Sigmund Freud was equally frugal in suggesting only two basic needs: the life and the death instincts. These ideas were the first to seriously challenge the time-honoured 'carrot and stick' method of motivation that pervaded every aspect of organizational life from armies at war to British weavers during the Industrial Revolution.

The first hint in the business world that there might be a more to motivation than rewards and redundancy came with Harvard Business School professor Elton Mayo's renowned Hawthorne studies. These were conducted between 1927 and 1932 at the Western Electric Hawthorne Works in Chicago. Starting out to see what effect illumination had on productivity, Mayo moved on to see how fatigue and monotony fitted into the equation by varying rest breaks, temperature, humidity and work hours, even providing a free meal at one point. Working with a team of six female Hawthorne employees, Mayo changed every parameter he could think of, including increasing and decreasing their working hours and rest breaks. Finally he returned to the original conditions. Every change resulted in an improvement in productivity, except when two 10-minute pauses morning and afternoon were expanded to six five-minute pauses. These frequent work pauses, the women felt, upset their work rhythm.

Mayo's conclusion was that showing 'someone upstairs cares' and engendering a sense of ownership and responsibility were important motivators that could be harnessed by management. After Mayo came a flurry of theories on motivation. William McDougall in his book, *The Energies of Men* (1932, Methuen), listed 18 basic needs that he referred to as instincts (eg curiosity, self-assertion, submission). H A Murray, Assistant Director of the Harvard Psychological Clinic, catalogued 20 core psychological needs, including achievement, affiliation and power.

The motivation theories most studied and applied by business school graduates are those espoused by Maslow (see Chapter 2) and these below.

Theory X and Theory Y

Douglas McGregor, an American social psychologist who taught at two top schools, Harvard and MIT, developed these theories to try to explain the assumptions about human behaviour that underlie management action.

Theory X makes the following assumptions:

- The average person has an inherent dislike of work and will avoid it if possible. So management needs to put emphasis on productivity, incentive schemes and the idea of a 'fair day's work'.

- Because of this dislike of work, most people must be coerced, controlled, directed and threatened with punishment to get them to achieve the company's goals.

- People prefer to be directed, want to avoid responsibility, have little ambition and really want a secure life above all.

But, while Theory X does explain some human behaviour, it does not provide a framework for understanding behaviour in the best businesses. McGregor and others have proposed an alternative.

Theory Y has as its basis the belief that:

- Physical or mental effort at work is as natural as either rest or play. Under the right conditions hard work can be a source of great satisfaction. Under the wrong conditions it can be a drudge, which will inspire little effort and less thought from those forced to participate.
- Once committed to a goal, most people at work are capable of a high degree of self-management.
- Job satisfaction and personal recognition are the highest 'rewards' that can be given, and will result in the greatest level of commitment to the task in hand.
- Under the right conditions most people will accept responsibility and even welcome more of it.
- Few people in business are being 'used' to anything like their capacity. Neither are they contributing creatively towards solving problems.

Typical Theory X bosses are likely to keep away from their employees as much as possible. However small the business, for example, they may make sure they have an office to themselves, and its door is kept tightly shut. Contact with others will be confined to giving instructions about work and complaining about poor performance. A Theory Y approach will involve collaborating over decisions rather than issuing orders and sharing feedback so that everyone can learn from both success and failure, rather than just reprimanding when things go wrong.

Hygiene and motivation theory

Frederick Herzberg, Professor of Psychology at Case Western Reserve University in Cleveland, discovered that distinctly separate factors were the cause of job satisfaction and job dissatisfaction. His research revealed that five factors stood out as strong determinants of job satisfaction.

- Motivators:
  - Achievement. People want to succeed, so if you can set goals that people can reach and better, they will be much more satisfied than if they are constantly missing targets.
  - Recognition. Everyone likes his or her hard work to be acknowledged. Not everyone wants that recognition made in the same way, however.
  - Responsibility. People like the opportunity to take responsibility for their own work and for the whole task. This helps them grow as individuals.
  - Advancement. Promotion or at any rate progress are key motivators. In a small firm, providing career prospects for key staff can be a fundamental reason for growth.

- – Attractiveness of the work itself (job interest). There is no reason why a job should be dull. You need to make people's jobs interesting and give them a say in how their work is done. This will encourage new ideas on how things can be done better.

When the reasons for dissatisfaction were analysed, they were found to be concerned with a different range of factors:

- Hygiene factors:
  - – Company policy. Rules, formal and informal, such as start and finish times, meal breaks, dress code.
  - – Supervision. To what extent are employees allowed to get on with the job, or do people have someone looking over their shoulders all day?
  - – Administration. Do things work well, or is paperwork in a muddle and supplies always come in late?
  - – Salary. Are employees getting at least the going rate and benefits comparable with others?
  - – Working conditions. Are people expected to work in substandard conditions with poor equipment and little job security?
  - – Interpersonal relationships. Is the atmosphere in work good or are people at daggers drawn?

Herzberg called these causes of dissatisfaction 'hygiene factors'. He reasoned that the lack of hygiene will cause disease, but the presence of hygienic conditions will not, of itself, produce good health. So the lack of adequate 'job hygiene' will cause dissatisfaction but hygienic conditions alone will not bring about job satisfaction; to do that you have to work on the determinants of job satisfaction.

Leadership vs management

However great the employees are, unless a business has effective leadership, nothing of great value can be made to happen. While the boss may have a pretty clear idea of what the business is all about and what makes it special and different, it may not be so clear to those who work further down. Employees often just keep their heads down and get on with the task in hand. While that's a useful trait it is not sufficient to make a business a great place to work. To make that happen the boss has to have a precise idea of where the business is heading and use his or her leadership skills to achieve results. (See 'Strategy', later in this chapter.)

Leadership and management are not the same thing, but you need both. A leader challenges the status quo, while a manager accepts it as a constraint. A boss usually has to be both a leader and a manager. Dozens of catchy phrases such as 'bottom up', 'top down', 'management by objectives' and 'crisis management' have been used to describe the many and various theories of how to manage.

American engineer Frederick Winslow Taylor (1856–1915), who is credited with coining the maxim 'Time is money', was one of the pioneers of the search for the 'one best way' to execute such basic managerial functions as selection, promotion, compensation, training and production. Taylor was followed by Henri Fayol (1841–1925), a successful managing director of a French mining company, who developed what he called the 14 principles of management, recognizing that his list was neither exhaustive nor universally applicable. He also set out what he saw as the five primary functions of a manager. Nearly a decade later, American social scientist Luther Gulick (1892–1993) and Lyndall Urwick (1891–1983), a founder of the British management consultancy profession, expanded Fayol's list to seven executive management activities summarized by the acronym POSDCORB:

- Planning: determine objectives in advance and the methods to achieve them.
- Organizing: establish a structure of authority for all work.
- Staffing: recruit, hire and train workers; maintain favourable working conditions.
- Directing: make decisions, issue orders and directives.
- Coordinating: interrelate all sectors of the organization.
- Reporting: inform hierarchy through reports, records and inspections.
- Budgeting: depend on fiscal planning, accounting and control.

By 1973 Canadian academic Henry Mintzberg (1939–), now Professor of Organizations at INSEAD in France, had further expanded the manager's tasks and responsibilities into 10 areas:

- Figurehead: performs ceremonial and symbolic duties as head of the organization.
- Leader: fosters a proper work atmosphere and motivates and develops subordinates.
- Liaison: develops and maintains a network of external contacts to gather information.
- Monitor: gathers internal and external information relevant to the organization.
- Disseminator: passes factual and value-based information to subordinates.
- Spokesperson: communicates to the outside world on performance and policies.
- Entrepreneur: designs and initiates change in the organization.
- Disturbance handler: deals with unexpected events and operational breakdowns.

- Resource allocator: controls and authorizes the use of organizational resources.
- Negotiator: intermediates with other organizations and individuals.

All of these attempts at formulating an overarching and universal approach to arriving at a single best definition of the role of management foundered on the limitations of the information flow from the front line upwards. Two management theorists, Tom Peters and Nancy Austin, suggest that managers in effective companies get the information they need by getting out of their offices and talking with people – employees, suppliers, other managers, and customers. They coined the approach as 'management by walking around', or MBWA (see Chapter 8) (1985, Peters and Austin).

Today the view of the role of a manager is best described as being contingent on the internal and external circumstances he or she finds themself in. Expanded into the rather grandiose title of 'contingency theory', its proponent, Fred Fiedler, a business and management psychologist at the University of Washington, first introduced what he called the contingency modelling of leadership in 1967.

Strategy

Joseph Lampel, Professor of Strategy at Cass Business School and author of *Strategy Bites Back* (2005, Financial Times Prentice Hall) tells the story of when he received an urgent request from one of his MBA students: could he please provide a clear and easy-to-use definition of strategy? 'My career,' wrote the student, 'may depend on it,' adding: 'besides, I would like to start the course with a better idea of what I am supposed to be looking out for.' Lampel goes on to explain that he was less surprised by the request than by the fact that it came before the course had even begun. He was used to being approached at the end of the course by students confessing that they still did not know exactly what strategy is.

Strategy, though a core subject in every business school, is less an academic discipline than an ever-shifting appraisal of how an organization should position itself to best meet the challenges it faces. Rather like the quote attributed to one governor of the Bank of England who said that the true meaning of Christmas would not be apparent until Easter, when it comes to estimating retail sales, successful strategies are really only recognizable after the event. The case below gives a flavour of the dimensions of how strategy is shaped: part marketing, part money, part people, part culture and mostly an appreciation of an ever-shifting and developing world.

Some of the basic tools of strategy fit squarely into marketing planning and as such are covered elsewhere in this book. The remaining core elements of the subject are as follows.

Strategic purpose

Business leaders, ably supported by their MBAs, have three major tasks: to determine the direction, chart the course and set the goals. The direction of a business has a number of components that can be best understood if thought of as being parts of a pyramid. See Figure 12.4.

FIGURE 12.4 The purpose pyramid

Vision

We said in the previous chapter that a vision is about stretching the organization's reach beyond its grasp. While few can see how the vision can be achieved, they can see that it would be great if it could be.

Microsoft's vision of a computer in every home, formed when few offices had one, is one example of a vision that has nearly been reached. In 1990 it might have raised a wry smile. After all, it was only a few decades before then that IBM had estimated the entire world demand for its computers as seven!

NASDAQ, the entrepreneurs' stock market, has as its vision: 'To build the world's first truly global securities market. A worldwide market of markets built on a worldwide network of networks linking pools of liquidity and connecting investors from all over the world, thus assuring the best possible price for securities at the lowest possible costs.' That certainly points beyond the horizon envisaged by business today.

Having a vision will make it easier to get employees to buy into a long-term commitment to a business by seeing they can have career opportunities and progression in an organization that knows where it is going.

Mission

A mission is a direction statement, intended to focus your attention on the essentials that encapsulate your specific competence(s) in relation to the market/customers you plan to serve. First, the mission should be narrow enough to give direction and guidance to everyone in the business. This concentration is the key to business success because it is only by focusing on specific needs that a small business can differentiate itself from its larger competitors. Nothing kills a business faster than trying to do too many different things too soon. Second, the mission should open up a large enough market to allow the business to grow and realize its potential. You can always add a bit on later.

In summary, the mission statement should explain:

● what business you are in and your purpose;

● what you want to achieve over the next one to three years, ie your strategic goal;

● how, ie your ethics, values and standards.

Above all, mission statements must be realistic, achievable – and brief.

Objectives

The milestones on the way to realizing the vision and mission are measured by the achievement of business objectives. These objectives 'cascade' through the organization from the top, where they are measures of profit, through to measures such as output, quality, reject rates, absenteeism and so forth.

Objective setting is a primary process in which clear performance measures are agreed with every employee. The achievement of specific objectives is the ultimate measure of effective leadership.

Balanced scorecard

The balanced scorecard, developed by Robert Kaplan and David Norton and published in a *Harvard Business Review* article in 1992, is a management process that sets out to align business activities to the vision and strategy of the organization, improve internal and external communications, and monitor organization performance against strategic goals. Its uniqueness was to add non-financial performance measures to traditional financial targets to give managers and directors a more 'balanced' view of organizational performance. Although Kaplan and Norton are credited with coining the phrase, the idea of a balanced scorecard originated with General Electric's work on performance measurement reporting in the 1950s and the work of French process engineers (who created the *tableau de bord* – literally, a 'dashboard' of performance measures) in the early part of the 20th century.

FIGURE 12.5   Balanced scorecard

Four perspectives are included in the management process, which in effect extends the range of management by objectives and value-based management into areas beyond purely financial target setting. A number of objectives, measures, targets and initiatives can be set to achieve specific key performance indicators (KPIs) for each perspective in terms of:

- Financial. These include KPIs for return on investment, cash flow, profit margins and shareholder value.

- Customer. Here the KPIs can be for customer retention rates, satisfaction levels, referrals and complaints.

- Internal business processes. These can include stock turn, accident rates, defects in production, reduction in the number of processes and improvements in communications.

- Learning and growth. KPIs here can include employee turnover, morale levels, training and development achievements and internal promotions vs new recruits.

The four perspectives are linked by a double feedback loop whose purpose is to ensure that KPIs are not in conflict with one another. For example, if customer satisfaction could be achieved by improving delivery times, achieving that by, say, increasing stock levels might conflict with a financial target of improving return on capital employed.

CASE STUDY   Alpharma

As well as having a clutch of MBAs at operating levels throughout the company, recent chairmen and CEOs of Alpharma also have MBAs. Gert W Munthe (1994–2000) has an MBA from Columbia and Peter G Tombros, chairman and a member of Alpharma's Board of Directors since 1995, received his MBA from the University of Pennsylvania in 1968. Other members of the top team with MBAs include Michael J Nestor, initially as President of the pharmaceutical business and later as President of the branded specialty pharmaceutical business where he established Alpharma's pain franchise. He has a Bachelor of Business Administration degree from Middle Tennessee State University and an MBA from Pepperdine University.

Alpharma's journey began in 1903, when a group of Norwegian pharmacists formed the A/S Apothekernes Laboratorium for Specialpræparater (Alpharma). The company grew rapidly as a manufacturer of pharmaceutical products and, in the years leading up to the First World War, production increased rapidly. By 1939 Alpharma was an important manufacturer of bandages and adhesive plasters, products considered vital to the Norwegian war effort. The next two decades saw a flurry of acquisitions leading to them becoming the largest manufacturer of bacitracin in the world, a strategy that laid the foundation for expansion into the United States.

In 1983 Alpharma acquired its biggest competitor, the Danish company A/S Dumex, financing the transaction through a public offer of shares in New York. This was the first time an American subsidiary of a European organization was listed in New York and with access to the largest capital market in the world they set about on an acquisition blitz. In 1987, they bought US company Barre-National, Inc., the largest manufacturer in the United States, and possibly the world, of liquid generic pharmaceuticals. The following year they bought the US pharmaceutical company NMC Laboratories, Inc., which specialized in generic medicinal ointments and creams. In May 2000, Alpharma acquired Roche's Medicinal Feed Additives business and in 2001 they acquired the American company, Purepac Pharmaceutical Co. Ltd., owned by Australian company F H Faulding. Purepac manufactured generics in tablet and capsule form for the North American market.

A few years earlier, around 1997 according to company sources, the pressure to meet shareholders' requirements for ever-increasing returns in a business with many different divisions serving diverse markets led to a need to monitor every company activity that impacted on EBIT (Earnings Before Interest and Tax).

Believing that the company could not meet shareholders' expectations with the management tools on hand the search was on for new ones. It was at this point that the company's Chief Executive Officer, who had an extensive network of contacts with external consulting firms began considering the Balanced Scorecard (BSC). Its simplicity, its function as a strategy evaluator and the ability to use non-financial indicators in addition to the financial ones was particularly attractive to a business whose culture was steeped in medical communications.

Once decided on, a project team of four from the company's Internal Control department was assembled to see how best to implement BSC. They formulated their findings in a handbook that was distributed company-wide at the end of June 1998, setting out company policy on all matters relating to the scorecard. Initially subsidiary divisions were encouraged to develop a scorecard, but the use of the concept was not compulsory until January 2001 when, for the first time, scorecard reporting was officially required in the strategic planning process.

Kaplan and Norton suggest that it takes about 25 to 26 months for a company to make the BSC a routine part of the management process and deliver value. By 2003 Alpharma Inc had become a global pharmaceutical company operating in 27 counties generating sales of $654 million a year.

On December 29, 2008, Alpharma, Inc. finally agreed to King Pharmaceuticals Inc's $1.6 billion cash takeover offer, ending the drug makers' months-long battle. That day King agreed to pay $37 a share for Alpharma, representing a 54 per cent premium to the Bridgewater, New Jersey company's stock price on 21 Aug, the last trading day before King's initial $33-per-share bid.

Online video courses and lectures

Accounting: Dr Ray Gregg Oral Roberts University, Tulsa, OK. A series of 37 lectures from the basics of debits and credits to capital budgets and investments: **www.youtube.com/playlist?list=PL31FC5F69A409A706**

Business strategy. Professor Carlo Alberto Carnevale Maffe of SDA Bocconi School of Management, Milan: **www.youtube.com/watch?v=a_1O-3xhKm4**

Corporate Finance Essentials: Prof Javier Estrada of IESE Business School offers this course each year. It consists of six sessions requiring no previous knowledge or preparation. Each session will consist of a video lecture of around 45–60 minutes and one or two recommended readings: **www.coursera.org/course/corpfinance**

Finance Fundamentals: Taught by Jim Stice and Kay Stice, professors at Marriott School of Management, Brigham Young University (US). You can watch this 3-hour 27-minute course as an introductory free trial at Lynda.com: **www.lynda.com/Business-Accounting-tutorials/Finance-Fundamentals/174917-2.html**

How to Build a Strategy for 'the Long Game'. Paul Schoemaker, research director for Wharton's Mack Institute for Innovation Management: **http://knowledge.wharton.upenn.edu/article/how-to-build-a-strategy-for-the-long-game**

Introduction to Financial Accounting: Contents include an introduction to the balance sheet, the income statement, cash flows and working capital assets and how to read an annual report. This course is presented as a combination of lecture videos, quizzes and discussion. The only required maths knowledge is addition, subtraction, multiplication, and division. Delivered four times a year by Wharton's faculty: **www.coursera.org/course/whartonaccounting**

The Five Competitive Forces That Shape Strategy, Professor Michael Porter, interviewed for the *Harvard Business Review*: **www.youtube.com/watch?v=mYF2_FBCvXw**

Online video case studies

Crowdfunding Case Studies with Fundit.ie: **www.youtube.com/watch?v=phX1q9CHmkY&feature=iv&src_vid=CejPet3MiMs&annotation_id=annotation_165899**

Endeca. Co-Founders Steve Papa and Pete Bell simulate the founding and early growth of their company, walking through key terms and legal due diligence. Harvard i-lab: **www.youtube.com/watch?v=0QTProGpc1o**

Facebook Strategy Revealed: Move Fast And Break Things! Business Insider: **www.businessinsider.com/henry-blodget-innovation-highlights-2010-2?IR=T**

How we helped IT contractor Ronan Moriarty understand his income. Crunch Accounting: **www.youtube.com/watch?v=cCja3dEpsXY&list=PLY1w7ViHqCO359V9apwhwoCPLFjwYCHBz&index=4**

How we're brightening up Greyworld's finances. Crunch Accounting: **www.youtube.com/watch?v=9NfghzMKXZQ&list=PLY1w7ViHqCO359V9apwhwoCPLFjwYCHBz&index=1**

INDEX